The Life and Times of Jesus: From Child to God

Compiled by Joseph Lumpkin

Using the Following Texts:

The Infancy Gospel of the Savior

Book of James, or Protevangelium

The Infancy Gospel of Thomas

The History of Joseph the Carpenter

Letters Between Pilate and Seneca

Letters Between Pilate and Herod

Letters between Pilate and Tiberius Caesar

The Life of Saint Issa (Jesus)

The Book Of Luke

Joseph Lumpkin

The Life and Times of Jesus: From Child to God

Copyright © 2009 by Joseph Lumpkin
All rights reserved.

Printed in the United States of America. No part of this book may be used or reproduced in any manner whatsoever without written permission except in the case of brief quotations embodied in critical articles and reviews.

Fifth Estate, Post Office Box 116,
Blountsville, AL 35031

First Edition
Cover Designed by An Quigley

Printed on acid-free paper

Library of Congress Control No: 2009943773

ISBN: 9781933580838

Fifth Estate, 2009

Joseph Lumpkin

Table of Contents

Introduction	7
Luke 1:1 - Luke 2:41	10
Infancy Narrative	18
Infancy Gospel Continued	25
Luke 2:42 – 2:52	61
Life of Saint Issa	62
Luke 3:1 – Luke 21:38	91
History of Joseph the Carpenter	143
Luke 22:1 – Luke 23:11	156
Letters of Pilate, Herod, Seneca, and Caesar	161
Luke 22:12 – 22:25	233
Luke 23:26 – Luke 24:53	241
Documents Used	246
Appendix Containing Infancy Gospels	265

Joseph Lumpkin

Introduction

God is born in human form. Ultimate power and authority reside in the hands of a child. Early Christians looked at their own children as they played, argued, loved, and fought and wondered what it would have been like to raise the Son of God. How would Jesus have acted as a baby, a toddler, a child, or a teenager?

How human was this "God-child," Jesus? Did he have the failings of their own children? Was he selfish and rash at the age of one? Was his stage of the "terrible twos" as horrible a stage as most? If Jesus were a normal youngster what would the outcome have been? For those who found themselves in the path of the young God's temper tantrum, devastating consequences, death or disfigurement could have followed.

Questions surrounding the nature of Jesus challenged the minds of Christians from the very beginning of the faith. Did Jesus mature and grow in wisdom, as most young men should? Did he discover his path in life and his calling or was he perfect and mature from the time of his birth? The Bible reports that the child Jesus "grew strong in spirit." Did that mean he was weaker in spirit as a child? These are the questions writers of early Christianity sought to address.

The texts presented in this little volume are those written by early believers struggling to make sense of the paradox of the man who is God. The scant information found in the Gospels regarding the first thirty years of his life gave rise to stories and folklore in an attempt to fill in gaps and answer questions regarding the life and times of Jesus.

Stories were told of the birth of Jesus and his early years. As he grew and began to venture out into the town to play with the other children, disagreements occurred between the strong willed deity and the children, parents, and teachers of the town. How does one discipline God?

Tales sprang from the imagination of believers about his deeds and misdeeds, his travels, and the process of maturing into the man who would save the lost.

Youth gives rise to arrogance and rash behavior, yet, age brings wisdom and self-control. With growing wisdom and guidance from his heavenly father and loving parents, Jesus began to realize his place in the universe as the compassionate rebel and the Messiah.

In the Gospel story, there is little information about the formative years of Jesus. Soon after his birth nothing more is heard of Jesus. The silence continued for almost a decade. Then, at the age of twelve the Bible tells us that Jesus had grown in strength and wisdom and was capable of discussing the Torah with adults in the temple. Again the Bible falls silent for the next eighteen years. Jesus next appeared around the age of thirty, ready to start his earthly ministry, and take on the yoke of Messiah.

What happened during the periods of silence? Did Jesus simply grow up in a tiny town doing manual labor as some suggest. Did he wake up one day, lay down his hammer and become the Great Physician, or did he mature into his rightful place over time by doing what he was born to do? Did he travel, teach, and heal as a young man?

These are the stories of Jesus' lost years. They are tales woven and stories told by early Christians, as they attempted to make sense of the paradox between Childhood and Godhood. These stories attempt to fill in the missing years in the Life of Jesus through the use of controversial and non-canonical texts.

Using the Book of Luke in the Holy Bible as a backdrop and source for our timeline, we will insert various texts, such as the Infancy Gospels, The Life of Saint Issa, The History of Joseph the Carpenter, as well as documents, such as the letters between Herod, Pilate, Seneca, and Caesar, in order to gain information and insight into the life of the most important and influential person in human history. Three separate Infancy Gospels were used. These stories overlap in time and content but each adds a piece to the puzzle. Combining all sources into a single document created the narrative used in this book.

The full Book of Luke is cited, but it is parsed within the timeline. This means that parts of the story will be repeated between Luke and the other sources. It was thought best to present the texts in full so the reader may witness the subtle, and sometimes not so subtle additions and differences.

Although the Infancy narrative used in the main body of the book represents a combined storyline from three Infancy Gospels, some readers will wish to read all of the Infancy Gospels in their entirety. The three Gospels are presented in the Appendix. Some books are questionable in pedigree, but all tell us what the writers were concerned with. Placing the dates of authorship informs us of what some Christians of that period believed the life of Jesus could have been like.

The Gospel of Luke not withstanding, the books and letters used here are not canon. Some may argue their validity, but there are many ancient documents used as historical sources that are not canon. Beyond this point, a broader picture emerges, which allows us a window into the thoughts, concerns, and beliefs of the people of ancient Christianity.

The reader is insightful and intelligent enough to decide what to believe or not believe about the specific accounts or documents used. Questions of reliability aside, these texts are some of the oldest sources left to draw upon in our quest for the missing years of Jesus.

The history and information pertaining to each document can be found at the end of the book. By arranging the book in this manner the reader is given information without interrupting the narrative developed by the concatenation of the various texts. To our knowledge, this is the first time these documents have been brought together to form a chronological narrative. The documents speak for themselves and the life and times of Jesus are revealed.

His Infancy

A Narrative Based on Three Infancy Gospels

The History of Mary

In the histories of the twelve tribes of Israel it is written that there was one Joakim, exceeding rich: and he offered his gifts twofold, saying: That which is of my great abundance shall be for the whole people, and that which is for my forgiveness shall be for the Lord, for a propitiation to me.

Now the great day of the Lord drew near and the children of Israel offered their gifts. And Reuben stood over against him saying: It is not lawful for you to offer your gifts first, forasmuch as you have gotten no offspring in Israel. And Joakim was very grieved, and went to the record of the twelve tribes of the people, saying: I will look upon the record of the twelve tribes of Israel, whether I only have not gotten offspring in Israel. And he searched, and found concerning all the righteous that they had raised up offspring in Israel. And he remembered the patriarch Abraham, how in the last days God gave him a son, even Isaac. And Joakim was very grieved, and showed not himself to his wife, but he took himself into the wilderness, and pitched his tent there, and fasted forty days and forty nights, saying within himself: I will not go down either for meat or for drink until the Lord my God visit me, and my prayer shall be to me meat and drink.

Now his wife Anna lamented with two lamentations, and bewailed herself with two wailings, saying: I will bewail my widowhood, and I will bewail my childlessness.

And the great day of the Lord drew near, and Judith her handmaid said to her: How long will you humble your soul? The great day of the Lord has come, and it is not lawful for you to mourn: but take this headband, which the mistress of my work gave me, and it is not lawful for me to put it on, forasmuch as I am a handmaid, and it has a mark of royalty. And Anna said: Get you from me. Look! I have done nothing, nor I will do so but the Lord has greatly humbled me: I suppose someone gave it to you in secret, and you have come to make me partaker in your sin. And Judith said: How shall I curse you, seeing the Lord has shut up your womb, to give you no fruit in Israel?

And Anna was very grieved and mourned with a great mourning because she was looked down on by all the tribes of Israel. And coming to herself she said: What shall I do? I will pray with weeping to the Lord my God that he may visit me. And she put off her mourning garments and cleansed and adorned her head and put on her bridal garments: and about the ninth hour she went down into the garden to walk there. And she saw a laurel-tree and sat down underneath it and besought the Lord saying: O God of our fathers, bless me, and listen to my prayer, as you did bless the womb of Sarah, and gave her a son, even Isaac.

And looking up to the heaven she spied a nest of sparrows in the laurel-tree, and made a lamentation within herself, saying: Woe to me, who begat me? And what womb brought me forth for I have become a curse before the children of Israel, and I am looked down on, and they have mocked me forth out of the temple of the Lord? Woe to me, to what am I similar? I am not similar to the fowls of the heaven, for even the fowls of the heaven are fruitful before you, O Lord. Woe to me, to what am I similar? I am not similar to the beasts of the earth, for even the beasts of the earth are fruitful before you, O Lord. Woe to me, to what am I similar? I am not similar to these waters, for even these waters are fruitful before you, O Lord. Woe to me, to what am I similar? I am not similar to this earth, for even this earth brings forth her fruits in due season and blesses you, O Lord.

And behold an angel of the Lord appeared, saying to her: Anna, Anna, the Lord has listened to your prayer, and you shall conceive and bear, and your offspring shall be spoken of in the whole world. And Anna said: As the Lord my God lives, if I bring forth either male or female, I will bring it for a gift to the Lord my God, and it shall be ministering to him all the days of its life.

And behold there came two messengers saying to her: Behold Joakim your husband comes with his flocks: for an angel of the Lord came down to him saying: Joakim, Joakim, the Lord God has listened to your prayer. Get you down here, for behold your wife Anna has conceived. And Joakim sat him down and called his herdsmen saying: Bring me here ten lambs without blemish and without spot, and they shall be for the Lord my God; and bring me twelve tender calves, and they shall be for the priests and for the assembly of the elders; and a hundred kids for the whole people.

And behold Joakim came with his flocks, and Anna stood at the gate and saw Joakim coming, and ran and hung upon his neck, saying: Now know I that the Lord God has greatly blessed me: for behold the widow is no more a widow, and she that was childless shall conceive. And Joakim rested the first day in his house.

And the next day he offered his gifts, saying in himself: If the Lord God be reconciled to me, the plate that is upon the forehead of the priest will make it manifest to me. And Joakim offered his gifts and looked earnestly upon the plate of the priest when he went up to the altar of the Lord, and he saw no sin in himself. And Joakim said: Now know I that the Lord is become propitious to me and has forgiven all my sins. And he went down from the temple of the Lord justified, and went to his house.

And her months were fulfilled, and in the ninth month Anna brought forth. And she said to the midwife: what have I brought forth? And she said: A female. And Anna said: My soul is magnified this day, and she laid herself down. And when the days were fulfilled, Anna purified herself and gave suck to the child and called her name Mary.

And day by day the child grew strong, and when she was six months old her mother stood her upon the ground to try if she would stand; and she walked seven steps and returned to her bosom. And she caught her up, saying: As the Lord my God lives, you shall walk no more upon this ground, until I bring you into the temple of the Lord. And she made a sanctuary in her bed chamber and suffered nothing common or unclean to pass through it. And she called for the daughters of the Hebrews that were undefiled, and they carried her here and thither.

And the first year of the child was fulfilled, and Joakim made a great feast and bade the priests and the scribes and the assembly of the elders and the whole people of Israel. And Joakim brought the child to the priests, and they blessed her, saying: God of our fathers, bless this child and give her a name renowned forever among all generations. And all the people said: So be it, so be it. Amen. And he brought her to the high priests, and they blessed her, saying: God of the high places, look upon this child, and bless her with the last blessing which has no successor.

And her mother caught her up into the sanctuary of her bedroom and gave her suck.

And Anna made a song to the Lord God, saying:

I will sing a hymn to the Lord my God, because he has visited me and taken away from me the ridicule of my enemies, and the Lord has given me a fruit of his righteousness, single and manifold before him. Who shall declare to the sons of Reuben that Anna gives suck? Listen, listen, you twelve tribes of Israel, that Anna gives suck. And she laid the child to rest in the bedroom of her sanctuary, and went forth and ministered to them. And when the feast was ended, they got them down rejoicing, and glorifying the God of Israel.

And to the child her months were added: and the child became two years old. And Joakim said: Let us bring her up to the temple of the Lord that we may pay the promise which we promised; lest the Lord require it of us and take it from us, and our gift become unacceptable. And Anna said: Let us wait until the third year, so that the child may not long after her father or mother. And Joakim said: Let us wait.

And the child became three years old, and Joakim said: Call for the daughters of the Hebrews that are undefiled, and let them take every one a lamp, and let them be burning, that the child turn not backward and her heart be taken captive away from the temple of the Lord. And they did so until they were gone up into the temple of the Lord.

And the priest received her and kissed her and blessed her and said: The Lord has magnified your name among all generations: in you in the latter days shall the Lord make manifest his redemption to the children of Israel. And he made her to sit upon the third step of the altar. And the Lord put grace upon her and she danced with her feet and all the house of Israel loved her.

And her parents got them down marveling, and praising the Lord God because the child was not turned away backward.

And Mary was in the temple of the Lord as a dove that is nurtured: and she received food from the hand of an angel.

And when she was twelve years old, there was a council of the priests, saying: Behold Mary is become twelve years old in the temple of the Lord. What then shall we do with her? Lest she pollute the sanctuary of the Lord. And they said to the high priest: You stand over the altar of the Lord. Enter in and pray concerning her: And whatsoever the Lord shall reveal to you, that let us do.

And the high priest took the vestment with the twelve bells and went in to the Holy of Holies and prayed concerning her. And lo, an angel of the Lord appeared saying to him: Zacharias, Zacharias, go forth and assemble them that are widowers of the people, and let them bring every man a rod, and to whomsoever the Lord shall show a sign, his wife shall she be. And the heralds went forth over all the country round about Judaea, and the trumpet of the Lord sounded, and all men ran thereto.

And Joseph cast down his adze and ran to meet them, and when they were gathered together they went to the high priest and took their rods with them. And he took the rods of them all and went into the temple and prayed. And when he had finished the prayer he took the rods and went forth and gave them back to them: and there was no sign upon them. But Joseph received the last rod: and lo, a dove came forth of the rod and flew upon the bead of Joseph. And the priest said to Joseph: Unto you has it fallen to take the virgin of the Lord and keep her for yourself. And Joseph refused, saying: I have sons, and I am an old man, but she is a girl: lest I became a laughing-stock to the children of Israel. And the priest said to Joseph: Hear the Lord your God, and remember what things God did to Dathan and Abiram and Korah, how the earth split and they were swallowed up because of their gainsaying. And now fear you, Joseph, lest it be so in your house. And Joseph was afraid, and took her to keep her for himself. And Joseph said to Mary: Lo, I have received you out of the temple of the Lord: and now do I leave you in my house, and I go away to build my buildings and I will come again to you. The Lord shall watch over you.

Now there was a council of the priests, and they said: Let us make a veil for the temple of the Lord. And the priest said: Call to me pure virgins of the tribe of David. And the officers departed and sought and found seven virgins. And the priests called to mind the child Mary, that she was of the tribe of David and was undefiled before God: and the officers went and fetched her. And they brought them into the temple of the Lord, and the priest said: Cast me lots, which of you shall weave the gold and the undefiled white and the fine linen and the silk and the hyacinthine, and the scarlet and the true purple. And the lot of the true purple and the scarlet fell to Mary, and she took them and went to her house.

And at that season Zacharias became dumb, and Samuel was in his place until the time when Zacharias spoke again. But Mary took the scarlet and began to spin it.

And she took the pitcher and went forth to fill it with water: and lo a voice saying: Hail, you that are highly favored; the Lord is with you: blessed are you among women.

And she looked about her upon the right hand and upon the left, to see from where this voice should be: and being filled with trembling she went to her house and set down the pitcher, and took the purple and sat down upon her seat and drew out the thread.

And behold an angel of the Lord stood before her saying: Fear not, Mary, for you have found grace before the Lord of all things, and you shall conceive of his word. And she, when she heard it, questioned in herself, saying: Shall I truly conceive of the living God, and bring forth after the manner of all women? And the angel of the Lord said: Not so, Mary, for a power of the Lord shall overshadow you: wherefore also that holy thing which shall be born of you shall be called the Son of the Highest. And you shall call his name Jesus: for he shall save his people from their sins. And Mary said: Behold the handmaid of the Lord is before him: be it to me according to your word.

And she made the purple and the scarlet and brought them to the priest. And the priest blessed her and said: Mary, the Lord God has magnified your name, and you shall be blessed among all generations of the earth. And Mary rejoiced and went away to Elizabeth her kinswoman: and she knocked at the door. And Elizabeth when she heard it cast down the scarlet wool and ran to the door and opened it, and when she saw Mary she blessed her and said: What is this to me that the mother of my Lord should come to me? For behold that which is in me leaped and blessed you. And Mary forgot the mysteries which Gabriel the archangel had told her, and she looked up to the heaven and said: Who am I, Lord, that all the generations of the earth do bless me? And she abode three months with Elizabeth, and day by day her womb grew: and Mary was afraid and departed to her house and hid herself from the children of Israel. Now she was sixteen years old when these mysteries came to pass.

Now it was the sixth month with her, and behold Joseph came from his building, and he entered into his house and found her great with child. And he smote his face, and cast himself down upon the ground on sackcloth and wept bitterly, saying: With what countenance shall I look to the Lord my God? And what prayer shall I make concerning this maiden? For I received her out of the temple of the Lord my God a virgin, and have not kept her safe. Who is he that has ensnared me? Who has done this evil in my house and has defiled the virgin? Is not the story of Adam repeated in me? For as at the hour of his giving thanks the serpent came and found Eve alone and deceived her, so has it befallen me also. And Joseph arose from off the sackcloth and called Mary and said to her, "Oh you that were cared for by God, why have you done this? You have forgotten the Lord your God. Why have you humbled your soul, you that were nourished up in the Holy of Holies and did receive food at the hand of an angel?" But she wept bitterly, saying: I am pure and I know not a man. And Joseph said to her: What then is that which is in your womb? And she said: As the Lord my God lives, I know not from where it is come to me.

Gospel of Luke from the Holy Bible

Luke.1

[1] Forasmuch as many have taken in hand to set forth in order a declaration of those things which are surely believed among us,
[2] Even as they delivered them to us, which from the beginning were eyewitnesses, and ministers of the word;
[3] It seemed good to me also, having had perfect understanding of all things from the very first, to write to you in order, most excellent Theophilus,
[4] That you might know the certainty of those things, wherein you have been instructed.
[5] There was in the days of Herod, the king of Judaea, a certain priest named Zacharias, of the course of Abia: and his wife was of the daughters of Aaron, and her name was Elisabeth.
[6] And they were both righteous before God, walking in all the commandments and ordinances of the Lord blameless.
[7] And they had no child, because that Elisabeth was barren, and they both were now well stricken in years.
[8] And it came to pass, that while he executed the priest's office before God in the order of his course,
[9] According to the custom of the priest's office, his lot was to burn incense when he went into the temple of the Lord.
[10] And the whole multitude of the people were praying without at the time of incense.
[11] And there appeared to him an angel of the Lord standing on the right side of the altar of incense.
[12] And when Zacharias saw him, he was troubled, and fear fell upon him.
[13] But the angel said to him, Fear not, Zacharias: for your prayer is heard; and your wife Elisabeth shall bear you a son, and you shall call his name John.
[14] And you shall have joy and gladness; and many shall rejoice at

his birth.

[15] For he shall be great in the sight of the Lord, and shall drink neither wine nor strong drink; and he shall be filled with the Holy Ghost, even from his mother's womb.

[16] And many of the children of Israel shall he turn to the Lord their God.

[17] And he shall go before him in the spirit and power of Elias, to turn the hearts of the fathers to the children, and the disobedient to the wisdom of the just; to make ready a people prepared for the Lord.

[18] And Zacharias said to the angel, Whereby shall I know this? for I am an old man, and my wife well stricken in years.

[19] And the angel answering said to him, I am Gabriel, that stands in the presence of God; and am sent to speak to you, and to show you these glad tidings.

[20] And, behold, you shall be dumb, and not able to speak, until the day that these things shall be performed, because you believe not my words, which shall be fulfilled in their season.

[21] And the people waited for Zacharias, and marveled that he tarried so long in the temple.

[22] And when he came out, he could not speak to them: and they perceived that he had seen a vision in the temple: for he beckoned to them, and remained speechless.

[23] And it came to pass, that, as soon as the days of his ministration were accomplished, he departed to his own house.

[24] And after those days his wife Elisabeth conceived, and hid herself five months, saying,

[25] Thus has the Lord dealt with me in the days wherein he looked on me, to take away my ridicule among men.

[26] And in the sixth month the angel Gabriel was sent from God to a city of Galilee, named Nazareth,

[27] To a virgin espoused to a man whose name was Joseph, of the house of David; and the virgin's name was Mary.

[28] And the angel came in to her, and said, Hail, you that are highly favored, the Lord is with you: blessed are you among women.

[29] And when she saw him, she was troubled at his saying, and cast in her mind what manner of salutation this should be.

[30] And the angel said to her, Fear not, Mary: for you have found favor with God.

[31] And, behold, you shall conceive in your womb, and bring forth a

son, and shall call his name JESUS.
[32] He shall be great, and shall be called the Son of the Highest: and the Lord God shall give to him the throne of his father David:
[33] And he shall reign over the house of Jacob forever; and of his kingdom there shall be no end.
[34] Then said Mary to the angel, How shall this be, seeing I know not a man?
[35] And the angel answered and said to her, The Holy Ghost shall come upon you, and the power of the Highest shall overshadow you: therefore also that holy thing which shall be born of you shall be called the Son of God.
[36] And, behold, your cousin Elisabeth, she has also conceived a son in her old age: and this is the sixth month with her, who was called barren.
[37] For with God nothing shall be impossible.
[38] And Mary said, Behold the handmaid of the Lord; be it to me according to your word. And the angel departed from her.
[39] And Mary arose in those days, and went into the hill country with haste, into a city of Juda;
[40] And entered into the house of Zacharias, and saluted Elisabeth.
[41] And it came to pass, that, when Elisabeth heard the salutation of Mary, the babe leaped in her womb; and Elisabeth was filled with the Holy Ghost:
[42] And she spoke out with a loud voice, and said, Blessed are you among women, and blessed is the fruit of your womb.
[43] And whence is this to me, that the mother of my Lord should come to me?
[44] For, lo, as soon as the voice of your salutation sounded in my ears, the babe leaped in my womb for joy.
[45] And blessed is she that believed: for there shall be a performance of those things which were told her from the Lord.
[46] And Mary said, My soul does magnify the Lord,
[47] And my spirit has rejoiced in God my Savior.
[48] For he has regarded the low estate of his handmaiden: for, behold, from now on all generations shall call me blessed.
[49] For he that is mighty has done to me great things; and holy is his name.
[50] And his mercy is on them that fear him from generation to generation.
[51] He has showed strength with his arm; he has scattered the proud

in the imagination of their hearts.

[52] He has put down the mighty from their seats, and exalted them of low degree.

[53] He has filled the hungry with good things; and the rich he has sent empty away.

[54] He has helped his servant Israel, in remembrance of his mercy;

[55] As he spoke to our fathers, to Abraham, and to his offspring for ever.

[56] And Mary abode with her about three months, and returned to her own house.

[57] Now Elisabeth's full time came that she should be delivered; and she brought forth a son.

[58] And her neighbors and her cousins heard how the Lord had showed great mercy upon her; and they rejoiced with her.

[59] And it came to pass, that on the eighth day they came to circumcise the child; and they called him Zacharias, after the name of his father.

[60] And his mother answered and said, Not so; but he shall be called John.

[61] And they said to her, There is none of your kindred that is called by this name.

[62] And they made signs to his father, how he would have him called.

[63] And he asked for a writing table, and wrote, saying, His name is John. And they marveled all.

[64] And his mouth was opened immediately, and his tongue loosed, and he spoke, and praised God.

[65] And fear came on all that dwelt round about them: and all these sayings were noised abroad throughout all the hill country of Judaea.

[66] And all they that heard them laid them up in their hearts, saying, What manner of child shall this be! And the hand of the Lord was with him.

[67] And his father Zacharias was filled with the Holy Ghost, and prophesied, saying,

[68] Blessed be the Lord God of Israel; for he has visited and redeemed his people,

[69] And has raised up a horn of salvation for us in the house of his servant David;

[70] As he spoke by the mouth of his holy prophets, which have been since the world began:

[71] That we should be saved from our enemies, and from the hand of all that hate us;
[72] To perform the mercy promised to our fathers, and to remember his holy covenant;
[73] The oath which he swore to our father Abraham,
[74] That he would grant to us, that we being delivered out of the hand of our enemies might serve him without fear,
[75] In holiness and righteousness before him, all the days of our life.
[76] And you, child, shall be called the prophet of the Highest: for you shall go before the face of the Lord to prepare his ways;
[77] To give knowledge of salvation to his people by the remission of their sins,
[78] Through the tender mercy of our God; whereby the dayspring from on high has visited us,
[79] To give light to them that sit in darkness and in the shadow of death, to guide our feet into the way of peace.
[80] And the child grew, and grew strong in spirit, and was in the deserts till the day of his showing to Israel.

Luke.2

[1] And it came to pass in those days, that there went out a decree from Caesar Augustus, that all the world should be taxed.
[2] (And this taxing was first made when Cyrenius was governor of Syria.)
[3] And all went to be taxed, every one into his own city.
[4] And Joseph also went up from Galilee, out of the city of Nazareth, into Judaea, to the city of David, which is called Bethlehem; (because he was of the house and lineage of David:)
[5] To be taxed with Mary his espoused wife, being great with child.
[6] And so it was, that, while they were there, the days were accomplished that she should be delivered.
[7] And she brought forth her firstborn son, and wrapped him in swaddling clothes, and laid him in a manger; because there was no room for them in the inn.
[8] And there were in the same country shepherds abiding in the field, keeping watch over their flock by night.
[9] And, lo, the angel of the Lord came upon them, and the glory of the Lord shone round about them: and they were very afraid.

[10] And the angel said to them, Fear not: for, behold, I bring you good tidings of great joy, which shall be to all people.
[11] For to you is born this day in the city of David a Savior, which is Christ the Lord.
[12] And this shall be a sign to you; You shall find the babe wrapped in swaddling clothes, lying in a manger.
[13] And suddenly there was with the angel a multitude of the heavenly host praising God, and saying,
[14] Glory to God in the highest, and on earth peace, good will toward men.
[15] And it came to pass, as the angels were gone away from them into heaven, the shepherds said one to another, Let us now go even to Bethlehem, and see this thing which is come to pass, which the Lord has made known to us.
[16] And they came with haste, and found Mary, and Joseph, and the babe lying in a manger.
[17] And when they had seen it, they made known abroad the saying which was told them concerning this child.
[18] And all they that heard it wondered at those things which were told them by the shepherds.
[19] But Mary kept all these things, and pondered them in her heart.
[20] And the shepherds returned, glorifying and praising God for all the things that they had heard and seen, as it was told to them.
[21] And when eight days were accomplished for the circumcising of the child, his name was called JESUS, which was so named of the angel before he was conceived in the womb.
[22] And when the days of her purification according to the law of Moses were accomplished, they brought him to Jerusalem, to present him to the Lord;
[23] (As it is written in the law of the Lord, Every male that opens the womb shall be called holy to the Lord;)
[24] And to offer a sacrifice according to that which is said in the law of the Lord, A pair of turtledoves, or two young pigeons.
[25] And, behold, there was a man in Jerusalem, whose name was Simeon; and the same man was just and devout, waiting for the consolation of Israel: and the Holy Ghost was upon him.
[26] And it was revealed to him by the Holy Ghost, that he should not see death, before he had seen the Lord's Christ.
[27] And he came by the Spirit into the temple: and when the parents brought in the child Jesus, to do for him after the custom of the law,

[28] Then took he him up in his arms, and blessed God, and said,
[29] Lord, now let you your servant depart in peace, according to your word:
[30] For my eyes have seen your salvation,
[31] Which you have prepared before the face of all people;
[32] A light to lighten the Gentiles, and the glory of your people Israel.
[33] And Joseph and his mother marveled at those things which were spoken of him.
[34] And Simeon blessed them, and said to Mary his mother, Behold, this child is set for the fall and rising again of many in Israel; and for a sign which shall be spoken against;
[35] (Yea, a sword shall pierce through your own soul also,) that the thoughts of many hearts may be revealed.
[36] And there was one Anna, a prophetess, the daughter of Phanuel, of the tribe of Aser: she was of a great age, and had lived with a husband seven years from her virginity;
[37] And she was a widow of about fourscore and four years, which departed not from the temple, but served God with fastings and prayers night and day.
[38] And she coming in that instant gave thanks likewise to the Lord, and spoke of him to all them that looked for redemption in Jerusalem.
[39] And when they had performed all things according to the law of the Lord, they returned into Galilee, to their own city Nazareth.
[40] And the child grew, and grew strong in spirit, filled with wisdom: and the grace of God was upon him.
[41] Now his parents went to Jerusalem every year at the feast of the Passover.

His Infancy – Continued

Jesus is born

And Joseph was very afraid and ceased from speaking to her, left her alone, and pondered what he should do with her. And Joseph said: If I hide her sin, I shall be found fighting against the law of the Lord: and if I manifest her to the children of Israel, I fear lest that which is in her be the offspring of an angel, and I shall be found delivering up innocent blood to the judgment of death. What then shall I do? I will let her go from me privately. And the night came upon him. And behold an angel of the Lord appeared to him in a dream, saying: Fear not this child, for that which is in her is of the Holy Ghost, and she shall bear a son and you shall call his name Jesus, for he shall save his people from their sins. And Joseph arose from sleep and glorified the God of Israel which had shown this favor to her: and he watched over her.

Now Annas the scribe came to him and said to him: Why did you not appear in our assembly? And Joseph said to him: I was weary with the journey, and I rested the first day. And Annas turned him about and saw Mary great with child. And he went hastily to the priest and said to him: Joseph, to whom you bear witness that he is righteous has sinned grievously. And the priest said: Wherein? And he said: The virgin whom he received out of the temple of the Lord, he has defiled her, and married her in secret marriage, and has not declared it to the children of Israel. (Stolen her – The act of sex is marriage.) And the priest answered and said: Has Joseph done this? And Annas the scribe said: Send officers, and you shall find the virgin great with child. And the officers went and found as he had said, and they brought her together with Joseph to the place of judgment. And the priest said: Mary, wherefore have you done this, and wherefore have you humbled your soul and forgotten the Lord your God, you that were nurtured in the Holy of Holies and did receive food at the hand of an angel and did hear the hymns and did dance before the Lord, wherefore have you done this?

But she wept bitterly, saying: As the Lord my God lives I am pure before him and I know not a man. And the priest said to Joseph: Why have you done this? And Joseph said: As the Lord my God lives I am pure as concerning her. And the priest said: Bear no false witness but speak the truth: you have married her by stealth and have not declared it to the children of Israel, and have not bowed your head under the mighty hand that your offspring should be blessed. And Joseph held his peace.

And the priest said: Restore the virgin whom you did receive out of the temple of the Lord. And Joseph was full of weeping. And the priest said: I will give you to drink of the water of the conviction of the Lord, and it will make manifest your sins before your eyes. And the priest took thereof and made Joseph drink and sent him into the hill-country. And he returned whole. He made Mary also drink and sent her into the hill-country. And she returned whole. And all the people were astonished, because sin appeared not in them. And the priest said: If the Lord God has not made your sin manifest, neither do I condemn you. And he let them go. And Joseph took Mary and departed to his house rejoicing, and glorifying the God of Israel.

In the three hundred and ninth year of the era of Alexander, Augustus put forth an edict, that every man should be enrolled in his native place. Joseph therefore arose, and taking Mary his spouse, went away to Jerusalem, and came to Bethlehem, to be enrolled along with his family in his native city.

And he saddled the she-ass, and set her upon it, and his son led it and Joseph followed after. And they drew near to Bethlehem within three miles: and Joseph turned himself about and saw her of a sad countenance and said within himself: Peradventure that which is within her pains her. And again Joseph turned himself about and saw her laughing, and said to her: Mary, what ails you that I see your face at one time laughing and at another time sad? And Mary said to Joseph: It is because I behold two peoples with my eyes, the one weeping and lamenting and the other rejoicing and exulting.

And they came to the midst of the way, and Mary said to him: Take me down from the ass, for that which is within me presses me, to come forth. And he took her down from the ass and said to her:

Where shall I take you to hide your shame? For the place is desert.

And having come to a cave, Mary told Joseph that the time of the birth was at hand, and that she could not go into the city; but, said she, let us go into this cave. This took place at sunset. And he found a cave there and brought her into it, and set his sons by her: and he went forth and sought for a midwife of the Hebrews in the country of Bethlehem. And Joseph went out in haste to go for a woman to be near her. When, therefore, he was busy about that, he saw an old Hebrew woman belonging to Jerusalem, and said: Come here my good woman, and go into this cave, in which there is a woman near her time.

And behold a woman coming down from the hill-country, and she said to me: Man, where go you? And I said: I seek a midwife of the Hebrews. And she answered and said to me: Are you of Israel? And I said to her: Yea. And she said: And who is she that brings forth in the cave? And I said: She that is betrothed to me. And she said to me: Is she not your wife? And I said to her: It is Mary that was nurtured up in the temple of the Lord: and I received her to wife by lot: and she is not my wife, but she has conception by the Holy Ghost.

And the midwife said to him: Is this the truth? And Joseph said to her: Come here and see. And the midwife went with him.

Therefore, after sunset, the old woman, and Joseph with her, came to the cave, and they both went in. And, behold, it was filled with lights more beautiful than the gleaming of lamps and candles, and more splendid than the light of the sun. The child, enwrapped in swaddling clothes, was sucking the breast of the Lady Mary, His mother, being placed in a stall. And when both were wondering at this light, the old woman asks the Lady Mary: Are you the mother of this Child? And when the Lady Mary gave her assent, she said: You are not at all like the daughters of Eve. The Lady Mary said: As my son has no equal among children, so his mother has no equal among women. The old woman replied: My mistress, I came to get payment; I have been for a long time affected with palsy. Our mistress the Lady Mary said to her: Place your hands upon the child. And the old woman did so, and was immediately cured. Then she went forth, saying: Henceforth I will be the attendant and servant of this child all the days of my life.

Then came shepherds; and when they had lighted a fire, and were rejoicing greatly, there appeared to them the hosts of heaven praising and celebrating God Most High. And while the shepherds were doing the same, the cave was at that time made like a temple of the upper world, since both heavenly and earthly voices glorified and magnified God on account of the birth of the Lord Christ. And when that old Hebrew woman saw the manifestation of those miracles, she thanked God, saying: I give You thanks, O God, the God of Israel, because my eyes have seen the birth of the Savior of the world.

And the time of circumcision on the eighth day was at hand, the child was to be circumcised according to the law. Therefore they circumcised Him in the cave. And the old Hebrew woman took the piece of skin; but some say that she took the navel-string, and laid it in a jar of old oil of nard. And she had a son, a dealer in unguents, and she gave it to him, saying: See that you do not sell this jar of ointment of nard (Himalayan spikenard), even although three hundred denarii should be offered you for it. And this is that jar which Mary the sinner bought and poured upon the head and feet of our Lord Jesus Christ, which thereafter she wiped with the hair of her head. Ten days after, they took Him to Jerusalem; and on the fortieth day after His birth they carried Him into the temple, and set Him before the Lord, and offered sacrifices for Him, according to the commandment of the law of Moses, which is: Every male that opens the womb shall be called the holy of God.

Then old Simeon saw Him shining like a pillar of light, when the Lady Mary, His virgin mother, rejoicing over Him, was carrying Him in her arms. And angels, praising Him, stood round Him in a circle, like lifeguards standing by a king. Simeon therefore went up in haste to the Lady Mary, and, with hands stretched out before her, said to the Lord Christ: Now, O my Lord, let Your servant depart in peace, according to Your word; for my eyes have seen Your compassion, which You have prepared for the salvation of all peoples, a light to all nations, and glory to Your people Israel. Hanna also, a prophetess, was present, and came up, giving thanks to God, and calling the Lady Mary blessed.

And it came to pass, when the Lord Jesus was born at Bethlehem of Judaea, in the time of King Herod, behold, magi came from the east to Jerusalem, as Zeraduscht (Zarathustra / Zoroaster) had predicted; and there were with them gifts of gold, frankincense, and myrrh. And they adored Him, and presented to Him their gifts. Then the Lady Mary took one of the swaddling-bands, and, on account of the smallness of her means, gave it to them; and they received it from her with the greatest marks of honor. And in the same hour there appeared to them an angel in the form of that star which had before guided them on their journey; and they went away, following the guidance of its light, until they arrived in their own country.

And their kings and chief men came together to them, asking what they had seen or done, how they had gone and come back, what they had brought with them. And they showed them that swathing-cloth which the Lady Mary had given them. Then they celebrated a feast, and, according to their custom, lighted a fire and worshipped it, and threw that swathing-cloth into it; and the fire laid hold of it, and enveloped it. And when the fire had gone out, they took out the swathing-cloth exactly as it had been before, just as if the fire had not touched it. Then they began to kiss it, and to put it on their heads and their eyes, saying: This truly is the truth without doubt. Assuredly it is a great thing that the fire was not able to burn or destroy it. Then they took it, and with the greatest honor laid it up among their treasures.

Now I, Joseph was walking, and I walked not. And I looked up to the air and saw the air in amazement. And I looked up to the pole of the heaven and saw it standing still, and the fowls of the heaven without motion. And I looked upon the earth and saw a dish set, and workmen lying by it, and their hands were in the dish: and they that were chewing chewed not, and they that were lifting the food lifted it not, and they that put it to their mouth put it not thereto, but the faces of all of them were looking upward. And behold there were sheep being driven, and they went not forward but stood still; and the shepherd lifted his hand to strike them with his staff, and his hand remained up. And I looked upon the stream of the river and saw the mouths of the kids upon the water and they drank not. And of a sudden all things moved onward in their course.

And they stood in the place of the cave: and behold a bright cloud overshadowing the cave. And the midwife said: My soul is magnified this day, because my eyes have seen marvelous things: for salvation is born to Israel. And immediately the cloud withdrew itself out of the cave, and a great light appeared in the cave so that our eyes could not endure it. And by little and little that light withdrew itself until the young child appeared: and it went and took the breast of its mother Mary.

And the midwife cried aloud and said: Great to me today is this day, in that I have seen this new sight. And the midwife went forth of the cave and Salome met her. And she said to her: Salome, Salome, a new sight have I to tell you. A virgin has brought forth, which her nature allows not. And Salome said: As the Lord my God lives, if I make not trial and prove her nature I will not believe that a virgin has brought forth.

And the midwife went in and said to Mary: Prepare yourself, for there is no small contention arisen concerning you. And Salome made trial and cried out and said: Woe to my iniquity and my unbelief, because I have tempted the living God, and lo, my hand falls away from me in fire. And she bowed her knees to the Lord, saying: O God of my fathers, remember that I am the offspring of Abraham and Isaac and Jacob: make me not a public example to the children of Israel, but restore me to the poor, for you know, Lord, that in your name did I perform my cures, and did receive my hire of you. And lo, an angel of the Lord appeared, saying to her: Salome, Salome, the Lord has listened to you: bring your hand near to the young child and take him up, and there shall be to you salvation and joy. And Salome came near and took him up, saying: I will do him worship, for a great king is born to Israel. And behold immediately Salome was healed: and she went forth of the cave justified. And lo, a voice saying: Salome, Salome, tell none of the marvels which you have seen, until the child enter into Jerusalem.

And the time of circumcision, that is, the eighth day, being at hand, the child was to be circumcised according to the law. Therefore they circumcised Him in the cave. And the old Hebrew woman took the piece of skin; but some say that she took the navel-string, and laid it in a jar of old oil of nard. And she had a son, a dealer in unguents, and she gave it to him, saying: See that you do not sell this jar of unguent of nard, even although three hundred denarii should be offered you for it. And this is that jar which Mary the sinner bought and poured upon the head and feet of our Lord Jesus Christ, which thereafter she wiped with the hair of her head. Ten days after, they took Him to Jerusalem; and on the fortieth day after His birth they carried Him into the temple, and set Him before the Lord, and offered sacrifices for Him, according to the command, which is the law of Moses, which is: Every male that opens the womb shall be called the holy of God.

Then old Simeon saw Him shining like a pillar of light, when the Lady Mary, His virgin mother, rejoicing over Him, was carrying Him in her arms. And angels, praising Him, stood round Him in a circle, like guards standing by a king, protecting his life. Simeon therefore went up in haste to the Lady Mary, and, with hands stretched out before her, said to the Lord Christ: Now, O my Lord, let Your servant depart in peace, according to Your word; for my eyes have seen Your compassion, which You have prepared for the salvation of all peoples, a light to all nations, and glory to Your people Israel. Hanna also, a prophetess, was present, and came up, giving thanks to God, and calling the Lady Mary blessed.

And behold, Joseph made him ready to go forth into Judaea. And there came a great tumult in Bethlehem of Judaea; for there came wise men, saying: Where is he that is born king of the Jews? For we have seen his star in the east and are come to worship him. And when Herod heard it he was troubled and sent officers to the wise men. And he sent for the high priests and questioned them, saying: How is it written concerning the Christ, where he is born? They say to him: In Bethlehem of Judaea: for so it is written. And he let them go. And he questioned the wise men, saying to them: What sign saw you concerning the king that is born? And the wise men said: We saw a very great star shining among those stars and dimming them so that the stars appeared not: and thereby knew we that a king was born to Israel, and we came to worship him. And Herod said: Go and seek for him, and if you find him, tell me, that I also may come and worship him. And the wise men went forth. And lo, the star which they saw in the east went before them until they entered into the cave: and it stood over the head of the cave. And the wise men saw the young child with Mary, his mother: and they brought out of their purse-bag gifts, gold-and frankincense and myrrh. And being warned by the angel that they should not enter into Judaea, they went into their own country by another way.

But when Herod perceived that he was mocked by the wise men, he was angry, and sent murderers, saying to them: Slay the children from two years old and under. And when Mary heard that the children were being slain, she was afraid, and took the young child and wrapped in swaddling clothes and laid him in an ox-manger.

But Elizabeth when she heard that they sought for John, took him and went up into the hill-country and looked about her where she should hide him: and there was no hiding-place. And Elizabeth groaned and said with a loud voice: mountain of God, receive you a mother with a child. For Elizabeth was not able to go up. And immediately the mountain split apart and took her in. And there was a light shining always for them: for an angel of the Lord was with them, keeping watch over them.

Now Herod sought for John, and sent officers to Zacharias, saying: Where have you hidden your son? And he answered and said to them: I am a minister of God and attend continually upon the temple of the Lord: I know not where my son is. And the officers departed and told Herod all these things. And Herod was angry and said: His son is to be king over Israel. And he sent to him again, saying: Say the truth: where is your son? For you know that your blood is under my hand. And the officers departed and told him all these things. And Zacharias said: I am a martyr of God if you shed my blood: for my spirit the Lord shall receive, because you shed innocent blood in the fore-court of the temple of the Lord.

And about the dawning of the day Zacharias was slain. And the children of Israel knew not that he was slain. But the priests entered in at the hour of the salutation, and the blessing of Zacharias met them not according to the manner. And the priests stood waiting for Zacharias, to salute him with the prayer, and to glorify the Most High. But as he delayed to come, they were all afraid: and one of them took courage and entered in: and he saw beside the altar congealed blood: and a voice saying: Zacharias has been slain, and his blood shall not be wiped out until his avenger come. And when he heard that word he was afraid, and went forth and told the priests. And they took courage and went in and saw that which was done: and the panels of the temple did wail: and they rent their clothes from the top to the bottom. And his body they found not, but his blood they found turned into stone. And they feared, and went forth and told all the people that Zacharias was slain. And all the tribes of the people heard it, and they mourned for him and lamented him three days and three nights. And after the three days the priests took counsel whom they should set in his place: and the lot came upon Symeon. Now he it was which was warned by the Holy Ghost that he should not see death until he should see the Christ in the flesh.

While all of this was transpiring, Joseph was reflecting on how best to set about his journey, morning came upon him after he had gone a very little way. And now he was approaching a great city, in which there was an idol, to which the other idols and gods of the Egyptians offered gifts and vows. And there stood before this idol a priest ministering to him, who, as often as Satan spoke from that idol, reported it to the inhabitants of Egypt and its territories. This priest had a son, three years old, beset by several demons; and he made many speeches and utterances; and when the demons seized him, he tore his clothes, and remained naked, and threw stones at the people. And there was a place of healing in that city dedicated to that idol. And when Joseph and the Lady Mary had come to the city, and had turned aside into that place of healing, the citizens were very much afraid; and all the chief men and the priests of the idols came together to that idol, and said to it: What agitation and commotion is this that has arisen in our land? The idol answered them: A God has come here in secret, who is God indeed; nor is any god besides Him worthy of divine worship, because He is truly the Son of God. And when this land became aware of His presence, it trembled at His arrival, and was moved and shaken; and we are exceedingly afraid from the greatness of His power. And in the same hour that idol fell down, and at its fall, all inhabitants of Egypt and others, ran together.

And the son of the priest, his usual disease having come upon him, entered the place of healing, and there he came upon Joseph and the

Lady Mary, from whom all others had fled. The Lady Mary had washed the cloths of the Lord Christ, and had spread them over some wood. That demoniac boy, therefore, came and took one of the cloths, and put it on his head. Then the demons, fleeing in the shape of ravens and serpents, began to go forth out of his mouth. The boy, being immediately healed at the command of the Lord Christ, began to praise God, and then to give thanks to the Lord who had healed him. And when his father saw him restored to health, My son, said he, what has happened to you? And by what means have you been healed? The son answered: When the demons had thrown me on the ground, I went into the place of healing, and there I found a respected woman with a boy, whose newly-washed cloths she had thrown on some wood: one of these I took up and put on my head, and the demons left me and fled. At this the father rejoiced greatly, and said: My son, it is possible that this boy is the Son of the living God who created the heavens and the earth: for when he came over to us, the idol was broken, and all the gods fell, and perished by the power of his magnificence.

Here was fulfilled the prophecy which says, Out of Egypt have I called my Son. Joseph indeed, and Mary, when they heard that that idol had fallen down and perished, trembled, and were afraid. Then they said: When we were in the land of Israel, Herod thought to put Jesus to death, and on that account slew all the children of Bethlehem and its confines; and there is no doubt that the Egyptians, as soon as they have heard that this idol has been broken, will burn us with fire.

Going out from there, they came to a place where there were robbers who had plundered several men of their baggage and clothes, and had bound them. Then the robbers heard a great noise, like the noise of a magnificent king going out of his city with his army, and his chariots and his drums; and at this the robbers were terrified, and left all their plunder. And their captives rose up, loosed each other's bonds, recovered their baggage, and went away. And when they saw Joseph and Mary coming up to the place, they said to them: Where is that king, at the hearing of the magnificent sound of whose approach the robbers have left us, so that we have escaped safe? Joseph answered them: He will come behind us.

Thereafter they came into another city, where there was a demoniac woman whom Satan, accursed and rebellious, had beset, when on one occasion she had gone out by night for water. She could neither bear clothes, nor live in a house; and as often as they tied her up with chains and leather straps, she broke them, and fled naked into waste places; and, standing in cross-roads and cemeteries, she kept throwing stones at people, and brought very heavy calamities upon her friends. And when the Lady Mary saw her, she pitied her; and upon this Satan immediately left her, and fled away in the form of a young man, saying: Woe to me from you, Mary, and from your son. So that woman was cured of her torment, and being restored to her senses, she blushed on account of her nakedness; and shunning the sight of men, went home to her friends. And after she put on her clothes, she gave an account of the matter to her father and her friends; and as they were the chief men of the city, they received the Lady Mary and Joseph with the greatest honor and hospitality.

On the day after, being supplied by them with provision for their journey, they went away, and on the evening of that day arrived at another town, in which they were celebrating a marriage; but, by the arts of accursed Satan and the work of enchanters, the bride had become dumb, and could not speak a word. And after the Lady Mary entered the town, carrying her son the Lord Christ, that dumb bride saw her, and stretched out her hands towards the Lord Christ, and drew Him to her, and took Him into her arms, and held Him close and kissed Him, and leaned over Him, moving His body back and forwards. Immediately the knot of her tongue was loosened, and her ears were opened; and she gave thanks and praise to God, because He had restored her to health. And that night the inhabitants of that town exulted with joy, and thought that God and His angels had come down to them.

There they remained three days, being held in great honor, and living splendidly. Thereafter, being supplied by them with provision for their journey, they went away and came to another city, in which, because it was very populous, they thought of passing the night. And there was in that city an excellent woman: and once, when she had gone to the river to bathe, lo, accursed Satan, in the form of a serpent, had leapt upon her, and twisted himself round her belly; and as often as night came on, he tyrannically tormented her. This woman, seeing the mistress, the Lady Mary, and the child, the Lord Christ, in her bosom, was struck with a longing for Him, and said to the mistress, the Lady Mary: O mistress, give me this child, that I may carry him, and kiss him. She therefore gave Him to the woman; and when He was brought to her, Satan let her go, and fled and left her, nor did the woman ever see him after that day. Then all who were present praised God Most High, and that woman bestowed on them liberal gifts

On the day after, the same woman took scented water to wash the Lord Jesus; and after she had washed Him, she took the water with which she had done it, and poured part of it on a girl who was living there, whose body was white with leprosy, and washed her with it. And as soon as this was done, the girl was cleansed from her leprosy. And the towns-people said: There is no doubt that Joseph and Mary and that boy are gods, not men. And when they were getting ready to go away from them, the girl who had labored under the leprosy came up to them, and asked them to let her go with them.

When they had given her permission, she went with them. And afterwards they came to a city, in which was the castle of a most illustrious prince, who kept a house for the entertainment of strangers. They turned into this place; and the girl went away to the prince's wife; and she found her weeping and sorrowful, and she asked why she was weeping. Do not be surprised, said she, at my tears; for I am overwhelmed by a great affliction, which as yet I have not endured to tell to any one. Perhaps, said the girl, if you reveal it and disclose it to me, I may have a remedy for it. Hide this secret, then, replied the princess, and tell it to no one. I was married to this prince, who is a king and ruler over many cities, and I lived long with him, but by me he had no son. And when at length I produced him a son, he was leprous; and as soon as he saw him, he turned away with loathing, and said to me: Either kill him, or give him to the nurse to be brought up in some place from which we shall never hear of him more. After this I can have nothing to do with you, and I will never see you more. On this account I know not what to do, and I am overwhelmed with grief. Alas! my son. Alas! my husband. Did I not say so? said the girl. I have found a cure for your disease, and I shall tell it you. For I too was a leper; but I was cleansed by God, who is Jesus, the son of the Lady Mary. And the woman asking her where this God was whom she had spoken of, Here, with you, said the girl;

He is living in the same house. But how is this possible? said she. Where is he? There, said the girl, are Joseph and Mary; and the child who is with them is called Jesus; and He it is who cured me of my disease and my torment. But by what means, said she, were you cured of your leprosy? Will you not tell me that? Why not? said the girl. I got from His mother the water in which He had been washed, and poured it over myself; and so I was cleansed from my leprosy. Then the princess rose up, and invited them to avail themselves of her hospitality. And she prepared a splendid banquet for Joseph in a great assembly of the men of the place. And on the following day she took scented water with which to wash the Lord Jesus, and thereafter poured the same water over her son, whom she had taken with her; and immediately her son was cleansed from his leprosy. Therefore, singing thanks and praises to God, she said: Blessed is the mother who bore you, O Jesus; do you so cleanse those who share the same nature with you with the water in which your body has been washed? Besides, she bestowed great gifts upon the mistress, the Lady Mary, and sent her away with great honor.

Coming thereafter to another city, they wished to spend the night in it. They turned aside, therefore, to the house of a man newly married, but who, under the influence of witchcraft, was not able to enjoy his wife; and when they had spent that night with him, his bond was loosed. And at daybreak, when they were girding themselves for their journey, the bridegroom would not let them go, and prepared for them a great banquet.

They set out, therefore, on the following day; and as they came near another city, they saw three women weeping as they came out of a cemetery. And when the Lady Mary beheld them, she said to the girl who accompanied her: Ask them what is the matter with them, or what calamity has befallen them. And to the girl's questions they made no reply, but asked in their turn: From where are you, and where are you going? For the day is already past, and night is coming on quickly. We are travelers, said the girl, and are seeking a house of entertainment in which we may pass the night. They said: Go with us, and spend the night with us. They followed them, therefore, and were brought into a new house with splendid decorations and furniture. Now it was winter; and the girl, going into the chamber of these women, found them again weeping and lamenting. There stood beside them a mule, covered with housings of cloth of gold, and sesame was put before him; and the women were kissing him, and giving him food. And the girl said: What is all the ado, my ladies, about this mule? They answered her with tears, and said: This mule, which you see, was our brother, born of the same mother with ourselves. And when our father died, and left us great wealth, and this only brother, we did our best to get him married, and were preparing his nuptials for him, after the manner of men. But some women, moved by mutual jealousy, bewitched him unknown to us; and one night, a little before daybreak, when the door of our house was shut, we saw that this our brother had been turned into a mule, as you now behold him. And we are sorrowful, as you see, having no father to comfort us: there is no wise man, or magician, or enchanter in the world that we have omitted to send for; but nothing has done us any good. And as often as our hearts are overwhelmed with grief, we rise and go away with our mother here, and weep at our father's grave, and come back again.

And when the girl heard these things, Be of good courage, said she, and weep not: for the cure of your calamity is near; yea, it is beside you, and in the middle of your own house. For I also was a leper; but when I saw that woman, and along with her that young child, whose name is Jesus, I sprinkled my body with the water with which His mother had washed Him, and I was cured. And I know that He can cure your affliction also. But rise, go to Mary my mistress; bring her into your house, and tell her your secret; and entreat and supplicate her to have pity on you. After the women had heard the girl's words, they went in haste to the Lady Mary, and brought her into their chamber, and sat down before her weeping, and saying: O our mistress, Lady Mary, have pity on your hand-maidens; for no one older than ourselves, and no head of the family, is left, neither father nor brother, to live with us; but this mule which you see was our brother, and women have made him such as you see by witchcraft. We beg you, therefore, to have pity on us. Then, grieving at their lot, the Lady Mary took up the Lord Jesus, and put Him on the mule's back; and she wept as well as the women, and said to Jesus Christ: Alas! my son, heal this mule by Your mighty power, and make him a man endowed with reason as he was before. And when these words were uttered by the Lady Mary, his form was changed, and the mule became a young man, free from every defect. Then he and his mother and his sisters adored the Lady Mary, and lifted the boy above their heads, and began to kiss Him, saying: Blessed is she that bore You, O Jesus, O Savior of the world; blessed are the eyes which enjoy the felicity of seeing You.

Moreover, both the sisters said to their mother: Our brother indeed, by the aid of the Lord Jesus Christ, and by the salutary intervention of this girl, who pointed out to us Mary and her son, has been raised to human form. Now, indeed, since our brother is unmarried, it would do very well for us to give him as his wife this girl, their servant. And having asked the Lady Mary, and obtained her consent, they made a splendid wedding for the girl; and their sorrow being changed into joy, and the beating of their breasts into dancing, they began to be glad, to rejoice, to exult, and sing, adorned, on account of their great joy, in most splendid and gorgeous attire. Then they began to recite songs and praises, and to say: O Jesus, son of David, who turn sorrows into gladness, and lamentations into joy! And Joseph and Mary remained there ten days. Thereafter they set out, treated with great honors by these people, who bade them farewell, and from bidding them farewell returned weeping, especially the girl.

And turning away from this place, they came to a desert; and hearing that it was infested with robbers, Joseph and the Lady Mary resolved to cross this region by night. But as they go along, behold, they see two robbers lying in the way, and along with them a great number of robbers, who were their associates, sleeping. Now those two robbers, into whose hands they had fallen, were Titus and Dumachus. Titus therefore said to Dumachus: I beg you to let these persons go freely, and so that our comrades may not see them. And as Dumachus refused, Titus said to him again: Take to yourself forty drachmas from me, and hold this as a pledge. At the same time he held out to him the belt which he had about his waist, to keep him from opening his mouth or speaking. And the Lady Mary, seeing that the robber had done them a kindness, said to him: The Lord God will sustain you by His right hand, and will grant you remission of your sins. And the Lord Jesus answered, and said to His mother: Thirty years from now, O my mother, the Jews will crucify me at Jerusalem, and these two robbers will be raised upon the cross along with me, Titus on my right hand and Dumachus on my left; and after that day Titus shall go before me into Paradise. And she said: God keep this from you, my son. And they went from there towards a city of idols, which, as they came near it, was changed into sand-hills.

Then they turned aside to that sycamore which is now called Matarea, and the Lord Jesus brought forth in Matarea a fountain in which the Lady Mary washed His shirt. And from the sweat of the Lord Jesus which she sprinkled there, balsam was produced in that region.

From there they came down to Memphis, and saw Pharaoh, and remained three years in Egypt; and the Lord Jesus did in Egypt very many miracles which are recorded neither in the Gospel of the Infancy nor in the perfect Gospel.

And as Jesus walked with Mary his mother through the midst of the marketplace of the city, he looked about and saw a master teaching his pupils. And behold twelve sparrows which were quarrelling one with another fell from the wall into the lap of the master who taught the boys. And when Jesus saw it he laughed and stood still. Now when that teacher saw him laughing, he said to his pupils in great anger: Go, bring him here to me. And when they had brought him, the master took hold on his ear and said: What saw you that you did laugh? And he said to him: Master, see, my hand is full of corn, and I showed it to them, and scattered the corn, which they are carrying away in danger: for this cause they fought with one another that they might partake of the corn. And Jesus left not the place until it was accomplished. And for this cause the master labored to cast him out of the city together with his mother.

(Other sources have a slightly different sequence of events and read as follows:

And behold, an angel of the Lord met with Mary and said to her: Take the child and return into the land of the Jews: for they are dead which sought his life. So Mary arose with Jesus, and they went into the city Nazareth, which is in the inheritance of her father. But when Joseph departed out of Egypt after the death of Herod, he took Jesus into the wilderness until there was quiet in Jerusalem from them that sought the life of the child. And he gave thanks to God for that he had given him understanding, and because he had found grace before the Lord God. Amen.)

And at the end of the three years He came back out of Egypt, and returned. And when they had arrived at Judaea, Joseph was afraid to enter it; but hearing that Herod was dead, and that Archelaus his son had succeeded him, he was afraid indeed, but he went into Judaea. And an angel of the Lord appeared to him, and said: O Joseph, go into the city of Nazareth, and there abide. Wonderful indeed, that the Lord of the world should be thus borne and carried about through the world!

And Mary arose with Jesus, and they went to the city of Capernaum which is of Tiberias, to the inheritance of her father. After these things an angel of the Lord came to Joseph and to Mary the mother of Jesus and said to them: Take the child, return into the land of Israel, for they are dead that sought the life of the child. And they arose and went to Nazareth where Joseph possessed the goods of his father.

Thereafter, going into the city of Bethlehem, they saw there many and grievous diseases infesting the eyes of the children, who were dying in consequence. And a woman was there with a sick son, whom, now very near death, she brought to the Lady Mary, who saw him as she was washing Jesus Christ. Then said the woman to her: O my Lady Mary, look on this son of mine, who is laboring under a grievous disease. And the Lady Mary listened to her, and said: Take a little of that water in which I have washed my son, and sprinkle him with it. She therefore took a little of the water, as the Lady Mary had told her, and sprinkled it over her son. And when this was done his illness abated; and after sleeping a little, he rose up from sleep safe and sound. His mother rejoicing at this, again took him to the Lady Mary. And she said to her: Give thanks to God, because He has healed this your son.

Now when Jesus was five years old there was a great rain on the earth, and the child Jesus walked about therein. And the rain was very terrible: and he gathered the water together into a pool and commanded with a word that it should become clear: and forthwith it did so.

Again, he took of the clay, which came of that pool and made thereof to the number of twelve sparrows. Now it was the Sabbath day when Jesus did this among the children of the Hebrews: and the children of the Hebrews went and said to Joseph his father: Lo, your son was playing with us and he took clay and made sparrows which it was not right to do on the Sabbath, and he has broken it. And Joseph went to the child Jesus, and said to him: Why have you done this which it was not right to do on the Sabbath? But Jesus spread forth and opened his hands and commanded the sparrows, saying: Go forth into the height and fly: you shall not meet death at any man's hands. And they flew and began to cry out and praise almighty God. But when the Jews saw what was done they were astonished and departed, proclaiming the signs which Jesus did.

But a Pharisee which was with Jesus took a branch of an olive tree and began to empty the pool which Jesus had made. And when Jesus saw it he was vexed and said to him: O you of Sodom, ungodly and ignorant, what hurt did the fountain of water do you, which I made? Lo, you shall become like a dry tree which has neither roots nor leaf nor fruit. And straightway he was dried up and fell to the earth and died: but his parents carried him away dead and reviled Joseph, saying: Behold what your son has done: teach him to pray and not to blaspheme.

There was in the same place another woman, a neighbor of her whose son had lately been restored to health. And as her son was laboring under the same disease, and his eyes were now almost blinded, she wept night and day. And the mother of the child that had been cured said to her: Why do you not take your son to the Lady Mary, as I did with mine when he was nearly dead? And he got well with that water with which the body of her son Jesus had been washed. And when the woman heard this from her, she too went and got some of the same water, and washed her son with it, and his body and his eyes were instantly made well. When she had brought her son to Mary, and disclosed to her all that had happened, the Lady Mary ordered to give thanks to God for her son's restoration to health, and to tell nobody of this matter.

There were in the same city two women, wives of one man, each having a son ill with fever. The one was called Mary, and her son's name was Cleopas. She rose and took up her son, and went to the Lady Mary, the mother of Jesus, and offering her a beautiful scarf, said: O my Lady Mary, accept this scarf, and for it give me one small bandage. Mary did so, and the mother of Cleopas went away, and made a shirt of it, and put it on her son. So he was cured of his disease; but the son of her rival died. Then there sprung up hatred between them; and as they did the house-work each week, and as it was the turn of Mary the mother of Cleopas, she heated the oven to bake bread; and going away to bring the lump that she had kneaded, she left her son Cleopas beside the oven. Her rival seeing, him alone and the oven was very hot with the fire blazing under it, seized him and threw him into the oven, and ran off. Mary coming back, and seeing her son Cleopas lying in the oven laughing, and the oven quite cold, as if no fire had ever come near it, knew that her rival had thrown him into the fire. She drew him out, therefore, and took him to the Lady Mary, and told her of what had happened to him. And she said: Keep silence, and tell nobody of the affair; for I am afraid for you if you divulge it. After this her rival went to the well to draw water; and seeing Cleopas playing beside the well, and nobody near, she seized him and threw him into the well, and went home herself. And some men who had gone to the well for water saw the boy sitting on the surface of the water; and so they went down and drew him out. And they were seized with a great admiration of that boy, and praised God. Then came his mother, and took him up, and went weeping to the Lady Mary, and said: O my lady, see what my rival has done to my son, and how she has thrown him into the well; she will be sure to destroy him some day or other. The Lady Mary said to her: God will avenge you on her. Thereafter, when her rival went to the well to draw water, her feet got entangled in the rope, and she fell into the well. Some men came to draw her out, but they found her skull fractured and her bones broken. Thus she died a miserable death, and in her came to pass that saying: They have dug a well deep, but have fallen into the pit which they had prepared.

Another woman there had twin sons who had fallen into disease, and one of them died, and the other was at his last breath. And his mother, weeping, lifted him up, and took him to the Lady Mary, and said: O my lady, aid me and comfort me. For I had two sons, and I have just buried the one, and the other is at the point of death. See how I am going to entreat and pray to God. And she began to say: O

Lord, You are compassionate, and merciful, and full of affection. You gave me two sons, of whom You have taken away the one: this one at least leave to me. Then the Lady Mary, seeing the fervor of her weeping, had compassion on her, and said: Put your son in my son's bed, and cover him with his clothes. And when she had put him in the bed in which Christ was lying, he had already closed his eyes in death; but as soon as the smell of the clothes of the Lord Jesus Christ reached the boy, he opened his eyes, and, calling on his mother with a loud voice, he asked for bread, and took it and sucked it. Then his mother said: O Lady Mary, now I know that the power of God dwells in you, so that your son heals those that partake of the same nature with himself, as soon as they have touched his clothes. This boy that was healed is he who in the Gospel is called Bartholomew.

Moreover, there was there a leprous woman, and she went to the Lady Mary, the mother of Jesus, and said: My lady, help me. And the Lady Mary answered: What help do you seek? Is it gold or silver? or is it that your body be made clean from the leprosy? And that woman asked: Who can grant me this? And the Lady Mary said to her: Wait a little, until I shall have washed my son Jesus, and put him to bed. The woman waited, as Mary had told her; and when she had put Jesus to bed, she held out to the woman the water in which she had washed His body, and said: Take a little of this water, and pour it over your body. And as soon as she had done so, she was cleansed, and gave praise and thanks to God.

Therefore, after staying with her three days, she went away; and coming to a city, saw there one of the chief men, who had married the daughter of another of the chief men. But when he saw the woman, he beheld between her eyes the mark of leprosy in the shape of a star; and so the marriage was dissolved, and became null and void. And when that woman saw them in this condition, weeping and overwhelmed with sorrow, she asked the cause of their grief. But they said: Inquire not into our condition, for to no one living can we tell our grief, and to none but ourselves can we disclose it. She urged them, however, and entreated them to entrust it to her, saying that she would perhaps be able to tell them of a remedy. And when they showed her the girl, and the sign of leprosy which appeared between her eyes, as soon as she saw it, the woman said: I also, whom you see here, labored under the same disease, when, on some business which happened to come in my way, I went to Bethlehem. There going into a cave, I saw a woman named Mary, whose son was he who was named Jesus; and when she saw that I was a leper. She took pity on me, and handed me the water with which she had washed her son's body. With it I sprinkled my body, and came out clean. Then the woman said to her: Will you not, Oh lady, rise and go with us, and show us the Lady Mary? And she assented; and they rose and went to the Lady Mary, carrying with them splendid gifts. And when they had gone in, and presented to her the gifts, they showed her the leprous girl whom they had brought. The Lady Mary therefore said: May the compassion of the Lord Jesus Christ descend upon you; and handing to them also a little of the water in which she had washed the body of Jesus Christ, she ordered the wretched woman to be bathed in it. And when this had been done, she was immediately cured; and they, and all standing by, praised God. Joyfully therefore they returned to their own city, praising the Lord for what He had done. And when the chief heard that his wife had been cured, he took her home, and made a second marriage, and gave thanks to God for the recovery of his wife's health.

There was there also a young woman afflicted by Satan; for that accursed wretch repeatedly appeared to her in the form of a huge dragon, and prepared to swallow her. He also sucked out all her blood, so that she was left like a corpse. As often as he came near her, she, with her hands clasped over her head, cried out, and said: Woe, woe's me, for nobody is near to free me from that accursed dragon. And her father and mother, and all who were about her or saw her, bewailed her lot; and men stood round her in a crowd, and all wept and lamented, especially when she wept, and said: Oh, my brethren and friends, is there no one to free me from that murderer? And the daughter of the chief who had been healed of her leprosy, hearing the girl's voice, went up to the roof of her castle, and saw her with her hands clasped over her head weeping, and all the crowds standing round her weeping as well. She therefore asked the demoniac's husband whether his wife's mother were alive. And when he answered that both her parents were living, she said: Send for her mother to come to me. And when she saw that he had sent for her, and she had come, she said: Is that deranged girl your daughter? Yes, O lady, said that sorrowful and weeping woman, she is my daughter. The chiefs daughter answered: Keep my secret, for I confess to you that I was formerly a leper; but now the Lady Mary, the mother of Jesus Christ, has healed me. But if you wish your daughter to be healed, take her to Bethlehem, and seek Mary the mother of Jesus, and believe that your daughter will be healed; I indeed believe that you will come back with joy, with your daughter healed. As soon as the woman heard the words of the chief's daughter, she led away her daughter in haste; and going to the place indicated, she went to the Lady Mary, and revealed to her the state of her daughter. And the Lady Mary hearing her words, gave her a little of the water in which she had washed the body of her son Jesus, and ordered her to pour it on the body of her daughter. She gave her also from the clothes of the Lord Jesus a swathing-cloth, saying: Take this cloth, and show it to your enemy as often as you shall see him. And she saluted them, and sent them away.

When, therefore, they had gone away from her, and returned to their own district, and the time was at hand at which Satan was wont to attack her, at this very time that accursed one appeared to her in the shape of a huge dragon, and the girl was afraid at the sight of him. And her mother said to her: Fear not, my daughter; allow him to come near you, and then show him the cloth which the Lady Mary has given us, and let us see what will happen. Satan, therefore, having come near in the likeness of a terrible dragon, the body of the girl shuddered for fear of him; but as soon as she took out the cloth, and placed it on her head, and covered her eyes with it, flames and live coals began to dart forth from it, and to be cast upon the dragon. O the great miracle which was done as soon as the dragon saw the cloth of the Lord Jesus, from which the fire darted, and was cast upon his head and eyes! He cried out with a loud voice: What have I to do with you, O Jesus, son of Mary? Where shall I fly from you? And with great fear he turned his back and departed from the girl, and never afterwards appeared to her. And the girl now had rest from him, and gave praise and thanks to God, and along with her all who were present at that miracle.

Another woman was living in the same place, whose son was tormented by Satan. He, Judas by name, as often as Satan seized him, used to bite all who came near him; and if he found no one near him, he used to bite his own hands and other limbs. The mother of this wretched creature, then, hearing the fame of the Lady Mary and her son Jesus, rose up and brought her son Judas with her to the Lady Mary. In the meantime, James and Joses had taken the child the Lord Jesus with them to play with the other children; and they had gone out of the house and sat down, and the Lord Jesus with them. And the demoniac Judas came up, and sat down at Jesus' right hand: then, being attacked by Satan in the same manner as usual, he wished to bite the Lord Jesus, but was not able; nevertheless he struck Jesus on the right side, whereupon He began to weep. And immediately Satan went forth out of that boy, fleeing like a mad dog. And this boy who struck Jesus, and out of whom Satan went forth in the shape of a dog, was Judas Iscariot, who betrayed Him to the Jews; and that same side on which Judas struck Him, the Jews ran him through with a lance.

And after some days as Jesus walked with Joseph through the city, there ran one of the children and smote Jesus on the arms: but Jesus said to him: So finish you your course. And immediately he fell to the earth and died. But they, when they saw this wonder, cried out saying: From where comes this child? And they said to Joseph: It is not right that such a child should be among us. And he departed and took him with him. And they said to him: Depart out of this place; and if you must be with us, teach him to pray and not to blaspheme: for our sons are put to death by him (or lose their senses). And Joseph called Jesus and began to admonish him, saying: Why blaspheme you? They that dwell in this place conceive hatred against us. But Jesus said: I know that these words are not mine but yours: yet for your sake I will hold my peace: But let them see and bear their own foolishness. And straightway they that spoke against Jesus were made blind, and as they walked to and fro they said: Every word that comes out of his mouth has fulfillment. And when Joseph saw what Jesus had done he took hold on him by his ear in anger: but Jesus was vexed and said to Joseph: It suffices you to see me and not to touch me. For you know not who I am, which if you knew, you would not grieve me. And albeit I am with you now, yet was I made before you.

There was therefore a man named Zacheus who heard all that Jesus said to Joseph, and he were astonished in himself and said: I have never beheld such a child that spoke so. And he came near to Joseph and said to him: You have a wise child: deliver him to me to learn letters, and when he is learned in the study of the letters, I will teach him reverently that he become not foolish. Joseph answered and said to him: No man is able to teach him but God only. Think you that this young child will be the occasion to us of little torment, my brother? Think you that he is worthy to receive a little cross?

But when Jesus heard Joseph saying these things, he said to Zacheus: Truly, O master, all things that proceed out of my mouth are true. And I am before all men, and I am Lord, but you are the children of strangers: for to me is given the glory of them or of the worlds but to you nothing is given: for I am before all worlds. And I know how many are the years of your life, and when you shall raise that standard that is the cross whereof my father spoke, then shall you understand that all things that proceed out of my mouth are true.

But the Jews which stood by and heard the words which Jesus spoke, were astonished and said: Now have we seen such wonders and heard such words from this child, as we have never heard neither shall hear from any other man, neither from the chief priests nor the doctors nor the Pharisees. Jesus answered and said to them: Why marvel you? Do you think it a thing incredible that I have told you the truth? I know when you were born, and your fathers: and if I should say more to you, I know when the world was created, and who sent me to you.

When the Jews heard the word which the child spoke, they were angry because they were not able to answer him. And the child turned himself about and rejoiced and said: I spoke to you a proverb; but I know that you are weak and know not anything.

Now that master said to Joseph: Bring him to me and I will teach him letters. And Joseph took the child Jesus and brought him to the house [of a certain master] where other children also were taught. But the master began to teach him the letters with sweet speech, and wrote for him the first line which goes from A to Z, and began to flatter him and to teach him and commanded him to say the letters: but the child held his peace. Then that teacher smote the child on the head and when the child received the blow, he said to him: I ought to teach you and not you to teach me. I know the letters which you would teach me, and I know that you are to me as vessels out of which comes nothing but sound, and neither wisdom nor salvation of the soul. And beginning the line he spoke all the letters from A even to Z fully with much quickness: and he looked upon the master and said: But you know not how to interpret A and B: how would you teach others? You hypocrite, if you know and canst tell me concerning A, then will I tell you concerning B. But when the teacher began to expound concerning the first letter, he was not able to give any answer.

Then said Jesus to Zacheus: Listen to me, O master and understand the first letter. Give ear to me, how that it has two lines eight quite unintelligible descriptive phrases follow. Now when Zacheus saw that he so divided the first letter he was confounded at such names, and at his teaching, and cried out and said: Woe is me, for I am confounded: I have brought shame to myself by means of this child. And he said to Joseph: I beg you earnestly, my brother, take him away from me: for I cannot look upon his face nor hear his mighty words. For this child is able to subdue the fire and to restrain the sea, for he was born before the worlds. What womb birthed him or what manner of mother brought him up I know not. O my friends, I have lost my wits, I am mocked, wretched man that I am. I said that I had a disciple, but he is found to be my master. I cannot overcome my shame, for I am old, and I cannot find wherewithal to answer him, so that I would now like to fall into heavy sickness and depart out of the world or go away from this city, for all men have seen my shame, that a child has ensnared me. What can I answer any man, or what words can I speak, for he has overcome me at the first letter! I am confounded, O you my friends and acquaintances, and I can find neither first nor last to answer him. And now I beg you brother Joseph, remove him from me and take him to your house, for either he is a sorcerer or a god, the Lord or an angel, and what to say I know not.

And Jesus turned himself to the Jews that were with Zacheus and said to them: Now let all them that see not see and let them understand which understand not, and let the deaf hear, and let them arise which have died by my means, and let me call them that are high to that which is higher, even as he that sent me to you has commanded me. And when the child Jesus ceased speaking, all the afflicted were made whole, as many as had been afflicted at his word. And they dare not speak to him.

Now on a day, when Jesus climbed up on a house with the children, he began to play with them: but one of the boys fell down through the door out of the upper chamber and died straightway. And when the children saw it they fled, all of them, but Jesus remained alone in the house. And when the parents of the child which had died came they spoke against Jesus saying: Of a truth you made him fall. But Jesus said: I never made him fall: nevertheless they accused him still. Jesus therefore came down from the house and stood over the dead child and cried with a loud voice, calling him by his name: Zeno, Zeno, arise and say if I made you fall. And suddenly he arose and said: Nay, Lord. And when his parents saw this great miracle which Jesus did, they glorified God, and worshipped Jesus.

And after a few days a certain boy of that village was splitting wood, and chopped his foot. And when much people came to him, Jesus also came with them. And he touched the foot which was hurt, and forthwith it was made whole. And Jesus said to him: Arise and chop the wood and remember me. But when the multitude that were with him saw the signs which were done they worshipped Jesus and said: of a truth we believe surely that you are God.

And when Jesus was six years old, his mother sent him to draw water. And when Jesus was come to the well there was much people there and they broke his pitcher. But he took the cloak which he had upon him and filled it with water and brought it to Mary his mother. And when his mother saw the miracle that Jesus did she kissed him and said: Lord, listen to me and save my son.

Now when it was seed (planting) time, Joseph went forth to sow corn, and Jesus followed after him. And when Joseph began to sow, Jesus put forth his hand and took of the corn so much as he could hold in his hand, and scattered it. Joseph therefore came at the time of harvest to reap his harvest. And Jesus also came and gathered the ears which he had sown, and they made a hundred measures of good corn: and he called the poor and the widows and fatherless and gave them the corn which he had gained, save that Joseph took a little thereof to his house for a blessing [of Jesus].

Now, when the Lord Jesus had completed seven years from His birth, on a certain day He was occupied with boys of His own age. For they were playing among clay, from which they were making images of asses, oxen, birds, and other animals; and each one boasting of his skill, was praising his own work. Then the Lord Jesus said to the boys: The images that I have made I will order to walk. The boys asked Him whether then he were the son of the Creator; and the Lord Jesus bade them walk. And they immediately began to leap; and then, when He had given them leave, they again stood still. And He had made figures of birds and sparrows, which flew when He told them to fly, and stood still when He told them to stand, and ate and drank when He handed them food and drink. After the boys had gone away and told this to their parents, their fathers said to them: My sons, take care not to keep company with him again, for he is a wizard: flee from him, therefore, and avoid him, and do not play with him again after this.

On a certain day the Lord Jesus, running about and playing with the boys, passed the shop of a dyer, whose name was Salem; and he had in his shop many pieces of cloth which he was to dye. The Lord Jesus then, going into his shop, took up all the pieces of cloth, and threw them into a tub full of indigo. And when Salem came and saw his cloths destroyed, he began to cry out with a loud voice, and to rebuke Jesus, saying: Why have you done this to me, O son of Mary? You have disgraced me before all my townsmen: for, seeing that every one wished the color that suited himself, you indeed have come and destroyed them all. The Lord Jesus answered: I shall change for you the color of any piece of cloth which you shall wish to be changed. And immediately He began to take the pieces of cloth out of the tub, each of them of that color which the dyer wished, until He had taken them all out. When the Jews saw this miracle and prodigy, they praised God.

And Joseph used to go about through the whole city, and take the Lord Jesus with him, when people sent for him in the way of his trade to make for them doors, and milk-pails, and beds, and chests; and the Lord Jesus was with him wherever he went. As often, therefore, as Joseph had to make anything a cubit or a span longer or shorter, wider or narrower, the Lord Jesus stretched His hand towards it; and as soon as He did so, it became such as Joseph wished. Nor was it necessary for him to make anything with his own hand, for Joseph was not very skilful in carpentry.

Now, on a certain day, the king of Jerusalem sent for him, and said: I wish you, Joseph, to make for me a throne to fit that place in which I usually sit. Joseph obeyed, and began the work immediately, and remained in the palace two years, until he finished the work of that throne. And when he had it carried to its place, he perceived that each side wanted two spans of the prescribed measure. And the king, seeing this, was angry with Joseph; and Joseph, being in great fear of the king, spent the night without supper, nor did he taste anything at all. Then, being asked by the Lord Jesus why he was afraid, Joseph said: Because I have spoiled all the work that I have been two years at. And the Lord Jesus said to him: Fear not, and do not lose heart; but do you take hold of one side of the throne; I shall take the other; and we shall put that to rights. And Joseph, having done as the Lord Jesus had said and each having drawn by his own side, the throne was put to rights, and brought to the exact measure of the place. And those that stood by and saw this miracle were struck with astonishment, and praised God. And the woods used in that throne were of those which are celebrated in the time of Solomon the son of David; that is, woods of many and various kinds.

On another day the Lord Jesus went out into the road, and saw the boys that had come together to play, and followed them; but the boys hid themselves from Him. The Lord Jesus, therefore, having come to the door of a certain house, and seen some women standing there, asked them where the boys had gone; and when they answered that there was no one there, He said again: Who are these whom you see in the furnace?' They replied that they were kids (young goats) of three years old. And the Lord Jesus cried out, and said: Come out here, O kids, to your Shepherd. Then the boys, in the form of kids, came out, and began to dance round Him; and the women, seeing this, were very much astonished, and were seized with trembling, and speedily, supplicated and adored the Lord Jesus, saying: O our Lord Jesus, son of Mary, You are of a truth that good Shepherd of Israel; have mercy on Your handmaidens who stand before You, and who have never doubted: for You have come, O our Lord, to heal, and not to destroy. And when the Lord Jesus answered that the sons of Israel were like the Ethiopians among the nations, the women said:

You, O Lord, know all things, nor is anything hid from You; now, indeed, we beg You, and ask You of Your affection to restore these boys Your servants to their former condition. The Lord Jesus therefore said: Come, boys, let us go and play. And immediately, while these women were standing by, the kids were changed into boys.

And Jesus came to be eight years old. Now Joseph was a builder and wrought ploughs and yokes for oxen. And on a day a certain rich man said to Joseph: Sir, make me a bed serviceable and comely. But Joseph was troubled because the beam which he had made ready for the work was short. Jesus said to him: Be not troubled, but take you hold of this beam by the one end and I by the other, and let us draw it out. And so it came to pass, and forthwith Joseph found it serviceable for that which he desired. And he said to Joseph: Behold, fashion that you will. But Joseph when he saw what was done embraced him and said: Blessed am I for that God has given me such a son.

And when Joseph saw that he had so great grace and that he increased in stature, he thought to deliver him over to learn letters. And he delivered him to another doctor that he should teach him. Then said that doctor to Joseph: What manner of letters would you teach this child? Joseph answered and said: Teach him first the letters of the Gentiles and after that the Hebrew. Now the doctor knew that he was of an excellent understanding, and received him gladly. And when he had written for him the first line, that is to say A and B, he taught him for the space of some hours: but Jesus held his peace and answered nothing. At the last Jesus said to the master: If you be truly a master and indeed know the letters, tell me the power of A and I will tell you the power of B. Then was the master filled with indignation and hit him on the head. But Jesus was angry and cursed him, and all of a sudden he fell down and died. But Jesus returned to his own home. And Joseph instructed Mary his mother that she should not let him go out of the court of the house.

After many days there came another doctor which was a friend of Joseph and said to him: Deliver him to me and I will teach him letters with much gentleness. And Joseph said to him: If you are able, take him and teach him, and it shall be done gladly. And when the doctor received Jesus, he went with fear and great boldness and took him rejoicing. And when he was come to the house of the doctor, he found a book lying in that place and took it and opened it, and read not those things which were written therein, but opened his mouth and spoke by the Holy Ghost and taught the law: and all that stood by listened attentively, and the teacher sat by him and heard him gladly and entreated him to continue teaching. And much people gathered together and heard all the holy doctrine which he taught and the beloved words which proceeded out of his mouth marveling that he being a little child spoke such things.

But when Joseph heard, he was afraid and ran to the place where Jesus was; and the master said to Joseph: Know my brother, that I received your child to teach him and instruct him, but he is filled with great grace and wisdom. Therefore behold now, take him to your house with joy, because the grace which he has is given him of the Lord. And when Jesus heard the master speak thus he was joyful and said: Now you have well said, O master: for your sake shall he rise again who was dead. And Joseph took him to his own home.

Now Joseph sent James to gather straw, and Jesus followed after him. And as James gathered straw, a viper bit him and he fell to the earth as dead by means of the venom. But when Jesus saw that, he breathed on his wound and forthwith James was made whole, and the viper died.

After a few days a child that was his neighbor died, and his mother mourned for him very much; and when Jesus heard, he went and stood over the child, and struck him on the breast and said: Child, I say to you, die not, but live. And immediately the child arose: and Jesus said to the mother of the child: Take up your son and give him suck, and remember me. But the multitudes when they saw that miracle said: Of a truth this child is from heaven, for now has he set free many souls from death and has saved all them that hoped in him.

Now in the month Adar, Jesus, after the manner of a king, assembled the boys together. They spread their clothes on the ground, and He sat down upon them. Then they put on His head a crown made of flowers, and, like chamber-servants, stood in His presence, on the right and on the left, as if He were a king. And whoever passed by that way was forcibly dragged by the boys, saying: Come here, and adore the king; then go your way.

In the meantime, while these things were going on, some men came up carrying a boy. For this boy had gone into the mountain with those of his own age to seek wood, and there he found a partridge's nest; and when he stretched out his hand to take the eggs from it, a venomous serpent bit him from the middle of the nest, so that he called out for help. His comrades accordingly went to him with haste, and found him lying on the ground like one dead. Then his relations came and took him up to carry him back to the city. And after they had come to that place where the Lord Jesus was sitting like a king, and the rest of the boys standing round Him like His servants, the boys went hastily forward to meet him who had been bitten by the serpent, and said to his relations: Come and salute the king. But when they were unwilling to go, on account of the sorrow in I which they were, the boys dragged them by force against their will. And when they had come up to the Lord Jesus, He asked them why they were carrying the boy. And when they answered that a serpent had bitten him, the Lord Jesus said to the boys: Let us go and kill that serpent. And the parents of the boy asked leave to go away, because their son was in the agony of death; but the boys answered them, saying: Did you not hear the king saying: Let us go kill the serpent? And will you not obey him? And so, against their will the boy was carried back. And when they came to the nest, the Lord Jesus said to the boys: Is this the serpent's place? They said that it was; and the serpent, at the call of the Lord, came forth without delay, and submitted itself to Him. And He said to it: Go away, and suck out all the poison which you have infused into this boy. And so the serpent crawled to the boy, and sucked out all its poison. Then the Lord Jesus cursed it, and immediately on this being done it burst apart; and the Lord Jesus stroked the boy with his hand, and he was healed. And he began to weep; but Jesus said: Do not weep, for by and by you shall be my disciple. And this is Simon the Canaanite, of whom mention is made in the Gospel.

On another day, Joseph sent his son James to gather wood, and the Lord Jesus went with him as his companion. And when they had come to the place where the wood was, and James had begun to gather it, behold, a venomous viper bit his band, so that he began to cry out and weep. The Lord Jesus then, seeing him in this condition, went up to him, and blew on the place where the viper had bitten him; and this being done, he was healed immediately.

Once upon a time the Lady Mary bad ordered the Lord Jesus to go and bring her water from the well. And when He had gone to get the water, the pitcher already full was knocked against something, and broken. And the Lord Jesus stretched out His handkerchief, and collected the water, and carried it to His mother; and she was astonished at it. And she hid and preserved in her heart all that she saw.

Again, on another day, the Lord Jesus was with the boys at a stream of water, and they had again made little fish-ponds. And the Lord Jesus had made twelve sparrows, and had arranged them round His fish-pond, three on each side. And it was the Sabbath-day. Then a Jew, the son of Hanan, coming up, and seeing them thus engaged, said in anger and great indignation: Do you make figures of clay on the Sabbath-day? And he ran quickly, and destroyed their fish-ponds. But when the Lord Jesus clapped His hands over the sparrows which He had made, they flew away chirping. Then the son of Hanan came up to the fish-pond of Jesus also, and kicked it with his shoes, and the water of it vanished away. And the Lord Jesus said to him: As that water has vanished away, so your life shall likewise vanish away. And immediately that boy dried up.

At another time, when the Lord Jesus was returning home with Joseph in the evening. He met a boy, who ran up against Him with so much force that He fell. And the Lord Jesus said to him: As you have thrown me down, so you shall fall and not rise again. And the same hour the boy fell down, and expired.

There was, moreover, at Jerusalem, a certain man named Zacchaeus, who taught boys. He said to Joseph: Why, O Joseph, do you not bring Jesus to learn his letters? Joseph agreed to do so, and reported the matter to the Lady Mary. They therefore took Him to the master; and he, as soon as he saw Him, wrote out the alphabet for Him, and told

The Life and Times of Jesus: From Child to God

Him to say Aleph. And when He had said Aleph, the master ordered Him to pronounce Beth. And the Lord Jesus said to him: Tell me first the meaning of the letter Aleph, and then I shall pronounce Beth. And when the master threatened to flog Him, the Lord Jesus explained to him the meanings of the letters Aleph and Beth; also which figures of the letter were straight, which crooked, which drawn round into a spiral, which marked with points, which without them, why one letter went before another; and many other things He began to recount and to elucidate which the master himself had never either heard or read in any book. The Lord Jesus, moreover, said to the master: Listen, and I shall say them to you. And He began clearly and distinctly to repeat Aleph, Beth, Gimel, Daleth, on to Tau. And the master was astonished, and said: I think that this boy was born before Noah. And turning to Joseph, be said: You have brought to me to be taught a boy more learned than all the masters. To the Lady Mary also said: This son of yours has no need of instruction.

Thereafter they took Him to another and a more learned master, who, when be saw Him, said: Say Aleph. And when He had said Aleph, the master ordered him to pronounce Beth. And the Lord Jesus answered him, and said: First tell me the meaning of the letter Aleph, and then I shall pronounce Beth. And when the master hereupon raised his hand and flogged Him, immediately his hand dried up, and he died. Then said Joseph, to the Lady Mary: From this time we shall not let him go out of the house, since every one who opposes him is struck dead.

And when He was twelve years old, they took Him to Jerusalem to the feast. And when the feast was finished, they indeed returned; but the Lord Jesus remained in the temple among the teachers and elders and learned men of the sons of Israel, to whom He put various questions upon the sciences, and gave answers in His turn. For He said to them: Whose son is the Messiahs? They answered Him: The son of David. Then, said He, does he in the Spirit call him his lord, when he says, The Lord said to my lord, Sit at my right hand, that I may put your enemies under your footsteps? Again the chief of the teachers said to Him: Hast you read the books? Both the books, said the Lord Jesus, and the things contained in the books. And He explained the books, and the law, and the precepts, and the statutes, and the mysteries, which are contained in the books of the prophets, things which the understanding of no creature attains to. That teacher therefore said: I hitherto have neither attained to nor heard of such knowledge: Who (what) do you think that boy will be?

And a philosopher who was there present, a skilful astronomer, asked the Lord Jesus whether He had studied astronomy. And the Lord Jesus answered him, and explained the number of the spheres, and of the heavenly bodies, their natures and operations; their opposition; their aspect, triangular, square, and sextile; their course, direct and retrograde; the twenty-fourths, and sixtieths of twenty-fourths; and other things beyond the reach of reason.

There was also among those philosophers one very skilled in treating of natural science, and he asked the Lord Jesus whether He had studied medicine. And He, in reply, explained to him physics and metaphysics, hyperphysics and hypophysics (theory and speculation), the powers likewise and humors of the body, and the effects of the same; also the number of members and bones, of veins, arteries, and nerves; also the effect of heat and dryness, of cold and moisture, and what these give rise to; what was the operation of the soul upon the body, and its perceptions and powers; what was the operation of the faculty of speech, of anger, of desire; lastly, their conjunction and disjunction, and other things beyond the reach of any created intellect. Then that philosopher rose up, and adored the Lord Jesus, and said: O Lord, from this time I will be your disciple and slave.

(Author's note:

It was thought that there were four basic fluids within the body. The balance and proportion of the fluids dictated health and disposition. Hippocrates of Cos or Hippokrates of Kos (ca. 460 BC – ca. 370 BC) is credited with the theory. The fluids or humors are:

Yellow Bile

Black Bile

Phlegm

Blood

Earth: black bile
Air: blood
Fire: yellow bile
Water: phlegm.

Too much earth made one melancholic; too much air, sanguine; too much fire, choleric; and too much water, phlegmatic.

Finally, each element/humor/season was associated with certain qualities. Thus yellow bile was thought of as hot and dry. Its opposite, phlegm (the mucus of colds,) was cold and moist. Black Bile was cold and dry, while its opposite, blood was hot and moist.)

While they were speaking to each other of these and other things, the Lady Mary came, after having gone about seeking Him for three days along with Joseph. She therefore, seeing Him sitting among the teachers asking them questions, and answering in His turn, said to Him: My son, why have you treated us thus? Behold, your father and I have sought you with great trouble. But He said: Why do you seek me? Do you not know that I ought to occupy myself in my Father's house? But they did not understand the words that He spoke to them. Then those teachers asked Mary whether He were her son; and when she signified that He was, they said: Blessed are you, O Mary, who have brought forth such a son. And returning with them to Nazareth, He obeyed them in all things. And His mother kept all these words of His in her heart. And the Lord Jesus advanced in stature, and in wisdom, and in favor with God and man.

And from this day He began to hide His miracles and mysteries and secrets, and to give attention to the law, until He completed His thirtieth year, when His Father publicly declared Him at the Jordan by this voice sent down from heaven: This is my beloved Son, in whom I am well pleased; the Holy Spirit being present in the form of a white dove.

This is He whom we adore with supplications, who has given us being and life, and who has brought us from our mothers' wombs; who for our sakes assumed a human body, and redeemed us, that He might embrace us in eternal compassion, and show to us His mercy according to His liberality, and beneficence, and generosity, and benevolence. To Him is glory, and beneficence, and power, and dominion from this time forth for evermore. Amen. Here ends the whole Gospel of the Infancy, with the aid of God Most High, according to what we have found in the original.

Gospel of Luke from the Holy Bible

Luke 2
[41] Now his parents went to Jerusalem every year at the feast of the Passover.
[42] And when he was twelve years old, they went up to Jerusalem after the custom of the feast.
[43] And when they had fulfilled the days, as they returned, the child Jesus tarried behind in Jerusalem; and Joseph and his mother knew not of it.
[44] But they, supposing him to have been in the company, went a day's journey; and they sought him among their kinsfolk and acquaintance.
[45] And when they found him not, they turned back again to Jerusalem, seeking him.
[46] And it came to pass, that after three days they found him in the temple, sitting in the midst of the doctors, both hearing them, and asking them questions.
[47] And all that heard him were astonished at his understanding and answers.
[48] And when they saw him, they were amazed: and his mother said to him, Son, why have you thus dealt with us? behold, your father and I have sought you sorrowing.
[49] And he said to them, How is it that you sought me? know you not that I must be about my Father's business?
[50] And they understood not the saying which he spoke to them.
[51] And he went down with them, and came to Nazareth, and was subject to them: but his mother kept all these sayings in her heart.
[52] And Jesus increased in wisdom and stature, and in favor with God and man.

This ends the quotation from the Holy Scripture.

The Life of Saint Issa
Best of the Sons of Men
Using the translation by Notovitch

CHAPTER I

1 The earth has trembled and the heavens have wept because of a great crime which has been committed in the land of Israel.

2 For they have tortured and there put to death the great and just Issa, in whom dwelt the soul of the universe,

3 Which was incarnate in a simple mortal in order to do good to men and to exterminate their evil thoughts.

4 And in order to bring back mankind, which has been degraded by his sins, to a life of peace, love, and happiness and to call him back to the one and indivisible Creator, whose mercy is infinite and without bounds.

5 Hear what the merchants from Israel relate to us on this subject.

CHAPTER II

1 The people of Israel, who dwelt on a fertile soil giving forth two crops a year and who possessed large flocks, had by their sins aroused the anger of God,

2 Who inflicted upon them a terrible chastisement by taking from them their land, their cattle, and their possessions. Israel was reduced to slavery by the powerful and rich pharaohs who then reigned in Egypt.

3 These treated the Israelites worse than animals, burdening them with difficult tasks and loading them with chains. They covered their bodies with whelps and wounds, without giving them food or permitting them to dwell beneath a roof,

4 to keep them in a state of continual terror and to deprive them of all human resemblance.

5 And in their great calamity, the people of Israel remembered their heavenly protector and, addressing themselves to him, they implored his grace and mercy.

6 An illustrious pharaoh then reigned in Egypt who had made himself famous by his numerous victories. The riches he gained had piled up, and there were vast palaces which his slaves had erected for him with their own hands.

7 This pharaoh had two sons, of whom the younger was called Mossa (Moses). Learned Israelites taught him diverse sciences.

8 And they loved Mossa (Moses) in Egypt for his goodness and the compassion which he showed to all those who suffered.

9 Seeing that in spite of the intolerable sufferings they were enduring the Israelites would not abandon their God to worship those made by the hand of man, which were gods of the Egyptian nation,

10 Mossa (Moses) believed in their invisible God, because He did not let their failing strength give way.

11 And the Israelite teachers excited the passion of Mossa and had conversations with him, praying him to intercede with the pharaoh his father in favor of their fellow believers.

12 Then the Prince Mossa went to his father, begging him to make better the fate of these unfortunates. But the pharaoh became angered against him and only augmented the torments endured by his slaves.

13 It happened that a short time after, a great evil visited Egypt. The pestilence came to decimate both the young and the old, the weak and the strong; and the pharaoh believed this was because his own gods were turning against him.

14 But the Prince Mossa told his father that it was the God of his slaves who was interceding in favor of these unfortunates in punishing the Egyptians.

15 The pharaoh then gave to Mossa his son an order to take all the slaves of the Jewish race, to conduct them outside the town, and to found at a great distance from the capital another city where he should dwell with them.

16 Mossa then made known to the Hebrew slaves that he had set them free in the name of their God, the God of Israel, and he went out with them from the city and from the land of Egypt.

17 He led them into the land they had lost by their many sins. There Mossa gave them laws, and enjoined them to pray always to the invisible Creator whose goodness is infinite.

18 On the death of Prince Mossa, the Israelites rigorously observed his laws, wherefore God made amends and rewarded them for the ills to which he had exposed them in Egypt.

19 Their kingdom became the most powerful of all the earth, their kings made themselves famous for their treasures, and a long peace reigned among the people of Israel.

CHAPTER III

1 The glory of the riches of Israel spread throughout the earth, and made neighboring nations envious.

2 For the Most High himself led the victorious arms of the Hebrews, and the pagans dared not attack them.

3 Unhappily, as man is not always true to himself, the fidelity of the Israelites to their God did not last long.

4 They began by forgetting all the favors which he had heaped upon them, seldom invoked his name, and sought the protection of magicians and sorcerers.

5 The kings and the captains substituted their own laws for those which Mossa had written down for them. The temple of God and the practice of worship were abandoned. The people gave themselves up to pleasure and lost their original purity.

6 Several centuries had elapsed since their departure from Egypt when God determined to exercise once more his chastisements upon them.

7 Strangers began to invade the land of Israel, devastating the country, ruining the villages, and carrying the inhabitants into captivity.

8 And there came at one time pagans from the country of Romeles, (birthplace of Romulus, modern day Rome) on the other side of the sea. They subdued the Hebrews and established among them military leaders who by delegation from Caesar ruled over them.

9 They destroyed the temples, they forced the inhabitants to cease worshipping the invisible God, and they compelled them to sacrifice victims to the pagan deities.

10 They made warriors of those who had been nobles, the women were torn away from their husbands, and the lower classes, were reduced to slavery and were sent by thousands beyond the seas.

11 As to the children, they were put to the sword. Soon in all the land of Israel nothing was heard but groans and lamentations.

12 In this extreme distress, the people remembered their great God. They implored his grace and besought him to forgive them; and our

Father, in his inexhaustible mercy, heard their prayer.

CHAPTER IV

1 It was at this time that the moment came when the all-merciful Judge elected to become incarnate in a human being.

2 And the Eternal Spirit, dwelling in a state of complete inaction (peace and stillness) and of supreme beatitude, awoke and detached itself for an indefinite period from the Eternal Being.

3 This was done to show forth in the guise of humanity the means of self-identification with Divinity and of attaining to eternal joy (bliss,)

4 And to demonstrate by example how man may attain moral purity and, by separating his soul from its mortal coil, the degree of perfection necessary to enter into the kingdom of heaven, which is unchangeable and where happiness reigns eternal.

5 Soon after, a marvelous child was born in the land of Israel, God himself speaking by the mouth of this infant of the frailty of the body and the grandeur of the soul.

6 The parents of the newborn child were poor people, belonging by birth to a family of noted piety, who, forgetting their ancient grandeur on earth, praised the name of the Creator and thanked him for the ills with which he saw fit to prove them.

7 To reward them for not turning aside from the way of truth, God blessed the firstborn of this family. He chose him for his elect and sent him to help those who had fallen into evil and to cure those who suffered.

8 The divine child, to whom was given the name of Issa (Jesus), began from his earliest years to speak of the one and indivisible God. He exhorted the souls of those gone astray to come to repentance and the purification of the sins of which they were culpable.

9 People came from all parts to hear him, and they marveled at the discourses proceeding from his childish mouth. All the Israelites were of one accord in saying that the Eternal Spirit dwelt in this child.

10 When Issa (Jesus) had attained the age of thirteen years, which is the period of life when an Israelite should take a wife,

11 the house where his parents earned their living by carrying on a modest trade began to be a place of meeting for rich and noble people, who were desirous of having the young Issa for a son-in-law, for he was already famous for his edifying discourses in the name of the Almighty.

12 Then it was that Issa left the parental house in secret, departed from Jerusalem, and with the merchants set out towards Sind, (a province of southeastern Pakistan)

13 with the aim of perfecting himself in the Divine Word and of studying the laws of the great Buddhas.

CHAPTER V

1 In the course of his fourteenth year, the young Issa, blessed of God, came on this side of Sind and established himself among the Aryas (Northern India) in the land beloved of God.

2 Fame spread the reputation of this marvelous child throughout the length of northern Sind, and when he crossed the country of the five rivers and the Rajputana, *(An area northwest of the Arāvalli Range including part of the Great Indian (Thar) Desert.)* These were the devotees of the god Jaine and they prayed Issa to dwell among them.

3 But he left the erring worshippers of Jaine and went to Juggernaut in the country of Orissa, where repose the mortal remains of Vyasa-Krishna and where the white priests of Brahma made him a Joyous welcome.

Joseph Lumpkin

(Juggernaut is the Hinduism form of Krishna worshiped in Puri, Orissa. Also called Jagannatha . Hindi from Sanskrit Jagannātha 'Lord of the world.')

4 They taught him to read and understand the Vedas, to cure by aid of prayer, to teach, to explain the holy scriptures to the people, and to drive out evil spirits from the bodies of men, restoring to them their sanity.

5 He passed six years at Juggernaut, at Rajagriha, at Benares, and in the other holy cities. Everyone loved him, for Issa lived in peace with the Vaisyas *(a member of the third of the four Hindu castes, comprising the merchants and farmers)* and the Sudras, *(a member of the worker caste, lowest of the four Hindu castes,)* whom he instructed in the holy scriptures.

6 But the Brahmans *(a member of the highest Hindu caste, that of the priesthood)* and the Kshatriyas *(a member of the second of the four great Hindu castes, the military caste. The traditional function of the Kshatriyas is to protect society by fighting in wartime and governing in peacetime,)* told him that they were forbidden by the great Para-Brahma to come near to those whom he had created from his side and his feet;

7 That the Vaisyas were only authorized to hear the reading of the Vedas, and this on festival days, and

8 that the Sudras were forbidden not only to assist at the reading of the Vedas, but also from contemplating them, for their condition was to serve in perpetuity as slaves to the Brahmans, the Kshatriyas, and even the Vaisyas.

9 "'Death only can set them free from their servitude' has said Para-Brahma. Leave them then and come and worship with us the gods, who will become very angry against you if you should disobey them."

10 But Issa listened not to their discourses and went to the Sudras, preaching against the commands of the Brahmans and the

Kshatriyas.

11 He spoke and preached against the act of a man claiming to himself the power to deprive his fellow beings of their rights of humanity; "for," said he, "God the Father makes no difference between his children; all to him are equally dear."

12 Issa denied the divine origin of the Vedas (scriptures) and the Puranas (written legends and folklore.) "For," he taught his followers, "a law has already been given to man to guide him in his actions, which are,

13 "Fear your God, bend the knee before him only, and bring to him alone the offerings which proceed from your gains."

14 Issa denied the Trimurti (the trinity of Brahma the creator, Vishnu the preserver, and Shiva the destroyer) and the incarnation of Para-Brahma in Vishnu, Siva, and other gods, for said he:

15 "The Judge Eternal, the Eternal Spirit, comprehends the one and indivisible soul of the universe, which alone creates, contains, and vivifies all.

Inasmuch as Jesus' closest disciple, John, begins his Gospel with a quote from the Vedas, "In the beginning was the Word . . . ," the authenticity of this passage may be questioned. (Notation added by Notovitch)

16 "He alone has willed and created, he alone has existed since all eternity, and his existence will have no end. He has no equal either in the heavens or on earth."

17 "The Great Creator has not shared his power with any living being, still less with inanimate objects, as they have taught to you; for he alone possesses omnipotence."

18 "He willed it and the world appeared. In a divine thought, he gathered together the waters, separating from them the dry portion of the globe. He is the principle of the mysterious existence of man, in

whom he has breathed a part of his Being. *(in-spired, to breathe into)*

19 "And he has subordinated to man the earth, the waters, the beasts, and all that he has created and that he himself preserves in immutable order, fixing for each thing the length of its duration."

20 "The anger of God will soon be let loose against man; for he has forgotten his Creator, he has filled his temples with abominations, and he worships a collection of creatures which God has made subordinate to him.

21 "For to do honor to stones and metals, he sacrifices human beings, in whom dwells a part of the spirit of the Most High."

22 "He humiliates those who work by the sweat of their brow in order to acquire the favor of an idle (shiftless) person seated at his sumptuous table (board)."

23 "Those who deprive their brethren of divine happiness shall be deprived of it themselves. The Brahmans and the Kshatriyas shall become the Sudras, and with the Sudras the Eternal (God) shall dwell everlastingly."

24 "Because in the day of the last judgment the Sudras and the Vaisyas (the two lowest classes) will be forgiven much because of their ignorance, while God, on the contrary, will punish with his wrath those who have usurped to themselves his rights."

25 The Vaisyas and the Sudras were filled with great admiration and asked Issa (Jesus) how they should pray so as not to lose their eternal joy (felicity).

26 "Worship not the idols, for they hear you not. Listen not to the Vedas, for their truth is counterfeit. Never put yourself in the first place and never humiliate your neighbor."

27 "Help the poor, support the weak, do ill to no one, and covet not that which you have not and which you see belongs to another."

Sir John Wodroofe notes: "The fourth Gospel opens grandly, 'In the beginning was the Word, and the Word was with God and the Word was God.' These are the very words of Veda. Prajapatir vai idam asit: In the beginning was Brahman. Tasya vag dvitya asit; with whom was the Vak or the Word... Vag vai paramam Brahma; and the word is Brahman" (The Garland Letters, 7th ed. [Pondicherry: Ganesh & Co., 1979] p.4)

CHAPTER VI

1 The white priests and the warriors, becoming acquainted with the discourses of Issa addressed to the Sudras, resolved upon his death and sent their servants to seek out the young prophet with this intent.

2 But Issa, warned of his danger by the Sudras, left the area of Juggernaut by night, reached the mountain, and established himself in the country of Gautamides, the birthplace of the great Buddha Sakyamuni, *(around Nepal?)* in the midst of a people worshipping the one and sublime Brahma.

3 After having perfected himself in the Pali language, the just Issa applied himself to the study of the sacred writings of the Sutras.

4 Six years after, Issa, whom the Buddha had elected to spread his holy word, had become a perfect teacher (expositor) of the sacred writings.

5 Then he left Nepal and the Himalayan mountains, descended into the valley of Rajputana, and went towards the west, preaching to diverse peoples the supreme perfection of man, (what a perfect man should be and do)

6 Which is, to do good to one's neighbor, being the sure means of merging oneself rapidly in the Eternal Spirit: "He who shall have regained his original purity," said Issa, "will die having obtained remission for his sins, and he will have the right to contemplate the

majesty of God."

7 In crossing pagan territories, the divine Issa taught that the worship of visible gods was contrary to the law of nature.

8 "For man," said he, "has not been permitted to see the image of God, and yet he has made a host of deities in the likeness of the Eternal."

(One may argue that as man has not seen God how could he make deities in His likeness. Possibly we should read this as, "Man made deities according to what His weak imagination envisioned God to look like.)

9 "Moreover, it is incompatible with the human conscience to make less matter of the splendor of divine purity than of animals and objects executed by the hand of man in stone or metal."

10 "The Eternal Lawgiver is one; there is no other God but he. He has not shared the world with anyone, neither has he informed anyone of his intentions."

11 "Even as a father would act towards his children, so will God judge men after their deaths according to the laws of his mercy. Never would he so humiliate his child as to transmigrate his soul, as in a purgatory, into the body of an animal."

12 "The heavenly law," said the Creator by the mouth of Issa, "is opposed to the immolation *(to kill as a sacrifice, especially by burning)* of human sacrifices to an image or to an animal; for I have consecrated to man all the animals and all that the earth contains."

13 "All things have been sacrificed to man, who is directly and intimately associated with me, his Father; therefore he who shall have stolen from me my child will be severely judged and chastised by the divine law."

14 "Man is nothing before the Eternal Judge, as the animal is nothing before man."

15 "Therefore I say to you, Leave your idols and perform no rites which separate you from your Father, associating you with the priests from whom the heavens have turned away."

16 "For it is they who have led you from the true God and whose superstitions and cruelties which help bring about the perversion of your soul and the loss of all moral sense."

CHAPTER VII

1 The words of Issa spread among the pagans in the midst of the countries he traversed, and the inhabitants forsook their idols.

2 But the priests tried to make Him pay who glorified the name of the true God in the presence of the people and ridiculed and demonstrated the nothingness of their idols.

3 And Issa made answer to them: "If your idols and your animals are powerful and really possessed of supernatural strength, then let them strike me to the earth."

4 "Work then a miracle," replied the priests, "and let your God confound our gods, if they inspire him with contempt."

5 But Issa then said: "The miracles of our God have been worked since the first day when the universe was created; they take place every day and at every moment. Whosoever does not see them is deprived of one of the finest gifts of life."

6 "And it is not against pieces of stone, metal, or wood, which are inanimate, that the anger of God will have full course; but it will fall on men, who, if they desire their salvation, must destroy all the idols they have made."

7 "Even as a stone and a grain of sand are nothing in the sight of man, but they wait patiently for the moment when he shall take and make use of them,

8 "so man must await the great favor that God shall accord him in his final judgment."

9 "But woe to you, you enemies of men, if it be not a favor that you await but rather the wrath of the Divinity-woe to you if you expect miracles to bear witness to his power.

10 "For it will not be the idols that he will annihilate in his anger but those who shall have erected them. Their hearts shall be consumed with eternal fire, and their lacerated bodies shall go to satiate the hunger of wild beasts."

11 "God will drive the impure from among his flocks, but he will take back to himself those who shall have gone astray through not having recognized the portion of spirituality within them."

12 Seeing the powerlessness of their priests, the pagans had still greater faith in the sayings of Issa and, fearing the anger of the Divine (God), broke their idols to pieces. As for the priests, they fled to escape the vengeance of the populace.

13 And Issa further taught the pagans not to strive to see the Eternal Spirit with their eyes but to endeavor to feel him in their hearts and by purity of soul to render themselves worthy of his favors.

14 He also said to them, "Abstain from consuming human sacrifices, but kill (sacrifice by fire) no creature to whom life has been given, for all things that exist have been created for the profit of man."

15 "Do not steal the goods of your neighbor, for that would be to deprive him of what he has acquired by the sweat of his brow."

16 "Deceive no one, so as not to be yourselves deceived. Endeavor to justify yourself prior to the last judgment, for then it will be too late."

17 "Do not give yourselves up to debauchery, for that would be to violate the laws of God."

18 "You shall attain to supreme happiness, not only in purifying yourselves, but also in guiding others in the way that shall permit them to gain original perfection."

CHAPTER VIII

1 The neighboring countries resounded with the prophecies of Issa, and when he entered into Persia the priests became alarmed and forbade the inhabitants to listen to him.

2 And when they saw all the villages welcoming him with joy and listening devoutly to his sermons, they gave orders to arrest him and had him brought before the high priest, where he underwent the following interrogation:

3 "Of what new God do you speak? Are you not aware, you unhappy man, that Saint Zoroaster is the only just one admitted to the privilege of communion with the Supreme Being,"

4 "who ordered the angels to put down in writing the word of God for the use of his people, laws that were given to Zoroaster in paradise?"

5 "Who then are you to dare here to blaspheme our God and to sow doubt in the hearts of believers?"

6 And Issa said to them: "It is not of a new God that I speak but of our Heavenly Father, who has existed since all time and who will still be after the end of all things.

7 "It is of him that I have discoursed to the people, who, like to innocent children, are not yet capable of comprehending God by the simple strength of their intelligence or of penetrating into his sublime and divine spirit."

8 "But even as a babe discovers its mother's breast in the darkness, so even your people, who have been led into error by your erroneous doctrine and your religious ceremonies, have recognized by instinct

their Father and it is the Father of whom I am the prophet."

9 "The Eternal Being has said to your people through the medium of my mouth: 'You shall not worship the sun, for it is but a part of the world which I have created for man."

10 "The sun rises in order to warm you during your work; it sets to allow you the rest, which I myself have appointed."

11 "It is to me, and to me alone, that you owe all that you possess, all that is to be found around you, above you, and below you."

12 "But," said the priests, "how could a people live according to the rules of justice if it had no teachers?"

13 Then Issa answered, "So long as the people had no priests, the natural law governed them, and they preserved the open honesty of their souls.

14 "Their souls were with God, and to commune with the Father they had recourse to the medium of no idol or animal, nor to the fire, as is practiced here."

15 "You contend that one must worship the sun, the spirit of good and of evil. Well, I say to you, your doctrine is a false one, the sun acting not spontaneously but according to the will of the invisible Creator who gave it birth"

16 "And who has willed it to be the star that should light the day, to warm the labor and the seedtime of man."

17 "The Eternal Spirit is the soul of all that is animate. You commit a great sin in dividing it into a spirit of evil and a spirit of good, for there is no God outside the good,"

18 "who, like to the father of a family, does but good to his children, forgiving all their faults if they repent them."

19 "The spirit of evil dwells on the earth in the hearts of those men who turn aside the children of God from the strait path."

20 "Therefore I say to you, Beware of the day of judgment, for God will inflict a terrible chastisement upon all those who shall have led his children astray from the right path and have filled them with superstitions and prejudices;"

21 "those who have blinded them that see, conveyed contagion to the healthy, and taught the worship of the things that God has subordinated to man for his good and to aid him in his work."

22 "Your doctrine is therefore the fruit of your errors; for desiring to bring near to you the God of truth, you have created for yourselves false gods."

23 After having listened to him, the magi determined to do him no harm. But at night, when all the town lay sleeping, they conducted him outside of the walls and abandoned him on the high road, in the hope that he would soon become a prey to the wild beasts.

24 But, protected by the Lord our God, Saint Issa continued his way undisturbed and unharmed.

CHAPTER IX

1 Issa, whom the Creator had elected to remind a depraved humanity of the true God, had reached his twenty-ninth year when he returned to the land of Israel.

2 Since his departure the pagans had inflicted still more atrocious sufferings on the Israelites, who were a prey to the deepest despondency.

3 Many among them had already begun to abandon the laws of their God and those of Mossa in the hope of appeasing their savage conquerors.

4 In the face of this evil, Issa exhorted his fellow citizens not to despair because the day of the redemption of sins was at hand, and he confirmed them in the belief which they had in the God of their fathers.

5 "Children, do not give yourselves up to despair," said the Heavenly Father by the mouth of Issa, "for I have heard your voice, and your cries have reached me."

6 "Do not weep, O my beloved ones! For your grief has touched the heart of your Father, and he has forgiven you, even as he forgave your forefathers."

7 "Do not abandon your families to plunge yourselves into debauchery, do not lose the nobility of your feelings, and do not worship idols who will remain deaf to your voices."

8 "Fill my temple with your hope and with your patience and abjure not the religion of your fathers; for I alone have guided them and have heaped them with benefits."

9 "You shall lift up those who have fallen, you shall give food to the hungry, and you shall come to the aid of the sick, so as to be all pure and just at the day of the last judgment which I prepare for you."

10 The Israelites came in crowds at the word of Issa, asking him where they should praise the Heavenly Father, seeing that the enemy had razed their temples to the ground and laid low their sacred vessels.

11 And Issa made answer to them that God had not in view temples erected by the hands of man, but he meant that the human heart was the true temple of God.

12 "Enter into your temple, into your heart. Illumine it with good thoughts and the patience and immovable confidence which you should have in your Father."

The Life and Times of Jesus: From Child to God

13 "And your sacred vessels, they are your hands and your eyes. See and do that which is agreeable to God, for in doing good to your neighbor you accomplish a rite which embellishes the temple wherein dwells he who gave you life."

14 "For God has created you in his own likeness; innocent, with pure souls and hearts filled with goodness, destined not for the conception of evil schemes but made to be sanctuaries of love and justice."

15 "Therefore I say to you, dirty not your hearts, for the Supreme Being dwells therein eternally."

16 "If you wish to accomplish works marked with love or piety, do them with an open heart and do not let your actions be governed by calculations (plans) or the hope of gain."

17 "For such actions would not help to your salvation, and you would fall into that state of moral degradation where theft, lying, and murder pass for generous deeds."

CHAPTER X

1 Saint Issa went from one town to another, strengthening the courage of the Israelites by the word of God, who were ready to succumb to the weight of their despair; and thousands of men followed him to hear him preach.

2 But the chiefs of the towns became afraid of him, and they made known to the principal governor who dwelt at Jerusalem that a man named Issa had arrived in the country; that he was stirring up the people against the authorities by his discourses; that the crowd listened to him with close attention, neglected the works of the state, and affirmed that before long it would be rid of its intrusive governors.

3 Then Pilate, governor of Jerusalem, ordered that they should seize Issa, the preacher, that they should bring him into the town and lead him before the judges. But in order not to excite the anger of the

populace, Pilate ordered the priests and the learned Hebrew elders to judge him in the temple.

4 Meanwhile Issa, continuing his preaching, arrived at Jerusalem; and, having learned of his arrival, all the inhabitants, knowing him already by reputation, went out to meet him.

5 They greeted him respectfully and opened to him the gates of their temple in order to hear from his mouth what he had said in the other cities of Israel.

6 And Issa said to them: "The human race perishes because of its lack of faith, for the darkness and the tempest have scattered the flocks of humanity and they have lost their shepherds.

7 "But the tempest will not last forever, and the darkness will not always obscure the light. The sky will become once more serene, the heavenly light will spread itself over the earth, and the flocks gone astray will gather around their shepherd."

8 "Do not strive to find straight paths in the darkness, or you will fall into a pit; but gather together your remaining strength, support one another, place your confidence in your God, and wait till light appears."

9 "He who sustains his neighbor, sustains himself; and whoever protects his family, protects the people and the state."

10 "For be sure that the day is at hand when you shall be delivered from the darkness; you shall be gathered together as one family; and your enemy, who ignores the favor (approval) of God, shall tremble with fear."

11 The priests and the elders who were listening to him were filled with admiration at his discourse and asked him if it were true that he had tried to stir up the people against the authorities of the country, as had been reported to the governor Pilate.

12 "Can one excite to insurrection men gone astray, whose door and path have been hidden and obscured?" replied Issa. "I have only warned the unfortunates, as I do here in this temple, that they may not further advance along the darkened way, for an abyss is open under their feet."

13 "Earthly power is not of long duration, and it is subject to many changes. What use is it that man should revolt against it, seeing that one power always succeeds to another power? And thus it will come to pass until the extinction of humanity."

14 "Don't you see that the mighty and the rich sow among the sons of Israel a spirit of rebellion against the eternal power of heaven?"

15 The elders then asked: "Who are you, and from what country do you come? We have not heard speak of you before, and we do not even know your name."

16 "I am an Israelite," replied Issa. "From the day of my birth I saw the walls of Jerusalem, and I heard the weeping of my brothers reduced to slavery and the lamentations of my sisters who were carried away by the pagans."

17 "And my soul was filled with sadness when I saw that my brethren had forgotten the true God. As a child, I left my father's house and went to dwell among other peoples."

18 "But having heard that my brethren were suffering still greater tortures, I have come back to the country where my parents dwell to remind my brothers of the faith of their forefathers, which teaches us patience on earth to obtain perfect and sublime happiness in heaven."

19 And the learned elders put to him this question: "It is said that you deny the laws of Mossa (Moses) and that you teach the people to forsake the temple of God?"

20 And Issa replied: "One cannot demolish that which has been given by our Heavenly Father, neither that which has been destroyed by sinners; but I have enjoined the purification of the heart from all

blemish, for it is the true temple of God."

21 "As for the laws of Mossa (Moses), I have endeavored to establish them in the hearts of men. And I say to you that you do not understand their real meaning, for it is not vengeance but mercy that they teach; but the sense (meaning) of these laws has been perverted."

CHAPTER XI

1 Having listened to Issa, the priests and the wise elders decided among themselves not to judge him, for he did harm to no one. And presenting themselves before Pilate, appointed governor of Jerusalem by the pagan king of the country of Romeles (Rome), they addressed him thus:

2 "We have seen the man whom you accuse of inciting our people to rebellion; we have heard his discourses, and we know him to be our compatriot."

3 "But the chiefs of the cities have made you false reports, for this is a just man who teaches the people the word of God. After having interrogated him, we dismissed him, that he might go in peace."

4 The governor then became enraged and sent near to Issa his servants in disguise, so that they might watch all his actions and report to the authorities the least word that he should address to the people.

5 In the meantime, Saint Issa continued to visit the neighboring towns, preaching the true ways of the Creator, exhorting the Hebrews to patience, and promising them a speedy deliverance.

6 And during all this time, many people followed him wherever he went, several never leaving him but becoming his servitors (attendant to their superior).

7 And Issa said: "Do not believe in miracles wrought by the hand of

man, for he who dominates over nature is alone capable of doing that which is supernatural, while man is powerless to stay the anger of the winds or to spread the rain.

8 "Nevertheless, there is one miracle which it is possible for man to accomplish. It is when, full of a sincere belief, he decides to root out from his heart all evil thoughts, and when to attain his end he forsakes the paths of iniquity.

9 "And all the things that are done without God are but errors, seductions, and enchantments, which only demonstrate to what an extent the soul of him who practices this is full of shamelessness, falsehood, and impurity."

10 "Put not your faith in oracles; God alone knows the future: he who has recourse to diviners profanes the temple which is in his heart and gives a proof of distrust towards his Creator."

11 "Faith in diviners and in their oracles destroys the innate simplicity of man and his childlike purity. An infernal power takes possession of him, forcing him to commit all sorts of crimes and to worship idols;"

12 "whereas the Lord our God, who has no equal, is one (unified), all-mighty, omniscient, and omnipresent. It is he who possesses all wisdom and all light."

13 "It is to him you must address yourselves to be consoled in your sorrows, helped in your works, and cured in your sickness. Whosoever shall have recourse to him shall not be denied."

14 "The secret of nature is in the hands of God. For the world, before it appeared, existed in the depth of the divine thought; it became material and visible by the will of the Most High."

15 "When you address yourselves to him, become again as children; for you know neither the past, the present, nor the future, and God is the Master of all time."

CHAPTER XII

1 The spies of the governor of Jerusalem said to him, "Righteous man, tell us if we shall perform the will of our Caesar or await our speedy deliverance. "

2 And Issa, having recognized them as people appointed to follow him, replied: "I have not said to you that you shall be delivered from Caesar. It is the soul plunged in error that shall have its deliverance."

3 "As there can be no family without a head, so there can be no order among a people without a Caesar; to him implicit obedience should be given, he alone being answerable for his acts before the supreme tribunal."

4 "Does Caesar possess a divine right?" further asked of him the spies. "And is he the best of mortals?"

5 "There should be no better among men, but there are also sufferers, whom those elected and charged with this mission should care for, by making use of the means conferred on them by the sacred law of our Heavenly Father."

6 "Mercy and justice are the highest attributes of a Caesar; his name will be illustrious if he adhere to them."

7 "But he who acts otherwise, who exceeds the limit of power that he has over his subordinates and goes so far as to put their lives in danger offends the great Judge and loses his dignity in the sight of man."

8 At this juncture, an old woman who had approached the group, the better to hear Issa, was pushed aside by one of the spies, who placed himself before her.

9 Then Issa held forth (his hand and said): "It is not good (meant) that

a son should set aside his mother to take her place. Whosoever respects not his mother, the most sacred being after his God, is unworthy of the name of son.

10 "Listen, then, to what I say to you: Respect woman, for she is the mother of the universe, and all the truth of divine creation lies in her."

11 "She is the basis of all that is good and beautiful, as she is also the germ of life and death. On her depends the whole existence of man, for she is his natural and moral support."

12 "She gives birth to you in the midst of suffering. By the sweat of her brow she rears you, and until her death you cause her the gravest anxieties. Bless her and worship her, for she is your one friend, your one support on earth."

13 "Respect her, uphold her. In acting thus you will win her love and her heart. You will find favor in the sight of God and many sins shall be forgiven you."

14 "In the same way, love your wives and respect them; for they will be mothers tomorrow, and each later on the ancestress of a race."

15 "Be lenient towards woman. Her love ennobles man, softens his hardened heart, tames the brute in him, and makes of him a lamb."

16 "The wife and the mother are the treasures beyond realms of appreciation given to you by God. They are the fairest ornaments of existence, and of them shall be born all the inhabitants of the world."

17 "Even as the God of armies separated of old the light from the darkness and the land from the waters, woman possesses the divine faculty of separating in a man good intentions from evil thoughts."

18 "Therefore I say to you, after God your best thoughts should belong to the women and the wives, woman being for you the temple wherein you will obtain the most easily perfect happiness."

19 "Acquire moral strength for yourselves in this temple. Here you will forget your sorrows and your failures, and you will recover the lost energy necessary to enable you to help your neighbor."

20 "Do not expose her to humiliation. In acting thus you would humiliate yourselves and lose the sentiment of love, without which nothing exists here below."

21 "Protect your wife, in order that she may protect you and all your family. All that you do for your wife, your mother, for a widow or another woman in distress, you will have done to your God."

CHAPTER XIII

1 Saint Issa taught the people of Israel thus for three years, in every town, in every village, by the waysides and on the plains; and all that he had predicted came to pass.

2 During all this time the disguised servants of Pilate watched him closely without hearing anything said like to the reports made against Issa in former years by the chiefs of the towns.

3 But the governor Pilate, becoming alarmed at the too great popularity of Saint Issa, who according to his adversaries sought to stir up the people to proclaim him king, ordered one of his spies to accuse him.

4 Then soldiers were commanded to proceed to his arrest, and they imprisoned him in a subterranean cell where they tortured him in various ways in the hope of forcing him to make a confession which should permit his being put to death.

5 The saint, thinking only of the perfect beatitude of his brethren, supported (endured) all his sufferings in the name of his Creator.

6 The servants of Pilate continued to torture him and reduced him to a state of extreme weakness; but God was with him and did not allow him to die.

7 Learning of the sufferings and the tortures, which their saint was enduring, the high priests and the wise elders went to pray the governor to set Issa at liberty in honor of an approaching festival.

8 But the governor straightway refused them this. They then prayed him to allow Issa to appear before the tribunal of the ancients so that he might be condemned or acquitted before the festival, and to this Pilate consented.

9 The next day the governor assembled together the chief captains, priests, wise elders, and lawyers so that they might judge Issa.

10 They brought him from his prison and seated him before the governor between two thieves to be judged at the same time as he, in order to show to the crowd that he was not the only one to be condemned.

11 And Pilate, addressing himself to Issa, said to him: "O man! is it true that you incite the people against the authorities with the intent of yourself becoming king of Israel?"

12 "One becomes not king at one's own will," replied Issa, "and they have lied who have told you that I stir up the people to rebellion. I have never spoken of other than the King of Heaven, and it is he I teach the people to worship."

13 "For the sons of Israel have lost their original purity; and if they have not recourse to the true God, they will be sacrificed and their temple shall fall into ruins."

14 "As temporal (earthly) power maintains order in a country, I teach them accordingly not to forget it. I say to them: 'Live conformably to your station and your fortune, so as not to disturb the public order.' And I have exhorted them also to remember that disorder reigns in their hearts and in their minds."

15 "Therefore the King of Heaven has punished them and suppressed their national kings. Nevertheless, I have said to them, 'If you become resigned to your destinies, as a reward the kingdom of heaven shall

be reserved for you."'

16 At this moment, the witnesses were brought forward, one of whom made the following deposition: "You have said to the people that the temporal (earthly) power is as nothing against that of the king who shall soon deliver the Israelites from the pagan yoke."

17 "Blessed are you," said Issa, "for having spoken the truth. The King of Heaven is greater and more powerful than the terrestrial law, and his kingdom surpasses all the kingdoms of the earth."

18 "And the time is not far off when, conforming to the divine will, the people of Israel shall purify them of their sins; for it has been said that a forerunner will come to proclaim the deliverance of the people, gathering them into one fold."

19 "And the governor, addressing himself to the judges, said: "Do you hear? The Israelite Issa confesses to the crime of which he is accused. Judge him, then, according to your laws, and pronounce against him capital punishment."

20 "We cannot condemn him," replied the priests and the elders. "You have just heard yourself that his allusions were made regarding the King of Heaven and that he has preached naught to the sons of Israel which could constitute an offense against the law."

21 The governor Pilate then sent for the witness who, at his instigation, had betrayed Issa. The man came and addressed Issa thus: "Did you not pass yourself off as the king of Israel when you said that he who reigns in the heavens had sent you to prepare his people?"

22 And Issa, having blessed him, said: "You shall be pardoned, for what you say does not come from you!" Then, addressing himself to the governor: "Why humiliate your dignity, and why teach your inferiors to live in falsehood, as without doing so you have power to condemn the innocent?"

23 At these words the governor became exceeding angry, ordering

the sentence of death to be passed on Issa and the acquittal of the two thieves.

24 The judges, having consulted together, said to Pilate: "We will not take upon our heads the great sin of condemning an innocent man and acquitting thieves. That would be against the law.

25 "Do then as you will." Saying this the priests and the wise elders went out and washed their hands in a sacred vessel, saying: "We are innocent of the death of this just man."

CHAPTER XIV

1 By the order of the governor, the soldiers then seized Issa and the two thieves, whom they led to the place of execution, where they nailed them to crosses erected on the ground.

2 All the day the bodies of Issa and the two thieves remained suspended, terrible to behold, under the guard of the soldiers; the people standing all around and the relatives of the sufferers were praying and weeping.

3 At sunset the sufferings of Issa came to an end. He lost consciousness, and the soul of this just man left his body to become absorbed in the Divinity.

4 Thus ended the earthly existence of the reflection of the Eternal Spirit under the form of a man who had saved hardened sinners and endured many sufferings.

Author's note: The following ending represents a divergence from mainline Christian Theology, which cannot be harmonized or reconciled. Under orders from Pilate the body of Issa (Jesus) is taken away. The "stolen body" theory is one of several explanations offered up by some who do not believe in the resurrection of Jesus.

5 Meanwhile, Pilate became afraid of his action and gave the body of the saint to his parents, who buried it near the spot of his execution.

The crowd came to pray over his tomb, and the air was filled with groans and lamentations.

6 Three days after, the governor sent his soldiers to carry away the body of Issa to bury it elsewhere, fearing otherwise a popular insurrection.

7 The next day the crowd found the tomb open and empty. At once the rumor spread that the supreme Judge had sent his angels to carry away the mortal remains of the saint in whom dwelt on earth a part of the Divine Spirit.

8 When this rumor reached the knowledge of Pilate, he became angered and forbade anyone, under the pain of slavery and death, to pronounce the name of Issa or to pray the Lord for him.

9 But the people continued to weep and to glorify aloud their Master; wherefore many were led into captivity, subjected to torture, and put to death.

10 And the disciples of Saint Issa abandoned the land of Israel and scattered themselves among the heathen, preaching that they should renounce their errors, bringing them to think about the salvation of their souls and of the perfect bliss (felicity) awaiting humanity in that immaterial (spiritual) world of light where, in repose (rest) and in all his purity, the Great Creator dwells in perfect majesty.

11 The pagans, their kings, and their warriors listened to the preachers, abandoned their absurd beliefs, and forsook their priests and their idols to celebrate the praise of the all-wise Creator of the universe, the King of kings, whose heart is filled with infinite mercy.

This ends the "Life of Saint Issa."

Gospel of Luke from the Holy Bible

Luke 3

[1] Now in the fifteenth year of the reign of Tiberius Caesar, Pontius Pilate being governor of Judaea, and Herod being tetrarch of Galilee, and his brother Philip tetrarch of Ituraea and of the region of Trachonitis, and Lysanias the tetrarch of Abilene,
[2] Annas and Caiaphas being the high priests, the word of God came to John the son of Zacharias in the wilderness.
[3] And he came into all the country about Jordan, preaching the baptism of repentance for the remission of sins;
[4] As it is written in the book of the words of Esaias the prophet, saying, The voice of one crying in the wilderness, Prepare you the way of the Lord, make his paths straight.
[5] Every valley shall be filled, and every mountain and hill shall be brought low; and the crooked shall be made straight, and the rough ways shall be made smooth;
[6] And all flesh shall see the salvation of God.
[7] Then said he to the multitude that came forth to be baptized of him, O generation of vipers, who has warned you to flee from the wrath to come?
[8] Bring forth therefore fruits worthy of repentance, and begin not to say within yourselves, We have Abraham to our father: for I say to you, That God is able of these stones to raise up children to Abraham.
[9] And now also the axe is laid to the root of the trees: every tree therefore which brings not forth good fruit is hewn down, and cast into the fire.
[10] And the people asked him, saying, What shall we do then?

[11] He answered and said to them, He that has two coats, let him impart to him that has none; and he that has meat, let him do likewise.
[12] Then came also publicans to be baptized, and said to him, Master, what shall we do?
[13] And he said to them, Exact no more than that which is appointed you.
[14] And the soldiers likewise demanded of him, saying, And what shall we do? And he said to them, Do violence to no man, neither accuse any falsely; and be content with your wages.
[15] And as the people were in expectation, and all men mused in their hearts of John, whether he were the Christ, or not;
[16] John answered, saying to them all, I indeed baptize you with water; but one mightier than I comes, the latchet of whose shoes I am not worthy to unloose: he shall baptize you with the Holy Ghost and with fire:
[17] Whose fan is in his hand, and he will thoroughly purge his floor, and will gather the wheat into his garner; but the chaff he will burn with fire unquenchable.
[18] And many other things in his exhortation preached he to the people.
[19] But Herod the tetrarch, being reproved by him for Herodias his brother Philip's wife, and for all the evils which Herod had done,
[20] Added yet this above all, that he shut up John in prison.
[21] Now when all the people were baptized, it came to pass, that Jesus also being baptized, and praying, the heaven was opened,
[22] And the Holy Ghost descended in a bodily shape like a dove upon him, and a voice came from heaven, which said, You are my beloved Son; in you I am well pleased.
[23] And Jesus himself began to be about thirty years of age, being (as was supposed) the son of Joseph, which was the son of Heli,
[24] Which was the son of Matthat, which was the son of Levi, which was the son of Melchi, which was the son of Janna, which was the son of Joseph,
[25] Which was the son of Mattathias, which was the son of Amos, which was the son of Naum, which was the son of Esli, which was the son of Nagge,
[26] Which was the son of Maath, which was the son of Mattathias, which was the son of Semei, which was the son of Joseph, which was the son of Juda,

[27] Which was the son of Joannes, which was the son of Rhesa, which was the son of Zerubabel, which was the son of Salathiel, which was the son of Neri,
[28] Which was the son of Melchi, which was the son of Addi, which was the son of Cosam, which was the son of Elmodam, which was the son of Er,
[29] Which was the son of Jose, which was the son of Eliezer, which was the son of Jorim, which was the son of Matthat, which was the son of Levi,
[30] Which was the son of Simeon, which was the son of Juda, which was the son of Joseph, which was the son of Jonan, which was the son of Eliakim,
[31] Which was the son of Melea, which was the son of Menan, which was the son of Mattatha, which was the son of Nathan, which was the son of David,
[32] Which was the son of Jesse, which was the son of Obed, which was the son of Boaz, which was the son of Salmon, which was the son of Naasson,
[33] Which was the son of Aminadab, which was the son of Aram, which was the son of Esrom, which was the son of Phares, which was the son of Juda,
[34] Which was the son of Jacob, which was the son of Isaac, which was the son of Abraham, which was the son of Thara, which was the son of Nachor,
[35] Which was the son of Saruch, which was the son of Ragau, which was the son of Phalec, which was the son of Heber, which was the son of Sala,
[36] Which was the son of Cainan, which was the son of Arphaxad, which was the son of Shem, which was the son of Noe, which was the son of Lamech,
[37] Which was the son of Mathusala, which was the son of Enoch, which was the son of Jared, which was the son of Maleleel, which was the son of Cainan,
[38] Which was the son of Enos, which was the son of Seth, which was the son of Adam, which was the son of God.

Luke 4

[1] And Jesus being full of the Holy Ghost returned from Jordan, and

was led by the Spirit into the wilderness,
[2] Being forty days tempted of the devil. And in those days he did eat nothing: and when they were ended, he afterward hungered.
[3] And the devil said to him, If you be the Son of God, command this stone that it be made bread.
[4] And Jesus answered him, saying, It is written, That man shall not live by bread alone, but by every word of God.
[5] And the devil, taking him up into a high mountain, showed to him all the kingdoms of the world in a moment of time.
[6] And the devil said to him, All this power will I give you, and the glory of them: for that is delivered to me; and to whomsoever I will I give it.
[7] If you therefore will worship me, all shall be yours.
[8] And Jesus answered and said to him, Get you behind me, Satan: for it is written, You shall worship the Lord your God, and him only shall you serve.
[9] And he brought him to Jerusalem, and set him on a pinnacle of the temple, and said to him, If you be the Son of God, cast yourself down from here:
[10] For it is written, He shall give his angels charge over you, to keep you:
[11] And in their hands they shall bear you up, lest at any time you dash your foot against a stone.
[12] And Jesus answering said to him, It is said, You shall not tempt the Lord your God.
[13] And when the devil had ended all the temptation, he departed from him for a season.
[14] And Jesus returned in the power of the Spirit into Galilee: and there went out a fame of him through all the region round about.
[15] And he taught in their synagogues, being glorified of all.
[16] And he came to Nazareth, where he had been brought up: and, as his custom was, he went into the synagogue on the Sabbath day, and stood up for to read.
[17] And there was delivered to him the book of the prophet Esaias. And when he had opened the book, he found the place where it was written,
[18] The Spirit of the Lord is upon me, because he has anointed me to preach the gospel to the poor; he has sent me to heal the brokenhearted, to preach deliverance to the captives, and recovering of sight to the blind, to set at liberty them that are bruised,

[19] To preach the acceptable year of the Lord.
[20] And he closed the book, and he gave it again to the minister, and sat down. And the eyes of all them that were in the synagogue were fastened on him.
[21] And he began to say to them, This day is this scripture fulfilled in your ears.
[22] And all bare him witness, and wondered at the gracious words which proceeded out of his mouth. And they said, Is not this Joseph's son?
[23] And he said to them, You will surely say to me this proverb, Physician, heal yourself: whatsoever we have heard done in Capernaum, do also here in your country.
[24] And he said, Truly I say to you, No prophet is accepted in his own country.
[25] But I tell you of a truth, many widows were in Israel in the days of Elias, when the heaven was shut up three years and six months, when great famine was throughout all the land;
[26] But to none of them was Elias sent, save to Sarepta, a city of Sidon, to a woman that was a widow.
[27] And many lepers were in Israel in the time of Eliseus the prophet; and none of them was cleansed, saving Naaman the Syrian.
[28] And all they in the synagogue, when they heard these things, were filled with wrath,
[29] And rose up, and thrust him out of the city, and led him to the brow of the hill whereon their city was built, that they might cast him down headlong.
[30] But he passing through the midst of them went his way,
[31] And came down to Capernaum, a city of Galilee, and taught them on the Sabbath days.
[32] And they were astonished at his doctrine: for his word was with power.
[33] And in the synagogue there was a man, which had a spirit of an unclean devil, and cried out with a loud voice,
[34] Saying, Let us alone; what have we to do with you, you Jesus of Nazareth? are you come to destroy us? I know you who you are; the Holy One of God.
[35] And Jesus rebuked him, saying, Hold your peace, and come out of him. And when the devil had thrown him in the midst, he came out of him, and hurt him not.
[36] And they were all amazed, and spoke among themselves,

saying, What a word is this! for with authority and power he commands the unclean spirits, and they come out.
[37] And the fame of him went out into every place of the country round about.
[38] And he arose out of the synagogue, and entered into Simon's house. And Simon's wife's mother was taken with a great fever; and they besought him for her.
[39] And he stood over her, and rebuked the fever; and it left her: and immediately she arose and ministered to them.
[40] Now when the sun was setting, all they that had any sick with divers diseases brought them to him; and he laid his hands on every one of them, and healed them.
[41] And devils also came out of many, crying out, and saying, You are Christ the Son of God. And he rebuking them suffered them not to speak: for they knew that he was Christ.
[42] And when it was day, he departed and went into a desert place: and the people sought him, and came to him, and stayed him, that he should not depart from them.
[43] And he said to them, I must preach the kingdom of God to other cities also: for therefore am I sent.
[44] And he preached in the synagogues of Galilee.

Luke 5

[1] And it came to pass, that, as the people pressed upon him to hear the word of God, he stood by the lake of Gennesaret,
[2] And saw two ships standing by the lake: but the fishermen were gone out of them, and were washing their nets.
[3] And he entered into one of the ships, which was Simon's, and prayed him that he would thrust out a little from the land. And he sat down, and taught the people out of the ship.
[4] Now when he had left speaking, he said to Simon, Launch out into the deep, and let down your nets for a draught.
[5] And Simon answering said to him, Master, we have toiled all the night, and have taken nothing: nevertheless at your word I will let down the net.
[6] And when they had this done, they enclosed a great multitude of fishes: and their net brake.
[7] And they beckoned to their partners, which were in the other

ship, that they should come and help them. And they came, and filled both the ships, so that they began to sink.

[8] When Simon Peter saw it, he fell down at Jesus' knees, saying, Depart from me; for I am a sinful man, O Lord.

[9] For he was astonished, and all that were with him, at the draught of the fishes which they had taken:

[10] And so was also James, and John, the sons of Zebedee, which were partners with Simon. And Jesus said to Simon, Fear not; from now on you shall catch men.

[11] And when they had brought their ships to land, they forsook all, and followed him.

[12] And it came to pass, when he was in a certain city, behold a man full of leprosy: who seeing Jesus fell on his face, and besought him, saying, Lord, if you will, you canst make me clean.

[13] And he put forth his hand, and touched him, saying, I will: be you clean. And immediately the leprosy departed from him.

[14] And he charged him to tell no man: but go, and show yourself to the priest, and offer for your cleansing, according as Moses commanded, for a testimony to them.

[15] But so much the more went there a fame abroad of him: and great multitudes came together to hear, and to be healed by him of their infirmities.

[16] And he withdrew himself into the wilderness, and prayed.

[17] And it came to pass on a certain day, as he was teaching, that there were Pharisees and doctors of the law sitting by, which were come out of every town of Galilee, and Judaea, and Jerusalem: and the power of the Lord was present to heal them.

[18] And, behold, men brought in a bed a man which was taken with a palsy: and they sought means to bring him in, and to lay him before him.

[19] And when they could not find by what way they might bring him in because of the multitude, they went on the housetop, and let him down through the tiling with his couch into the midst before Jesus.

[20] And when he saw their faith, he said to him, Man, your sins are forgiven you.

[21] And the scribes and the Pharisees began to reason, saying, Who is this which speaks blasphemies? Who can forgive sins, but God alone?

[22] But when Jesus perceived their thoughts, he answering said to

them, What reason you in your hearts?

[23] Whether is easier, to say, Your sins be forgiven you; or to say, Rise up and walk?

[24] But that you may know that the Son of man has power on earth to forgive sins, (he said to the sick of the palsy,) I say to you, Arise, and take up your couch, and go into your house.

[25] And immediately he rose up before them, and took up that whereon he lay, and departed to his own house, glorifying God.

[26] And they were all amazed, and they glorified God, and were filled with fear, saying, We have seen strange things to day.

[27] And after these things he went forth, and saw a publican, named Levi, sitting at the receipt of custom: and he said to him, Follow me.

[28] And he left all, rose up, and followed him.

[29] And Levi made him a great feast in his own house: and there was a great company of publicans and of others that sat down with them.

[30] But their scribes and Pharisees murmured against his disciples, saying, Why do you eat and drink with publicans and sinners?

[31] And Jesus answering said to them, They that are whole need not a physician; but they that are sick.

[32] I came not to call the righteous, but sinners to repentance.

[33] And they said to him, Why do the disciples of John fast often, and make prayers, and likewise the disciples of the Pharisees; but your eat and drink?

[34] And he said to them, Can you make the children of the bridechamber fast, while the bridegroom is with them?

[35] But the days will come, when the bridegroom shall be taken away from them, and then shall they fast in those days.

[36] And he spoke also a parable to them; No man puts a piece of a new garment upon an old; if otherwise, then both the new makes a rent, and the piece that was taken out of the new agrees not with the old.

[37] And no man puts new wine into old bottles; else the new wine will burst the bottles, and be spilled, and the bottles shall perish.

[38] But new wine must be put into new bottles; and both are preserved.

[39] No man also having drunk old wine straightway desires new: for he said, The old is better.

Luke 6

[1] And it came to pass on the second Sabbath after the first, that he went through the corn fields; and his disciples plucked the ears of corn, and did eat, rubbing them in their hands.
[2] And certain of the Pharisees said to them, Why do you that which is not lawful to do on the Sabbath days?
[3] And Jesus answering them said, Have you not read so much as this, what David did, when he was hungry, and they which were with him;
[4] How he went into the house of God, and did take and eat the shewbread, and gave also to them that were with him; which it is not lawful to eat but for the priests alone?
[5] And he said to them, That the Son of man is Lord also of the Sabbath.
[6] And it came to pass also on another Sabbath, that he entered into the synagogue and taught: and there was a man whose right hand was withered.
[7] And the scribes and Pharisees watched him, whether he would heal on the Sabbath day; that they might find an accusation against him.
[8] But he knew their thoughts, and said to the man which had the withered hand, Rise up, and stand forth in the midst. And he arose and stood forth.
[9] Then said Jesus to them, I will ask you one thing; Is it lawful on the Sabbath days to do good, or to do evil? to save life, or to destroy it?
[10] And looking round about upon them all, he said to the man, Stretch forth your hand. And he did so: and his hand was restored whole as the other.
[11] And they were filled with madness; and communed one with another what they might do to Jesus.
[12] And it came to pass in those days, that he went out into a mountain to pray, and continued all night in prayer to God.
[13] And when it was day, he called to him his disciples: and of them he chose twelve, whom also he named apostles;
[14] Simon, (whom he also named Peter,) and Andrew his brother, James and John, Philip and Bartholomew,
[15] Matthew and Thomas, James the son of Alphaeus, and Simon called Zelotes,

[16] And Judas the brother of James, and Judas Iscariot, which also was the traitor.
[17] And he came down with them, and stood in the plain, and the company of his disciples, and a great multitude of people out of all Judaea and Jerusalem, and from the sea coast of Tyre and Sidon, which came to hear him, and to be healed of their diseases;
[18] And they that were vexed with unclean spirits: and they were healed.
[19] And the whole multitude sought to touch him: for there went virtue out of him, and healed them all.
[20] And he lifted up his eyes on his disciples, and said, Blessed be you poor: for yours is the kingdom of God.
[21] Blessed are you that hunger now: for you shall be filled. Blessed are you that weep now: for you shall laugh.
[22] Blessed are you, when men shall hate you, and when they shall separate you from their company, and shall ridicule you, and cast out your name as evil, for the Son of man's sake.
[23] Rejoice you in that day, and leap for joy: for, behold, your reward is great in heaven: for in the like manner did their fathers to the prophets.
[24] But woe to you that are rich! for you have received your consolation.
[25] Woe to you that are full! for you shall hunger. Woe to you that laugh now! for you shall mourn and weep.
[26] Woe to you, when all men shall speak well of you! for so did their fathers to the false prophets.
[27] But I say to you which hear, Love your enemies, do good to them which hate you,
[28] Bless them that curse you, and pray for them which despitefully use you.
[29] And to him that strikes you on the one cheek offer also the other; and him that takes away your cloak forbid not to take your coat also.
[30] Give to every man that asks of you; and of him that takes away your goods ask them not again.
[31] And as you would that men should do to you, do you also to them likewise.
[32] For if you love them which love you, what thank have you? for sinners also love those that love them.
[33] And if you do good to them which do good to you, what thank have you? for sinners also do even the same.

[34] And if you lend to them of whom you hope to receive, what thank have you? for sinners also lend to sinners, to receive as much again.
[35] But love you your enemies, and do good, and lend, hoping for nothing again; and your reward shall be great, and you shall be the children of the Highest: for he is kind to the unthankful and to the evil.
[36] Be you therefore merciful, as your Father also is merciful.
[37] Judge not, and you shall not be judged: condemn not, and you shall not be condemned: forgive, and you shall be forgiven:
[38] Give, and it shall be given to you; good measure, pressed down, and shaken together, and running over, shall men give into your bosom. For with the same measure that you mete withal it shall be measured to you again.
[39] And he spoke a parable to them, Can the blind lead the blind? shall they not both fall into the ditch?
[40] The disciple is not above his master: but every one that is perfect shall be as his master.
[41] And why behold you the mote that is in your brother's eye, but perceive not the beam that is in your own eye?
[42] Either how canst you say to your brother, Brother, let me pull out the mote that is in your eye, when you yourself behold not the beam that is in your own eye? You hypocrite, cast out first the beam out of your own eye, and then shall you see clearly to pull out the mote that is in your brother's eye.
[43] For a good tree brings not forth corrupt fruit; neither does a corrupt tree bring forth good fruit.
[44] For every tree is known by his own fruit. For of thorns men do not gather figs, nor of a bramble bush gather they grapes.
[45] A good man out of the good treasure of his heart brings forth that which is good; and an evil man out of the evil treasure of his heart brings forth that which is evil: for of the abundance of the heart his mouth speaks.
[46] And why call you me, Lord, Lord, and do not the things which I say?
[47] Whosoever comes to me, and hears my sayings, and does them, I will show you to whom he is like:
[48] He is like a man which built a house, and dug deep, and laid the foundation on a rock: and when the flood arose, the stream beat vehemently upon that house, and could not shake it: for it was

founded upon a rock.
[49] But he that hears, and does not, is like a man that without a foundation built a house upon the earth; against which the stream did beat vehemently, and immediately it fell; and the ruin of that house was great.

Luke 7

[1] Now when he had ended all his sayings in the audience of the people, he entered into Capernaum.
[2] And a certain centurion's servant, who was dear to him, was sick, and ready to die.
[3] And when he heard of Jesus, he sent to him the elders of the Jews, beseeching him that he would come and heal his servant.
[4] And when they came to Jesus, they besought him instantly, saying, That he was worthy for whom he should do this:
[5] For he loves our nation, and he has built us a synagogue.
[6] Then Jesus went with them. And when he was now not far from the house, the centurion sent friends to him, saying to him, Lord, trouble not yourself: for I am not worthy that you should enter under my roof:
[7] Therefore neither thought I myself worthy to come to you: but say in a word, and my servant shall be healed.
[8] For I also am a man set under authority, having under me soldiers, and I say to one, Go, and he goes; and to another, Come, and he comes; and to my servant, Do this, and he does it.
[9] When Jesus heard these things, he marveled at him, and turned him about, and said to the people that followed him, I say to you, I have not found so great faith, no, not in Israel.
[10] And they that were sent, returning to the house, found the servant whole that had been sick.
[11] And it came to pass the day after, that he went into a city called Nain; and many of his disciples went with him, and much people.
[12] Now when he came near to the gate of the city, behold, there was a dead man carried out, the only son of his mother, and she was a widow: and much people of the city was with her.
[13] And when the Lord saw her, he had compassion on her, and said to her, Weep not.

[14] And he came and touched the bier: and they that bare him stood still. And he said, Young man, I say to you, Arise.
[15] And he that was dead sat up, and began to speak. And he delivered him to his mother.
[16] And there came a fear on all: and they glorified God, saying, That a great prophet is risen up among us; and, That God has visited his people.
[17] And this rumor of him went forth throughout all Judaea, and throughout all the region round about.
[18] And the disciples of John showed him of all these things.
[19] And John calling to him two of his disciples sent them to Jesus, saying, Are you he that should come? or look we for another?
[20] When the men were come to him, they said, John Baptist has sent us to you, saying, Are you he that should come? or look we for another?
[21] And in that same hour he cured many of their infirmities and plagues, and of evil spirits; and to many that were blind he gave sight.
[22] Then Jesus answering said to them, Go your way, and tell John what things you have seen and heard; how that the blind see, the lame walk, the lepers are cleansed, the deaf hear, the dead are raised, to the poor the gospel is preached.
[23] And blessed is he, whoever shall not be offended in me.
[24] And when the messengers of John were departed, he began to speak to the people concerning John, What went you out into the wilderness for to see? A reed shaken with the wind?
[25] But what went you out for to see? A man clothed in soft raiment? Behold, they which are gorgeously appareled, and live delicately, are in kings' courts.
[26] But what went you out for to see? A prophet? Yea, I say to you, and much more than a prophet.
[27] This is he, of whom it is written, Behold, I send my messenger before your face, which shall prepare your way before you.
[28] For I say to you, Among those that are born of women there is not a greater prophet than John the Baptist: but he that is least in the kingdom of God is greater than he.
[29] And all the people that heard him, and the publicans, justified God, being baptized with the baptism of John.
[30] But the Pharisees and lawyers rejected the counsel of God against themselves, being not baptized of him.

[31] And the Lord said, Whereunto then shall I liken the men of this generation? and to what are they like?
[32] They are like to children sitting in the marketplace, and calling one to another, and saying, We have piped to you, and you have not danced; we have mourned to you, and you have not wept.
[33] For John the Baptist came neither eating bread nor drinking wine; and you say, He has a devil.
[34] The Son of man is come eating and drinking; and you say, Behold a gluttonous man, and a winebibber, a friend of publicans and sinners!
[35] But wisdom is justified of all her children.
[36] And one of the Pharisees desired him that he would eat with him. And he went into the Pharisee's house, and sat down to meat.
[37] And, behold, a woman in the city, which was a sinner, when she knew that Jesus sat at meat in the Pharisee's house, brought an alabaster box of ointment,
[38] And stood at his feet behind him weeping, and began to wash his feet with tears, and did wipe them with the hairs of her head, and kissed his feet, and anointed them with the ointment.
[39] Now when the Pharisee which had bidden him saw it, he spoke within himself, saying, This man, if he were a prophet, would have known who and what manner of woman this is that touched him: for she is a sinner.
[40] And Jesus answering said to him, Simon, I have somewhat to say to you. And he said, Master, say on.
[41] There was a certain creditor which had two debtors: the one owed five hundred pence, and the other fifty.
[42] And when they had nothing to pay, he frankly forgave them both. Tell me therefore, which of them will love him most?
[43] Simon answered and said, I suppose that he, to whom he forgave most. And he said to him, You have rightly judged.
[44] And he turned to the woman, and said to Simon, See you this woman? I entered into your house, you gave me no water for my feet: but she has washed my feet with tears, and wiped them with the hairs of her head.
[45] You gave me no kiss: but this woman since the time I came in has not ceased to kiss my feet.
[46] My head with oil you did not anoint: but this woman has anointed my feet with ointment.
[47] Therefore I say to you, Her sins, which are many, are forgiven;

for she loved much: but to whom little is forgiven, the same loves little.
[48] And he said to her, Your sins are forgiven.
[49] And they that sat at meat with him began to say within themselves, Who is this that forgives sins also?
[50] And he said to the woman, Your faith has saved you; go in peace.

Luke 8

[1] And it came to pass afterward, that he went throughout every city and village, preaching and showing the glad tidings of the kingdom of God: and the twelve were with him,
[2] And certain women, which had been healed of evil spirits and infirmities, Mary called Magdalene, out of whom went seven devils,
[3] And Joanna the wife of Chuza Herod's steward, and Susanna, and many others, which ministered to him of their substance.
[4] And when much people were gathered together, and were come to him out of every city, he spoke by a parable:
[5] A sower went out to sow his seed: and as he sowed, some fell by the way side; and it was trodden down, and the fowls of the air devoured it.
[6] And some fell on a rock; and as soon as it was sprung up, it withered away, because it lacked moisture.
[7] And some fell among thorns; and the thorns sprang up with it, and choked it.
[8] And other fell on good ground, and sprang up, and bare fruit a hundredfold. And when he had said these things, he cried, He that has ears to hear, let him hear.
[9] And his disciples asked him, saying, What might this parable be?
[10] And he said, Unto you it is given to know the mysteries of the kingdom of God: but to others in parables; that seeing they might not see, and hearing they might not understand.
[11] Now the parable is this: The seed is the word of God.
[12] Those by the way side are they that hear; then comes the devil, and takes away the word out of their hearts, lest they should believe and be saved.
[13] They on the rock are they, which, when they hear, receive the word with joy; and these have no root, which for a while believe, and

in time of temptation fall away.
[14] And that which fell among thorns are they, which, when they have heard, go forth, and are choked with cares and riches and pleasures of this life, and bring no fruit to perfection.
[15] But that on the good ground are they, which in an honest and good heart, having heard the word, keep it, and bring forth fruit with patience.
[16] No man, when he has lighted a candle, covers it with a vessel, or puts it under a bed; but sets it on a candlestick, that they which enter in may see the light.
[17] For nothing is secret, that shall not be made manifest; neither any thing hid, that shall not be known and come abroad.
[18] Take heed therefore how you hear: for whoever has, to him shall be given; and whoever has not, from him shall be taken even that which he seems to have.
[19] Then came to him his mother and his brethren, and could not come at him for the press.
[20] And it was told him by certain which said, Your mother and your brethren stand without, desiring to see you.
[21] And he answered and said to them, My mother and my brethren are these which hear the word of God, and do it.
[22] Now it came to pass on a certain day, that he went into a ship with his disciples: and he said to them, Let us go over to the other side of the lake. And they launched forth.
[23] But as they sailed he fell asleep: and there came down a storm of wind on the lake; and they were filled with water, and were in jeopardy.
[24] And they came to him, and awoke him, saying, Master, master, we perish. Then he arose, and rebuked the wind and the raging of the water: and they ceased, and there was a calm.
[25] And he said to them, Where is your faith? And they being afraid wondered, saying one to another, What manner of man is this! for he commands even the winds and water, and they obey him.
[26] And they arrived at the country of the Gadarenes, which is over against Galilee.
[27] And when he went forth to land, there met him out of the city a certain man, which had devils a long time, and ware no clothes, neither abode in any house, but in the tombs.
[28] When he saw Jesus, he cried out, and fell down before him, and with a loud voice said, What have I to do with you, Jesus, you Son of

God most high? I beg you, torment me not.

[29] (For he had commanded the unclean spirit to come out of the man. For oftentimes it had caught him: and he was kept bound with chains and in fetters; and he brake the bands, and was driven of the devil into the wilderness.)

[30] And Jesus asked him, saying, What is your name? And he said, Legion: because many devils were entered into him.

[31] And they besought him that he would not command them to go out into the deep.

[32] And there was there a herd of many swine feeding on the mountain: and they besought him that he would suffer them to enter into them. And he suffered them.

[33] Then went the devils out of the man, and entered into the swine: and the herd ran violently down a steep place into the lake, and were choked.

[34] When they that fed them saw what was done, they fled, and went and told it in the city and in the country.

[35] Then they went out to see what was done; and came to Jesus, and found the man, out of whom the devils were departed, sitting at the feet of Jesus, clothed, and in his right mind: and they were afraid.

[36] They also which saw it told them by what means he that was possessed of the devils was healed.

[37] Then the whole multitude of the country of the Gadarenes round about besought him to depart from them; for they were taken with great fear: and he went up into the ship, and returned back again.

[38] Now the man out of whom the devils were departed besought him that he might be with him: but Jesus sent him away, saying,

[39] Return to your own house, and show how great things God has done to you. And he went his way, and published throughout the whole city how great things Jesus had done to him.

[40] And it came to pass, that, when Jesus was returned, the people gladly received him: for they were all waiting for him.

[41] And, behold, there came a man named Jairus, and he was a ruler of the synagogue: and he fell down at Jesus' feet, and besought him that he would come into his house:

[42] For he had one only daughter, about twelve years of age, and she lay a dying. But as he went the people thronged him.

[43] And a woman having an issue of blood twelve years, which had spent all her living on physicians, neither could be healed of any,

[44] Came behind him, and touched the border of his garment: and

immediately her issue of blood stanched.
[45] And Jesus said, Who touched me? When all denied, Peter and they that were with him said, Master, the multitude throng you and press you, and say you, Who touched me?
[46] And Jesus said, Somebody has touched me: for I perceive that virtue is gone out of me.
[47] And when the woman saw that she was not hid, she came trembling, and falling down before him, she declared to him before all the people for what cause she had touched him and how she was healed immediately.
[48] And he said to her, Daughter, be of good comfort: your faith has made you whole; go in peace.
[49] While he yet spoke, there comes one from the ruler of the synagogue's house, saying to him, Your daughter is dead; trouble not the Master.
[50] But when Jesus heard it, he answered him, saying, Fear not: believe only, and she shall be made whole.
[51] And when he came into the house, he suffered no man to go in, save Peter, and James, and John, and the father and the mother of the maiden.
[52] And all wept, and bewailed her: but he said, Weep not; she is not dead, but sleeps.
[53] And they laughed him to scorn, knowing that she was dead.
[54] And he put them all out, and took her by the hand, and called, saying, Maid, arise.
[55] And her spirit came again, and she arose straightway: and he commanded to give her meat.
[56] And her parents were astonished: but he charged them that they should tell no man what was done.

Luke 9

[1] Then he called his twelve disciples together, and gave them power and authority over all devils, and to cure diseases.
[2] And he sent them to preach the kingdom of God, and to heal the sick.
[3] And he said to them, Take nothing for your journey, neither staves, nor scrip (purse-bag), neither bread, neither money; neither have two coats apiece.

[4] And whatsoever house you enter into, there abide, and from there depart.
[5] And whoever will not receive you, when you go out of that city, shake off the very dust from your feet for a testimony against them.
[6] And they departed, and went through the towns, preaching the gospel, and healing every where.
[7] Now Herod the tetrarch heard of all that was done by him: and he was perplexed, because that it was said of some, that John was risen from the dead;
[8] And of some, that Elias had appeared; and of others, that one of the old prophets was risen again.
[9] And Herod said, John have I beheaded: but who is this, of whom I hear such things? And he desired to see him.
[10] And the apostles, when they were returned, told him all that they had done. And he took them, and went aside privately into a desert place belonging to the city called Bethsaida.
[11] And the people, when they knew it, followed him: and he received them, and spoke to them of the kingdom of God, and healed them that had need of healing.
[12] And when the day began to wear away, then came the twelve, and said to him, Send the multitude away, that they may go into the towns and country round about, and lodge, and get victuals: for we are here in a desert place.
[13] But he said to them, Give you them to eat. And they said, We have no more but five loaves and two fishes; except we should go and buy meat for all this people.
[14] For they were about five thousand men. And he said to his disciples, Make them sit down by fifties in a company.
[15] And they did so, and made them all sit down.
[16] Then he took the five loaves and the two fishes, and looking up to heaven, he blessed them, and brake, and gave to the disciples to set before the multitude.
[17] And they did eat, and were all filled: and there was taken up of fragments that remained to them twelve baskets.
[18] And it came to pass, as he was alone praying, his disciples were with him: and he asked them, saying, Whom say the people that I am?
[19] They answering said, John the Baptist; but some say, Elias; and others say, that one of the old prophets is risen again.
[20] He said to them, But whom say you that I am? Peter answering

said, The Christ of God.

[21] And he directly charged them, and commanded them to tell no man that thing;

[22] Saying, The Son of man must suffer many things, and be rejected of the elders and chief priests and scribes, and be slain, and be raised the third day.

[23] And he said to them all, If any man will come after me, let him deny himself, and take up his cross daily, and follow me.

[24] For whoever will save his life shall lose it: but whoever will lose his life for my sake, the same shall save it.

[25] For what is a man advantaged, if he gain the whole world, and lose himself, or be cast away?

[26] For whoever shall be ashamed of me and of my words, of him shall the Son of man be ashamed, when he shall come in his own glory, and in his Father's, and of the holy angels.

[27] But I tell you of a truth, there be some standing here, which shall not taste of death, till they see the kingdom of God.

[28] And it came to pass about eight days after these sayings, he took Peter and John and James, and went up into a mountain to pray.

[29] And as he prayed, the fashion of his countenance was altered, and his raiment was white and glistering.

[30] And, behold, there talked with him two men, which were Moses and Elias:

[31] Who appeared in glory, and spoke of his decease which he should accomplish at Jerusalem.

[32] But Peter and they that were with him were heavy with sleep: and when they were awake, they saw his glory, and the two men that stood with him.

[33] And it came to pass, as they departed from him, Peter said to Jesus, Master, it is good for us to be here: and let us make three tabernacles; one for you, and one for Moses, and one for Elias: not knowing what he said.

[34] While he thus spoke, there came a cloud, and overshadowed them: and they feared as they entered into the cloud.

[35] And there came a voice out of the cloud, saying, This is my beloved Son: hear him.

[36] And when the voice was past, Jesus was found alone. And they kept it close, and told no man in those days any of those things which they had seen.

[37] And it came to pass, that on the next day, when they were come

down from the hill, much people met him.
[38] And, behold, a man of the company cried out, saying, Master, I beg you, look on my son: for he is my only child.
[39] And, lo, a spirit takes him, and he suddenly cries out; and it tears him that he foams again, and bruising him hardly departs from him.
[40] And I besought your disciples to cast him out; and they could not.
[41] And Jesus answering said, O faithless and perverse generation, how long shall I be with you, and suffer you? Bring your son here.
[42] And as he was yet a coming, the devil threw him down, and tare him. And Jesus rebuked the unclean spirit, and healed the child, and delivered him again to his father.
[43] And they were all amazed at the mighty power of God. But while they wondered every one at all things which Jesus did, he said to his disciples,
[44] Let these sayings sink down into your ears: for the Son of man shall be delivered into the hands of men.
[45] But they understood not this saying, and it was hid from them, that they perceived it not: and they feared to ask him of that saying.
[46] Then there arose a reasoning among them, which of them should be greatest.
[47] And Jesus, perceiving the thought of their heart, took a child, and set him by him,
[48] And said to them, Whosoever shall receive this child in my name receives me: and whoever shall receive me receives him that sent me: for he that is least among you all, the same shall be great.
[49] And John answered and said, Master, we saw one casting out devils in your name; and we forbade him, because he follows not with us.
[50] And Jesus said to him, Forbid him not: for he that is not against us is for us.
[51] And it came to pass, when the time was come that he should be received up, he steadfastly set his face to go to Jerusalem,
[52] And sent messengers before his face: and they went, and entered into a village of the Samaritans, to make ready for him.
[53] And they did not receive him, because his face was as though he would go to Jerusalem.
[54] And when his disciples James and John saw this, they said, Lord, will you that we command fire to come down from heaven, and consume them, even as Elias did?

[55] But he turned, and rebuked them, and said, You know not what manner of spirit you are of.
[56] For the Son of man is not come to destroy men's lives, but to save them. And they went to another village.
[57] And it came to pass, that, as they went in the way, a certain man said to him, Lord, I will follow you whithersoever you goest.
[58] And Jesus said to him, Foxes have holes, and birds of the air have nests; but the Son of man has not where to lay his head.
[59] And he said to another, Follow me. But he said, Lord, suffer me first to go and bury my father.
[60] Jesus said to him, Let the dead bury their dead: but go you and preach the kingdom of God.
[61] And another also said, Lord, I will follow you; but let me first go bid them farewell, which are at home at my house.
[62] And Jesus said to him, No man, having put his hand to the plough, and looking back, is fit for the kingdom of God.

Luke 10

[1] After these things the Lord appointed another seventy also, and sent them two and two before his face into every city and place, where he himself would come.
[2] Therefore said he to them, The harvest truly is great, but the laborers are few: pray you therefore the Lord of the harvest, that he would send forth laborers into his harvest.
[3] Go your ways: behold, I send you forth as lambs among wolves.
[4] Carry neither purse, nor scrip (purse-bag), nor shoes: and salute no man by the way.
[5] And into whatsoever house you enter, first say, Peace be to this house.
[6] And if the son of peace be there, your peace shall rest on it: if not, it shall turn to you again.
[7] And in the same house remain, eating and drinking such things as they give: for the laborer is worthy of his hire. Go not from house to house.
[8] And into whatsoever city you enter, and they receive you, eat such things as are set before you:
[9] And heal the sick that are therein, and say to them, The kingdom of God is come near to you.

[10] But into whatsoever city you enter, and they receive you not, go your ways out into the streets of the same, and say,

[11] Even the very dust of your city, which clings to us, we do wipe off against you: notwithstanding be you sure of this, that the kingdom of God is come near to you.

[12] But I say to you, that it shall be more tolerable in that day for Sodom, than for that city.

[13] Woe to you, Chorazin! woe to you, Bethsaida! for if the mighty works had been done in Tyre and Sidon, which have been done in you, they had a great while ago repented, sitting in sackcloth and ashes.

[14] But it shall be more tolerable for Tyre and Sidon at the judgment, than for you.

[15] And you, Capernaum, which are exalted to heaven, shall be thrust down to hell.

[16] He that hears you hears me; and he that despises you despises me; and he that despises me despises him that sent me.

[17] And the seventy returned again with joy, saying, Lord, even the devils are subject to us through your name.

[18] And he said to them, I beheld Satan as lightning fall from heaven.

[19] Behold, I give to you power to tread on serpents and scorpions, and over all the power of the enemy: and nothing shall by any means hurt you.

[20] Notwithstanding in this rejoice not, that the spirits are subject to you; but rather rejoice, because your names are written in heaven.

[21] In that hour Jesus rejoiced in spirit, and said, I thank you, O Father, Lord of heaven and earth, that you have hid these things from the wise and prudent, and have revealed them to babes: even so, Father; for so it seemed good in your sight.

[22] All things are delivered to me of my Father: and no man knows who the Son is, but the Father; and who the Father is, but the Son, and he to whom the Son will reveal him.

[23] And he turned him to his disciples, and said privately, Blessed are the eyes which see the things that you see:

[24] For I tell you, that many prophets and kings have desired to see those things which you see, and have not seen them; and to hear those things which you hear, and have not heard them.

[25] And, behold, a certain lawyer stood up, and tempted him, saying, Master, what shall I do to inherit eternal life?

[26] He said to him, What is written in the law? how read you?
[27] And he answering said, You shall love the Lord your God with all your heart, and with all your soul, and with all your strength, and with all your mind; and your neighbor as yourself.
[28] And he said to him, You have answered right: this do, and you shall live.
[29] But he, willing to justify himself, said to Jesus, And who is my neighbor?
[30] And Jesus answering said, A certain man went down from Jerusalem to Jericho, and fell among thieves, which stripped him of his raiment, and wounded him, and departed, leaving him half dead.
[31] And by chance there came down a certain priest that way: and when he saw him, he passed by on the other side.
[32] And likewise a Levite, when he was at the place, came and looked on him, and passed by on the other side.
[33] But a certain Samaritan, as he journeyed, came where he was: and when he saw him, he had compassion on him,
[34] And went to him, and bound up his wounds, pouring in oil and wine, and set him on his own beast, and brought him to an inn, and took care of him.
[35] And on the morrow when he departed, he took out two pence, and gave them to the host, and said to him, Take care of him; and whatsoever you spend more, when I come again, I will repay you.
[36] Which now of these three, think you, was neighbor to him that fell among the thieves?
[37] And he said, He that showed mercy on him. Then said Jesus to him, Go, and do you likewise.
[38] Now it came to pass, as they went, that he entered into a certain village: and a certain woman named Martha received him into her house.
[39] And she had a sister called Mary, which also sat at Jesus' feet, and heard his word.
[40] But Martha was cumbered about much serving, and came to him, and said, Lord, do you not care that my sister has left me to serve alone? bid her therefore that she help me.
[41] And Jesus answered and said to her, Martha, Martha, you are careful and troubled about many things:
[42] But one thing is needful: and Mary has chosen that good part, which shall not be taken away from her.

Luke 11

[1] And it came to pass, that, as he was praying in a certain place, when he ceased, one of his disciples said to him, Lord, teach us to pray, as John also taught his disciples.
[2] And he said to them, When you pray, say, Our Father which are in heaven, Hallowed be your name. Your kingdom come. Your will be done, as in heaven, so in earth.
[3] Give us day by day our daily bread.
[4] And forgive us our sins; for we also forgive every one that is indebted to us. And lead us not into temptation; but deliver us from evil.
[5] And he said to them, Which of you shall have a friend, and shall go to him at midnight, and say to him, Friend, lend me three loaves;
[6] For a friend of mine in his journey is come to me, and I have nothing to set before him?
[7] And he from within shall answer and say, Trouble me not: the door is now shut, and my children are with me in bed; I cannot rise and give you.
[8] I say to you, Though he will not rise and give him, because he is his friend, yet because of his importunity he will rise and give him as many as he needs.
[9] And I say to you, Ask, and it shall be given you; seek, and you shall find; knock, and it shall be opened to you.
[10] For every one that asks receives; and he that seeks finds; and to him that knocks it shall be opened.
[11] If a son shall ask bread of any of you that is a father, will he give him a stone? or if he ask a fish, will he for a fish give him a serpent?
[12] Or if he shall ask an egg, will he offer him a scorpion?
[13] If you then, being evil, know how to give good gifts to your children: how much more shall your heavenly Father give the Holy Spirit to them that ask him?
[14] And he was casting out a devil, and it was dumb. And it came to pass, when the devil was gone out, the dumb spoke; and the people wondered.
[15] But some of them said, He casts out devils through Beelzebub the chief of the devils.
[16] And others, tempting him, sought of him a sign from heaven.

[17] But he, knowing their thoughts, said to them, Every kingdom divided against itself is brought to desolation; and a house divided against a house falls.
[18] If Satan also be divided against himself, how shall his kingdom stand? because you say that I cast out devils through Beelzebub.
[19] And if I by Beelzebub cast out devils, by whom do your sons cast them out? therefore shall they be your judges.
[20] But if I with the finger of God cast out devils, no doubt the kingdom of God is come upon you.
[21] When a strong man armed keeps his palace, his goods are in peace:
[22] But when a stronger than he shall come upon him, and overcome him, he takes from him all his armor wherein he trusted, and divides his spoils.
[23] He that is not with me is against me: and he that gathered not with me scatters.
[24] When the unclean spirit is gone out of a man, he walks through dry places, seeking rest; and finding none, he said, I will return to my house from where I came out.
[25] And when he comes, he finds it swept and garnished.
[26] Then goes he, and takes to him seven other spirits more wicked than himself; and they enter in, and dwell there: and the last state of that man is worse than the first.
[27] And it came to pass, as he spoke these things, a certain woman of the company lifted up her voice, and said to him, Blessed is the womb that bare you, and the breasts which you have sucked.
[28] But he said, Yea rather, blessed are they that hear the word of God, and keep it.
[29] And when the people were gathered thick together, he began to say, This is an evil generation: they seek a sign; and there shall no sign be given it, but the sign of Jonas the prophet.
[30] For as Jonas was a sign to the Ninevites, so shall also the Son of man be to this generation.
[31] The queen of the south shall rise up in the judgment with the men of this generation, and condemn them: for she came from the utmost parts of the earth to hear the wisdom of Solomon; and, behold, a greater than Solomon is here.
[32] The men of Nineve shall rise up in the judgment with this generation, and shall condemn it: for they repented at the preaching of Jonas; and, behold, a greater than Jonas is here.

[33] No man, when he has lighted a candle, puts it in a secret place, neither under a bushel, but on a candlestick, that they which come in may see the light.
[34] The light of the body is the eye: therefore when your eye is single, your whole body also is full of light; but when your eye is evil, your body also is full of darkness.
[35] Take heed therefore that the light which is in you be not darkness.
[36] If your whole body therefore be full of light, having no part dark, the whole shall be full of light, as when the bright shining of a candle does give you light.
[37] And as he spoke, a certain Pharisee besought him to dine with him: and he went in, and sat down to meat.
[38] And when the Pharisee saw it, he marveled that he had not first washed before dinner.
[39] And the Lord said to him, Now do you Pharisees make clean the outside of the cup and the platter; but your inward part is full of ravening and wickedness.
[40] You fools, did not he that made that which is without make that which is within also?
[41] But rather give alms of such things as you have; and, behold, all things are clean to you.
[42] But woe to you, Pharisees! for you tithe mint and rue and all manner of herbs, and pass over judgment and the love of God: these ought you to have done, and not to leave the other undone.
[43] Woe to you, Pharisees! for you love the uppermost seats in the synagogues, and greetings in the markets.
[44] Woe to you, scribes and Pharisees, hypocrites! for you are as graves which appear not, and the men that walk over them are not aware of them.
[45] Then answered one of the lawyers, and said to him, Master, thus saying you ridicule us also.
[46] And he said, Woe to you also, you lawyers! for you lade men with burdens grievous to be borne, and you yourselves touch not the burdens with one of your fingers.
[47] Woe to you! for you build the sepulchers of the prophets, and your fathers killed them.
[48] Truly you bear witness that you allow the deeds of your fathers: for they indeed killed them, and you build their sepulchers.
[49] Therefore also said the wisdom of God, I will send them

prophets and apostles, and some of them they shall slay and persecute:
[50] That the blood of all the prophets, which was shed from the foundation of the world, may be required of this generation;
[51] From the blood of Abel to the blood of Zacharias, which perished between the altar and the temple: truly I say to you, It shall be required of this generation.
[52] Woe to you, lawyers! for you have taken away the key of knowledge: you entered not in yourselves, and them that were entering in you hindered.
[53] And as he said these things to them, the scribes and the Pharisees began to urge him vehemently, and to provoke him to speak of many things:
[54] Laying wait for him, and seeking to catch something out of his mouth, that they might accuse him.

Luke 12

[1] In the mean time, when there were gathered together an innumerable multitude of people, insomuch that they walked one upon another, he began to say to his disciples first of all, Beware you of the leaven of the Pharisees, which is hypocrisy.
[2] For there is nothing covered, that shall not be revealed; neither hid, that shall not be known.
[3] Therefore whatsoever you have spoken in darkness shall be heard in the light; and that which you have spoken in the ear in closets shall be proclaimed upon the housetops.
[4] And I say to you my friends, Be not afraid of them that kill the body, and after that have no more that they can do.
[5] But I will forewarn you whom you shall fear: Fear him, which after he has killed has power to cast into hell; yea, I say to you, Fear him.
[6] Are not five sparrows sold for two farthings, and not one of them is forgotten before God?
[7] But even the very hairs of your head are all numbered. Fear not therefore: you are of more value than many sparrows.
[8] Also I say to you, Whosoever shall confess me before men, him shall the Son of man also confess before the angels of God:
[9] But he that denies me before men shall be denied before the

angels of God.

[10] And whoever shall speak a word against the Son of man, it shall be forgiven him: but to him that blasphemes against the Holy Ghost it shall not be forgiven.

[11] And when they bring you to the synagogues, and to magistrates, and powers, take you no thought how or what thing you shall answer, or what you shall say:

[12] For the Holy Ghost shall teach you in the same hour what you ought to say.

[13] And one of the company said to him, Master, speak to my brother, that he divide the inheritance with me.

[14] And he said to him, Man, who made me a judge or a divider over you?

[15] And he said to them, Take heed, and beware of covetousness: for a man's life consists not in the abundance of the things which he possesses.

[16] And he spoke a parable to them, saying, The ground of a certain rich man brought forth plentifully:

[17] And he thought within himself, saying, What shall I do, because I have no room where to bestow my fruits?

[18] And he said, This will I do: I will pull down my barns, and build greater; and there will I bestow all my fruits and my goods.

[19] And I will say to my soul, Soul, you have much goods laid up for many years; take your ease, eat, drink, and be merry.

[20] But God said to him, You fool, this night your soul shall be required of you: then whose shall those things be, which you have provided?

[21] So is he that laid up treasure for himself, and is not rich toward God.

[22] And he said to his disciples, Therefore I say to you, Take no thought for your life, what you shall eat; neither for the body, what you shall put on.

[23] The life is more than meat, and the body is more than raiment.

[24] Consider the ravens: for they neither sow nor reap; which neither have storehouse nor barn; and God feeds them: how much more are you better than the fowls?

[25] And which of you with taking thought can add to his stature one cubit?

[26] If you then be not able to do that thing which is least, why take you thought for the rest?

[27] Consider the lilies how they grow: they toil not, they spin not; and yet I say to you, that Solomon in all his glory was not arrayed like one of these.
[28] If then God so clothe the grass, which is to day in the field, and tomorrow is cast into the oven; how much more will he clothe you, O you of little faith?
[29] And seek not what you shall eat, or what you shall drink, neither be you of doubtful mind.
[30] For all these things do the nations of the world seek after: and your Father knows that you have need of these things.
[31] But rather seek you the kingdom of God; and all these things shall be added to you.
[32] Fear not, little flock; for it is your Father's good pleasure to give you the kingdom.
[33] Sell that you have, and give alms; provide yourselves bags which wax not old, a treasure in the heavens that fails not, where no thief approaches, neither moth corrupts.
[34] For where your treasure is, there will your heart be also.
[35] Let your loins be girded about, and your lights burning;
[36] And you yourselves like to men that wait for their lord, when he will return from the wedding; that when he comes and knocks, they may open to him immediately.
[37] Blessed are those servants, whom the lord when he comes shall find watching: truly I say to you, that he shall prepare himself, and make them to sit down to meat, and will come forth and serve them.
[38] And if he shall come in the second watch, or come in the third watch, and find them so, blessed are those servants.
[39] And this know, that if the goodman of the house had known what hour the thief would come, he would have watched, and not have suffered his house to be broken through.
[40] Be you therefore ready also: for the Son of man comes at an hour when you think not.
[41] Then Peter said to him, Lord, speak you this parable to us, or even to all?
[42] And the Lord said, Who then is that faithful and wise steward, whom his lord shall make ruler over his household, to give them their portion of meat in due season?
[43] Blessed is that servant, whom his lord when he comes shall find so doing.
[44] Of a truth I say to you, that he will make him ruler over all that

he has.

[45] But and if that servant say in his heart, My lord delays his coming; and shall begin to beat the menservants and maidens, and to eat and drink, and to be drunken;

[46] The lord of that servant will come in a day when he looks not for him, and at an hour when he is not aware, and will cut him asunder, and will appoint him his portion with the unbelievers.

[47] And that servant, which knew his lord's will, and prepared not himself, neither did according to his will, shall be beaten with many stripes.

[48] But he that knew not, and did commit things worthy of stripes, shall be beaten with few stripes. For to whomsoever much is given, of him shall be much required: and to whom men have committed much, of him they will ask the more.

[49] I am come to send fire on the earth; and what will I if it be already kindled?

[50] But I have a baptism to be baptized with; and how am I straitened till it be accomplished!

[51] Suppose you that I am come to give peace on earth? I tell you, Nay; but rather division:

[52] For from now on there shall be five in one house divided, three against two, and two against three.

[53] The father shall be divided against the son, and the son against the father; the mother against the daughter, and the daughter against the mother; the mother-in-law against her daughter-in-law, and the daughter-in-law against her mother-in-law.

[54] And he said also to the people, When you see a cloud rise out of the west, straightway you say, There comes a shower; and so it is.

[55] And when you see the south wind blow, you say, There will be heat; and it comes to pass.

[56] You hypocrites, you can discern the face of the sky and of the earth; but how is it that you do not discern this time?

[57] Yea, and why even of yourselves judge you not what is right?

[58] When you go with your adversary to the magistrate, as you are in the way, give diligence that you may be delivered from him; lest he turn you over to the judge, and the judge deliver you to the officer, and the officer cast you into prison.

[59] I tell you, you shall not depart from there, till you have paid the very last mite.

Luke 13

[1] There were present at that season some that told him of the Galilaeans, whose blood Pilate had mingled with their sacrifices.
[2] And Jesus answering said to them, Suppose you that these Galilaeans were sinners above all the Galilaeans, because they suffered such things?
[3] I tell you, Nay: but, except you repent, you shall all likewise perish.
[4] Or those eighteen, upon whom the tower in Siloam fell, and slew them, think you that they were sinners above all men that dwelt in Jerusalem?
[5] I tell you, Nay: but, except you repent, you shall all likewise perish.
[6] He spoke also this parable; A certain man had a fig tree planted in his vineyard; and he came and sought fruit thereon, and found none.
[7] Then said he to the dresser of his vineyard, Behold, these three years I come seeking fruit on this fig tree, and find none: cut it down; why cumbereth it the ground?
[8] And he answering said to him, Lord, let it alone this year also, till I shall dig about it, and dung it:
[9] And if it bear fruit, well: and if not, then after that you shall cut it down.
[10] And he was teaching in one of the synagogues on the Sabbath.
[11] And, behold, there was a woman which had a spirit of infirmity eighteen years, and was bowed together, and could in no wise lift up herself.
[12] And when Jesus saw her, he called her to him, and said to her, Woman, you are loosed from your infirmity.
[13] And he laid his hands on her: and immediately she was made straight, and glorified God.
[14] And the ruler of the synagogue answered with indignation, because that Jesus had healed on the Sabbath day, and said to the people, There are six days in which men ought to work: in them therefore come and be healed, and not on the Sabbath day.
[15] The Lord then answered him, and said, You hypocrite, does not each one of you on the Sabbath loose his ox or his ass from the stall, and lead him away to watering?

[16] And ought not this woman, being a daughter of Abraham, whom Satan has bound, lo, these eighteen years, be loosed from this bond on the Sabbath day?
[17] And when he had said these things, all his adversaries were ashamed: and all the people rejoiced for all the glorious things that were done by him.
[18] Then said he, Unto what is the kingdom of God like? and whereunto shall I resemble it?
[19] It is like a grain of mustard seed, which a man took, and cast into his garden; and it grew, and grew a great tree; and the fowls of the air lodged in the branches of it.
[20] And again he said, Whereunto shall I liken the kingdom of God?
[21] It is like leaven, which a woman took and hid in three measures of meal, till the whole was leavened.
[22] And he went through the cities and villages, teaching, and journeying toward Jerusalem.
[23] Then said one to him, Lord, are there few that be saved? And he said to them,
[24] Strive to enter in at the strait gate: for many, I say to you, will seek to enter in, and shall not be able.
[25] When once the master of the house is risen up, and has shut the door, and you begin to stand without, and to knock at the door, saying, Lord, Lord, open to us; and he shall answer and say to you, I know you not whence you are:
[26] Then shall you begin to say, We have eaten and drunk in your presence, and you have taught in our streets.
[27] But he shall say, I tell you, I know you not from where you are; depart from me, all you workers of iniquity.
[28] There shall be weeping and gnashing of teeth, when you shall see Abraham, and Isaac, and Jacob, and all the prophets, in the kingdom of God, and you yourselves thrust out.
[29] And they shall come from the east, and from the west, and from the north, and from the south, and shall sit down in the kingdom of God.
[30] And, behold, there are last which shall be first, and there are first which shall be last.
[31] The same day there came certain of the Pharisees, saying to him, Get you out, and depart from here: for Herod will kill you.
[32] And he said to them, Go you, and tell that fox, Behold, I cast out devils, and I do cures to day and tomorrow, and the third day I shall

be perfected.

[33] Nevertheless I must walk today, and tomorrow, and the day following: for it cannot be that a prophet perish out of Jerusalem.

[34] O Jerusalem, Jerusalem, which kill the prophets, and stone them that are sent to you; how often would I have gathered your children together, as a hen does gather her brood under her wings, and you would not!

[35] Behold, your house is left to you desolate: and truly I say to you, You shall not see me, until the time come when you shall say, Blessed is he that comes in the name of the Lord.

Luke 14

[1] And it came to pass, as he went into the house of one of the chief Pharisees to eat bread on the Sabbath day, that they watched him.

[2] And, behold, there was a certain man before him which had the dropsy.

[3] And Jesus answering spoke to the lawyers and Pharisees, saying, Is it lawful to heal on the Sabbath day?

[4] And they held their peace. And he took him, and healed him, and let him go;

[5] And answered them, saying, Which of you shall have an ass or an ox fallen into a pit, and will not straightway pull him out on the Sabbath day?

[6] And they could not answer him again to these things.

[7] And he put forth a parable to those which were bidden, when he marked how they chose out the chief rooms; saying to them,

[8] When you are bidden of any man to a wedding, sit not down in the highest room; lest a more honorable man than you be bidden of him;

[9] And he that bade you and him come and say to you, Give this man place; and you begin with shame to take the lowest room.

[10] But when you are bidden, go and sit down in the lowest room; that when he that bade you comes, he may say to you, Friend, go up higher: then shall you have worship in the presence of them that sit at meat with you.

[11] For whoever exalts himself shall be abased; and he that humbles himself shall be exalted.

[12] Then said he also to him that bade him, When you make a

dinner or a supper, call not your friends, nor your brethren, neither your kinsmen, nor your rich neighbors; lest they also bid you again, and a recompense be made you.
[13] But when you make a feast, call the poor, the maimed, the lame, the blind:
[14] And you shall be blessed; for they cannot recompense you: for you shall be recompensed at the resurrection of the just.
[15] And when one of them that sat at meat with him heard these things, he said to him, Blessed is he that shall eat bread in the kingdom of God.
[16] Then said he to him, A certain man made a great supper, and bade many:
[17] And sent his servant at supper time to say to them that were bidden, Come; for all things are now ready.
[18] And they all with one consent began to make excuse. The first said to him, I have bought a piece of ground, and I must needs go and see it: I pray you have me excused.
[19] And another said, I have bought five yoke of oxen, and I go to prove them: I pray you have me excused.
[20] And another said, I have married a wife, and therefore I cannot come.
[21] So that servant came, and showed his lord these things. Then the master of the house being angry said to his servant, Go out quickly into the streets and lanes of the city, and bring in here the poor, and the maimed, and the halt, and the blind.
[22] And the servant said, Lord, it is done as you have commanded, and yet there is room.
[23] And the lord said to the servant, Go out into the highways and hedges, and compel them to come in, that my house may be filled.
[24] For I say to you, That none of those men which were bidden shall taste of my supper.
[25] And there went great multitudes with him: and he turned, and said to them,
[26] If any man come to me, and hate not his father, and mother, and wife, and children, and brethren, and sisters, yea, and his own life also, he cannot be my disciple.
[27] And whoever does not bear his cross, and come after me, cannot be my disciple.
[28] For which of you, intending to build a tower, sits not down first, and counts the cost, whether he have sufficient to finish it?

[29] Lest haply, after he has laid the foundation, and is not able to finish it, all that behold it begin to mock him,
[30] Saying, This man began to build, and was not able to finish.
[31] Or what king, going to make war against another king, sits not down first, and consults whether he be able with ten thousand to meet him that comes against him with twenty thousand?
[32] Or else, while the other is yet a great way off, he sends an ambassador, and desires conditions of peace.
[33] So likewise, whoever he be of you that forsakes not all that he has, he cannot be my disciple.
[34] Salt is good: but if the salt have lost its savor, wherewith shall it be seasoned?
[35] It is neither fit for the land, nor yet for the dunghill; but men cast it out. He that has ears to hear, let him hear.

Luke 15

[1] Then drew near to him all the publicans and sinners for to hear him.
[2] And the Pharisees and scribes murmured, saying, This man receives sinners, and eats with them.
[3] And he spoke this parable to them, saying,
[4] What man of you, having a hundred sheep, if he lose one of them, does not leave the ninety and nine in the wilderness, and go after that which is lost, until he find it?
[5] And when he has found it, he laid it on his shoulders, rejoicing.
[6] And when he comes home, he calls together his friends and neighbors, saying to them, Rejoice with me; for I have found my sheep which was lost.
[7] I say to you, that likewise joy shall be in heaven over one sinner that repents, more than over ninety and nine just persons, which need no repentance.
[8] Either what woman having ten pieces of silver, if she lose one piece, does not light a candle, and sweep the house, and seek diligently till she find it?
[9] And when she has found it, she calls her friends and her neighbors together, saying, Rejoice with me; for I have found the piece which I had lost.
[10] Likewise, I say to you, there is joy in the presence of the angels of

God over one sinner that repents.

[11] And he said, A certain man had two sons:

[12] And the younger of them said to his father, Father, give me the portion of goods that falls to me. And he divided to them his living.

[13] And not many days after the younger son gathered all together, and took his journey into a far country, and there wasted his substance with riotous living.

[14] And when he had spent all, there arose a mighty famine in that land; and he began to be in want.

[15] And he went and joined himself to a citizen of that country; and he sent him into his fields to feed swine.

[16] And he would fain have filled his belly with the husks that the swine did eat: and no man gave to him.

[17] And when he came to himself, he said, How many hired servants of my father's have bread enough and to spare, and I perish with hunger!

[18] I will arise and go to my father, and will say to him, Father, I have sinned against heaven, and before you,

[19] And am no more worthy to be called your son: make me as one of your hired servants.

[20] And he arose, and came to his father. But when he was yet a great way off, his father saw him, and had compassion, and ran, and fell on his neck, and kissed him.

[21] And the son said to him, Father, I have sinned against heaven, and in your sight, and am no more worthy to be called your son.

[22] But the father said to his servants, Bring forth the best robe, and put it on him; and put a ring on his hand, and shoes on his feet:

[23] And bring here the fatted calf, and kill it; and let us eat, and be merry:

[24] For this my son was dead, and is alive again; he was lost, and is found. And they began to be merry.

[25] Now his elder son was in the field: and as he came and drew near to the house, he heard music and dancing.

[26] And he called one of the servants, and asked what these things meant.

[27] And he said to him, Your brother is come; and your father has killed the fatted calf, because he has received him safe and sound.

[28] And he was angry, and would not go in: therefore came his father out, and entreated him.

[29] And he answering said to his father, Lo, these many years do I

serve you, neither transgressed I at any time your commandment: and yet you never gave me a kid, that I might make merry with my friends:
[30] But as soon as this your son was come, which has devoured your living with harlots, you have killed for him the fatted calf.
[31] And he said to him, Son, you are ever with me, and all that I have is yours.
[32] It was meet that we should make merry, and be glad: for this your brother was dead, and is alive again; and was lost, and is found.

Luke 16

[1] And he said also to his disciples, There was a certain rich man, which had a steward; and the same was accused to him that he had wasted his goods.
[2] And he called him, and said to him, How is it that I hear this of you? give an account of your stewardship; for you may be no longer steward.
[3] Then the steward said within himself, What shall I do? for my lord takes away from me the stewardship: I cannot dig; to beg I am ashamed.
[4] I am resolved what to do, that, when I am put out of the stewardship, they may receive me into their houses.
[5] So he called every one of his lord's debtors to him, and said to the first, How much owe you to my lord?
[6] And he said, An hundred measures of oil. And he said to him, Take your bill, and sit down quickly, and write fifty.
[7] Then said he to another, And how much owe you? And he said, An hundred measures of wheat. And he said to him, Take your bill, and write fourscore.
[8] And the lord commended the unjust steward, because he had done wisely: for the children of this world are in their generation wiser than the children of light.
[9] And I say to you, Make to yourselves friends of the mammon of unrighteousness; that, when you fail, they may receive you into everlasting habitations.
[10] He that is faithful in that which is least is faithful also in much: and he that is unjust in the least is unjust also in much.
[11] If therefore you have not been faithful in the unrighteous

mammon, who will commit to your trust the true riches?
[12] And if you have not been faithful in that which is another man's, who shall give you that which is your own?
[13] No servant can serve two masters: for either he will hate the one, and love the other; or else he will hold to the one, and despise the other. You cannot serve God and mammon.
[14] And the Pharisees also, who were covetous, heard all these things: and they derided him.
[15] And he said to them, You are they which justify yourselves before men; but God knows your hearts: for that which is highly esteemed among men is abomination in the sight of God.
[16] The law and the prophets were until John: since that time the kingdom of God is preached, and every man presses into it.
[17] And it is easier for heaven and earth to pass, than one tittle of the law to fail.
[18] Whosoever puts away his wife, and marries another, commits adultery: and whoever marries her that is put away from her husband commits adultery.
[19] There was a certain rich man, which was clothed in purple and fine linen, and fared sumptuously every day:
[20] And there was a certain beggar named Lazarus, which was laid at his gate, full of sores,
[21] And desiring to be fed with the crumbs which fell from the rich man's table: moreover the dogs came and licked his sores.
[22] And it came to pass, that the beggar died, and was carried by the angels into Abraham's bosom: the rich man also died, and was buried;
[23] And in hell he lift up his eyes, being in torments, and sees Abraham afar off, and Lazarus in his bosom.
[24] And he cried and said, Father Abraham, have mercy on me, and send Lazarus, that he may dip the tip of his finger in water, and cool my tongue; for I am tormented in this flame.
[25] But Abraham said, Son, remember that you in your lifetime received your good things, and likewise Lazarus evil things: but now he is comforted, and you are tormented.
[26] And beside all this, between us and you there is a great gulf fixed: so that they which would pass from here to you cannot; neither can they pass to us, that would come from there.
[27] Then he said, I pray you therefore, father, that you would send him to my father's house:

[28] For I have five brethren; that he may testify to them, lest they also come into this place of torment.
[29] Abraham said to him, They have Moses and the prophets; let them hear them.
[30] And he said, Nay, father Abraham: but if one went to them from the dead, they will repent.
[31] And he said to him, If they hear not Moses and the prophets, neither will they be persuaded, though one rose from the dead.

Luke 17

[1] Then said he to the disciples, It is impossible but that offences will come: but woe to him, through whom they come!
[2] It were better for him that a millstone were hanged about his neck, and he be cast into the sea, than that he should offend one of these little ones.
[3] Take heed to yourselves: If your brother trespass against you, rebuke him; and if he repent, forgive him.
[4] And if he trespass against you seven times in a day, and seven times in a day turn again to you, saying, I repent; you shall forgive him.
[5] And the apostles said to the Lord, Increase our faith.
[6] And the Lord said, If you had faith as a grain of mustard seed, you might say to this sycamore tree, Be you plucked up by the root, and be you planted in the sea; and it should obey you.
[7] But which of you, having a servant plowing or feeding cattle, will say to him by and by, when he is come from the field, Go and sit down to meat?
[8] And will not rather say to him, Make ready wherewith I may sup, and prepare yourself, and serve me, till I have eaten and drunken; and afterward you shall eat and drink?
[9] Does he thank that servant because he did the things that were commanded him? I think not.
[10] So likewise you, when you shall have done all those things which are commanded you, say, We are unprofitable servants: we have done that which was our duty to do.
[11] And it came to pass, as he went to Jerusalem, that he passed through the midst of Samaria and Galilee.
[12] And as he entered into a certain village, there met him ten men

that were lepers, which stood afar off:

[13] And they lifted up their voices, and said, Jesus, Master, have mercy on us.

[14] And when he saw them, he said to them, Go show yourselves to the priests. And it came to pass, that, as they went, they were cleansed.

[15] And one of them, when he saw that he was healed, turned back, and with a loud voice glorified God,

[16] And fell down on his face at his feet, giving him thanks: and he was a Samaritan.

[17] And Jesus answering said, Were there not ten cleansed? but where are the nine?

[18] There are not found that returned to give glory to God, save this stranger.

[19] And he said to him, Arise, go your way: your faith has made you whole.

[20] And when he was demanded of the Pharisees, when the kingdom of God should come, he answered them and said, The kingdom of God comes not with observation:

[21] Neither shall they say, Lo here! or, lo there! for, behold, the kingdom of God is within you.

[22] And he said to the disciples, The days will come, when you shall desire to see one of the days of the Son of man, and you shall not see it.

[23] And they shall say to you, See here; or, see there: go not after them, nor follow them.

[24] For as the lightning, that lightens out of the one part under heaven, shines to the other part under heaven; so shall also the Son of man be in his day.

[25] But first must he suffer many things, and be rejected of this generation.

[26] And as it was in the days of Noe, so shall it be also in the days of the Son of man.

[27] They did eat, they drank, they married wives, they were given in marriage, until the day that Noe entered into the ark, and the flood came, and destroyed them all.

[28] Likewise also as it was in the days of Lot; they did eat, they drank, they bought, they sold, they planted, they built;

[29] But the same day that Lot went out of Sodom it rained fire and brimstone from heaven, and destroyed them all.

[30] Even thus shall it be in the day when the Son of man is revealed.
[31] In that day, he which shall be on the housetop, and his stuff in the house, let him not come down to take it away: and he that is in the field, let him likewise not return back.
[32] Remember Lot's wife.
[33] Whosoever shall seek to save his life shall lose it; and whoever shall lose his life shall preserve it.
[34] I tell you, in that night there shall be two men in one bed; the one shall be taken, and the other shall be left.
[35] Two women shall be grinding together; the one shall be taken, and the other left.
[36] Two men shall be in the field; the one shall be taken, and the other left.
[37] And they answered and said to him, Where, Lord? And he said to them, Wheresoever the body is, thither will the eagles be gathered together.

Luke 18

[1] And he spoke a parable to them to this end, that men ought always to pray, and not to faint;
[2] Saying, There was in a city a judge, which feared not God, neither regarded man:
[3] And there was a widow in that city; and she came to him, saying, Avenge me of my adversary.
[4] And he would not for a while: but afterward he said within himself, Though I fear not God, nor regard man;
[5] Yet because this widow troubleth me, I will avenge her, lest by her continual coming she weary me.
[6] And the Lord said, Hear what the unjust judge said.
[7] And shall not God avenge his own elect, which cry day and night to him, though he bear long with them?
[8] I tell you that he will avenge them speedily. Nevertheless when the Son of man comes, shall he find faith on the earth?
[9] And he spoke this parable to certain which trusted in themselves that they were righteous, and despised others:
[10] Two men went up into the temple to pray; the one a Pharisee, and the other a publican.
[11] The Pharisee stood and prayed thus with himself, God, I thank

you, that I am not as other men are, extortioners, unjust, adulterers, or even as this publican.
[12] I fast twice in the week, I give tithes of all that I possess.
[13] And the publican, standing afar off, would not lift up so much as his eyes to heaven, but smote upon his breast, saying, God be merciful to me a sinner.
[14] I tell you, this man went down to his house justified rather than the other: for every one that exalts himself shall be abased; and he that humbles himself shall be exalted.
[15] And they brought to him also infants, that he would touch them: but when his disciples saw it, they rebuked them.
[16] But Jesus called them to him, and said, Suffer the little children to come to me, and forbid them not: for of such is the kingdom of God.
[17] Truly I say to you, Whosoever shall not receive the kingdom of God as a little child shall in no wise enter therein.
[18] And a certain ruler asked him, saying, Good Master, what shall I do to inherit eternal life?
[19] And Jesus said to him, Why call you me good? none is good, save one, that is, God.
[20] You know the commandments, Do not commit adultery, Do not kill, Do not steal, Do not bear false witness, Honor your father and your mother.
[21] And he said, All these have I kept from my youth up.
[22] Now when Jesus heard these things, he said to him, Yet lack you one thing: sell all that you have, and distribute to the poor, and you shall have treasure in heaven: and come, follow me.
[23] And when he heard this, he was very sorrowful: for he was very rich.
[24] And when Jesus saw that he was very sorrowful, he said, How hardly shall they that have riches enter into the kingdom of God!
[25] For it is easier for a camel to go through a needle's eye, than for a rich man to enter into the kingdom of God.
[26] And they that heard it said, Who then can be saved?
[27] And he said, The things which are impossible with men are possible with God.
[28] Then Peter said, Lo, we have left all, and followed you.
[29] And he said to them, Truly I say to you, There is no man that has left house, or parents, or brethren, or wife, or children, for the kingdom of God's sake,

[30] Who shall not receive manifold more in this present time, and in the world to come life everlasting.
[31] Then he took to him the twelve, and said to them, Behold, we go up to Jerusalem, and all things that are written by the prophets concerning the Son of man shall be accomplished.
[32] For he shall be delivered to the Gentiles, and shall be mocked, and spitefully entreated, and spit on:
[33] And they shall scourge him, and put him to death: and the third day he shall rise again.
[34] And they understood none of these things: and this saying was hid from them, neither knew they the things which were spoken.
[35] And it came to pass, that as he was come near to Jericho, a certain blind man sat by the way side begging:
[36] And hearing the multitude pass by, he asked what it meant.
[37] And they told him, that Jesus of Nazareth passed by.
[38] And he cried, saying, Jesus, you Son of David, have mercy on me.
[39] And they which went before rebuked him, that he should hold his peace: but he cried so much the more, You Son of David, have mercy on me.
[40] And Jesus stood, and commanded him to be brought to him: and when he was come near, he asked him,
[41] Saying, What will you that I shall do to you? And he said, Lord, that I may receive my sight.
[42] And Jesus said to him, Receive your sight: your faith has saved you.
[43] And immediately he received his sight, and followed him, glorifying God: and all the people, when they saw it, gave praise to God.

Luke 19

[1] And Jesus entered and passed through Jericho.
[2] And, behold, there was a man named Zacchaeus, which was the chief among the publicans, and he was rich.
[3] And he sought to see Jesus who he was; and could not for the press, because he was little of stature.
[4] And he ran before, and climbed up into a sycamore tree to see him: for he was to pass that way.

[5] And when Jesus came to the place, he looked up, and saw him, and said to him, Zacchaeus, make haste, and come down; for to day I must abide at your house.
[6] And he made haste, and came down, and received him joyfully.
[7] And when they saw it, they all murmured, saying, he was gone to be a guest with a man that is a sinner.
[8] And Zacchaeus stood, and said to the Lord; Behold, Lord, the half of my goods I give to the poor; and if I have taken any thing from any man by false accusation, I restore him fourfold.
[9] And Jesus said to him, This day is salvation come to this house, forsomuch as he also is a son of Abraham.
[10] For the Son of man is come to seek and to save that which was lost.
[11] And as they heard these things, he added and spoke a parable, because he was near to Jerusalem, and because they thought that the kingdom of God should immediately appear.
[12] He said therefore, A certain nobleman went into a far country to receive for himself a kingdom, and to return.
[13] And he called his ten servants, and delivered them ten pounds, and said to them, Occupy till I come.
[14] But his citizens hated him, and sent a message after him, saying, We will not have this man to reign over us.
[15] And it came to pass, that when he was returned, having received the kingdom, then he commanded these servants to be called to him, to whom he had given the money, that he might know how much every man had gained by trading.
[16] Then came the first, saying, Lord, your pound has gained ten pounds.
[17] And he said to him, Well, you good servant: because you have been faithful in a very little, have you authority over ten cities.
[18] And the second came, saying, Lord, your pound has gained five pounds.
[19] And he said likewise to him, Be you also over five cities.
[20] And another came, saying, Lord, behold, here is your pound, which I have kept laid up in a napkin:
[21] For I feared you, because you are an austere man: you take up that you lay not down, and reap that you did not sow.
[22] And he said to him, Out of your own mouth will I judge you, you wicked servant. You knew that I was an austere man, taking up that I laid not down, and reaping that I did not sow:

[23] Therefore then gave not you my money into the bank, that at my coming I might have required my own with usury?
[24] And he said to them that stood by, Take from him the pound, and give it to him that has ten pounds.
[25] (And they said to him, Lord, he has ten pounds.)
[26] For I say to you, That to every one which has shall be given; and from him that has not, even that he has shall be taken away from him.
[27] But those my enemies, which would not that I should reign over them, bring here, and slay them before me.
[28] And when he had thus spoken, he went before, ascending up to Jerusalem.
[29] And it came to pass, when he was come near to Bethphage and Bethany, at the mount called the mount of Olives, he sent two of his disciples,
[30] Saying, Go you into the village over against you; in the which at your entering you shall find a colt tied, whereon yet never man sat: loose him, and bring him here.
[31] And if any man ask you, Why do you loose him? thus shall you say to him, Because the Lord has need of him.
[32] And they that were sent went their way, and found even as he had said to them.
[33] And as they were loosing the colt, the owners thereof said to them, Why loose you the colt?
[34] And they said, The Lord has need of him.
[35] And they brought him to Jesus: and they cast their garments upon the colt, and they set Jesus thereon.
[36] And as he went, they spread their clothes in the way.
[37] And when he was come near, even now at the descent of the mount of Olives, the whole multitude of the disciples began to rejoice and praise God with a loud voice for all the mighty works that they had seen;
[38] Saying, Blessed be the King that comes in the name of the Lord: peace in heaven, and glory in the highest.
[39] And some of the Pharisees from among the multitude said to him, Master, rebuke your disciples.
[40] And he answered and said to them, I tell you that, if these should hold their peace, the stones would immediately cry out.
[41] And when he was come near, he beheld the city, and wept over it,

[42] Saying, If you had known, even you, at least in this your day, the things which belong to your peace! but now they are hid from your eyes.
[43] For the days shall come on you, that your enemies shall cast a trench about you, and compass you round, and keep you in on every side,
[44] And shall lay you even with the ground, and your children within you; and they shall not leave in you one stone upon another; because you knew not the time of your visitation.
[45] And he went into the temple, and began to cast out them that sold therein, and them that bought;
[46] Saying to them, It is written, My house is the house of prayer: but you have made it a den of thieves.
[47] And he taught daily in the temple. But the chief priests and the scribes and the chief of the people sought to destroy him,
[48] And could not find what they might do: for all the people were very attentive to hear him.

Luke 20

[1] And it came to pass, that on one of those days, as he taught the people in the temple, and preached the gospel, the chief priests and the scribes came upon him with the elders,
[2] And spoke to him, saying, Tell us, by what authority do you these things? or who is he that gave you this authority?
[3] And he answered and said to them, I will also ask you one thing; and answer me:
[4] The baptism of John, was it from heaven, or of men?
[5] And they reasoned with themselves, saying, If we shall say, From heaven; he will say, Why then believed you him not?
[6] But and if we say, Of men; all the people will stone us: for they be persuaded that John was a prophet.
[7] And they answered, that they could not tell where it was.
[8] And Jesus said to them, Neither tell I you by what authority I do these things.
[9] Then began he to speak to the people this parable; A certain man planted a vineyard, and let it forth to husbandmen, and went into a far country for a long time.
[10] And at the season he sent a servant to the husbandmen, that they

should give him of the fruit of the vineyard: but the husbandmen beat him, and sent him away empty.
[11] And again he sent another servant: and they beat him also, and entreated him shamefully, and sent him away empty.
[12] And again he sent a third: and they wounded him also, and cast him out.
[13] Then said the lord of the vineyard, What shall I do? I will send my beloved son: it may be they will reverence him when they see him.
[14] But when the husbandmen saw him, they reasoned among themselves, saying, This is the heir: come, let us kill him, that the inheritance may be ours.
[15] So they cast him out of the vineyard, and killed him. What therefore shall the lord of the vineyard do to them?
[16] He shall come and destroy these husbandmen, and shall give the vineyard to others. And when they heard it, they said, God forbid.
[17] And he beheld them, and said, What is this then that is written, The stone which the builders rejected, the same is become the head of the corner?
[18] Whosoever shall fall upon that stone shall be broken; but on whomsoever it shall fall, it will grind him to powder.
[19] And the chief priests and the scribes the same hour sought to lay hands on him; and they feared the people: for they perceived that he had spoken this parable against them.
[20] And they watched him, and sent forth spies, which should feign themselves just men, that they might take hold of his words, that so they might deliver him to the power and authority of the governor.
[21] And they asked him, saying, Master, we know that you say and teach rightly, neither accept you the person of any, but teach the way of God truly:
[22] Is it lawful for us to give tribute to Caesar, or no?
[23] But he perceived their craftiness, and said to them, Why tempt you me?
[24] Show me a penny. Whose image and superscription has it? They answered and said, Caesar's.
[25] And he said to them, Render therefore to Caesar the things which be Caesar's, and to God the things which be God's.
[26] And they could not take hold of his words before the people: and they marveled at his answer, and held their peace.
[27] Then came to him certain of the Sadducees, which deny that

there is any resurrection; and they asked him,
[28] Saying, Master, Moses wrote to us, If any man's brother die, having a wife, and he die without children, that his brother should take his wife, and raise up offspring to his brother.
[29] There were therefore seven brethren: and the first took a wife, and died without children.
[30] And the second took her to wife, and he died childless.
[31] And the third took her; and in like manner the seven also: and they left no children, and died.
[32] Last of all the woman died also.
[33] Therefore in the resurrection whose wife of them is she? for seven had her to wife.
[34] And Jesus answering said to them, The children of this world marry, and are given in marriage:
[35] But they which shall be accounted worthy to obtain that world, and the resurrection from the dead, neither marry, nor are given in marriage:
[36] Neither can they die any more: for they are equal to the angels; and are the children of God, being the children of the resurrection.
[37] Now that the dead are raised, even Moses showed at the bush, when he called the Lord the God of Abraham, and the God of Isaac, and the God of Jacob.
[38] For he is not a God of the dead, but of the living: for all live to him.
[39] Then certain of the scribes answering said, Master, you have well said.
[40] And after that they dare not ask him any question at all.
[41] And he said to them, How say they that Christ is David's son?
[42] And David himself said in the book of Psalms, The LORD said to my Lord, Sit you on my right hand,
[43] Till I make your enemies your footstool.
[44] David therefore called him Lord, how is he then his son?
[45] Then in the audience of all the people he said to his disciples,
[46] Beware of the scribes, which desire to walk in long robes, and love greetings in the markets, and the highest seats in the synagogues, and the chief rooms at feasts;
[47] Which devour widows' houses, and for a show make long prayers: the same shall receive greater damnation.

Luke.21

[1] And he looked up, and saw the rich men casting their gifts into the treasury.
[2] And he saw also a certain poor widow casting in thither two mites.
[3] And he said, Of a truth I say to you, that this poor widow has cast in more than they all:
[4] For all these have of their abundance cast in to the offerings of God: but she of her penury has cast in all the living that she had.
[5] And as some spoke of the temple, how it was adorned with goodly stones and gifts, he said,
[6] As for these things which you behold, the days will come, in the which there shall not be left one stone upon another, that shall not be thrown down.
[7] And they asked him, saying, Master, but when shall these things be? and what sign will there be when these things shall come to pass?
[8] And he said, Take heed that you be not deceived: for many shall come in my name, saying, I am Christ; and the time draws near: go you not therefore after them.
[9] But when you shall hear of wars and commotions, be not terrified: for these things must first come to pass; but the end is not by and by.
[10] Then said he to them, Nation shall rise against nation, and kingdom against kingdom:
[11] And great earthquakes shall be in divers places, and famines, and pestilences; and fearful sights and great signs shall there be from heaven.
[12] But before all these, they shall lay their hands on you, and persecute you, delivering you up to the synagogues, and into prisons, being brought before kings and rulers for my name's sake.
[13] And it shall turn to you for a testimony.
[14] Settle it therefore in your hearts, not to meditate before what you shall answer:
[15] For I will give you a mouth and wisdom, which all your adversaries shall not be able to gainsay nor resist.
[16] And you shall be betrayed both by parents, and brethren, and kinsfolks, and friends; and some of you shall they cause to be put to death.
[17] And you shall be hated of all men for my name's sake.
[18] But there shall not a hair of your head perish.

[19] In your patience possess you your souls.
[20] And when you shall see Jerusalem compassed with armies, then know that the desolation thereof is near.
[21] Then let them which are in Judaea flee to the mountains; and let them which are in the midst of it depart out; and let not them that are in the countries enter there.
[22] For these be the days of vengeance, that all things which are written may be fulfilled.
[23] But woe to them that are with child, and to them that give suck, in those days! for there shall be great distress in the land, and wrath upon this people.
[24] And they shall fall by the edge of the sword, and shall be led away captive into all nations: and Jerusalem shall be trodden down of the Gentiles, until the times of the Gentiles be fulfilled.
[25] And there shall be signs in the sun, and in the moon, and in the stars; and upon the earth distress of nations, with perplexity; the sea and the waves roaring;
[26] Men's hearts failing them for fear, and for looking after those things which are coming on the earth: for the powers of heaven shall be shaken.
[27] And then shall they see the Son of man coming in a cloud with power and great glory.
[28] And when these things begin to come to pass, then look up, and lift up your heads; for your redemption draws near.
[29] And he spoke to them a parable; Behold the fig tree, and all the trees;
[30] When they now shoot forth, you see and know of your own selves that summer is now near at hand.
[31] So likewise you, when you see these things come to pass, know you that the kingdom of God is near at hand.
[32] Truly I say to you, This generation shall not pass away, till all be fulfilled.
[33] Heaven and earth shall pass away: but my words shall not pass away.
[34] And take heed to yourselves, lest at any time your hearts be overcharged with surfeiting, and drunkenness, and cares of this life, and so that day come upon you unawares.
[35] For as a snare shall it come on all them that dwell on the face of the whole earth.
[36] Watch you therefore, and pray always, that you may be

accounted worthy to escape all these things that shall come to pass, and to stand before the Son of man.

[37] And in the day time he was teaching in the temple; and at night he went out, and abode in the mount that is called the mount of Olives.

[38] And all the people came early in the morning to him in the temple, for to hear him.

Authors Note: The text entitled, The History of Joseph the Carpenter" is included here because it purports to be an account told by Jesus himself to his disciples at the time they were on the Mount of Olives.

The History of Joseph the Carpenter

IN the name of God, of one essence and three persons.
The History of the death of our father, the holy old man, Joseph the carpenter.
May his blessings and prayers preserve us all, O brethren! Amen. His whole life was one hundred and eleven years, and his departure from this world happened on the twenty-sixth of the month Abib. May his prayer preserve us! Amen.

And, indeed, it was our Lord Jesus Christ Himself who related this history to His holy disciples on the Mount of Olives, telling about all Joseph's labor, and the end of his days. And the holy apostles have preserved this conversation, and have left it written down in the library at Jerusalem. May their prayers preserve us! Amen.

1. One day, when the Savior, our Master and God, the Savior Jesus Christ, was sitting along with His disciples, they were all assembled on the Mount of Olives. He said to them: My brethren and friends, sons of the Father who has chosen you from all men, you know that I have often told you that I must be crucified, and must die for the salvation of Adam and his posterity, and that I shall rise from the dead. Now I shall commit to you the doctrine of the holy gospel formerly announced to you, that you may declare it throughout the whole world. And I shall endow you with power from on high, and fill you with the Holy Spirit. And you shall declare to all nations repentance and remission of sins. For a single cup of water, if a man shall find it in the world to come, is greater and better than all the wealth of this whole world. And as much ground as one foot can

occupy in the house of my Father, is greater and more excellent than all the riches of the earth. Yes, a single hour in the joyful dwelling of the pious is more blessed and more precious than a thousand years among sinners: inasmuch as their weeping and lamentation shall not come to an end, and their tears shall not cease, nor shall they find consolation for themselves and rest at any time for ever. And now, my honored members, go and declare to all nations, and tell them, and say to them: Truly the Savior diligently inquires into the inheritance which is due, and is the administrator of justice. And the angels will cast down their enemies, and will fight for them in the day of conflict. And He will examine every single foolish and idle word which men speak, and they shall give an account of it. For as no one shall escape death, so also the works of every man shall be laid open on the Day of Judgment, whether they have been good or evil. Tell them also this word which I have said to you today: Let not the strong man glory in his strength, nor the rich man in his riches; but let him who wishes to glory, glory in the Lord.

2. There was a man whose name was Joseph, who sprung from a family of Bethlehem, which was a town of Judah, and it was the city of King David. This same man, being well furnished with wisdom and learning, was made a priest in the temple of the Lord. He was, skilful in his trade, which was that of a carpenter. And after the manner of all men, he married a wife. Moreover, he begot for himself sons and daughters, four sons, namely, and two daughters. Now these are their names; Judas, Justus, James, and Simon. The names of the two daughters were Assia and Lydia. At length the wife of righteous Joseph, a woman intent on the divine glory in all her works, departed this life. But Joseph, that righteous man, my father after the flesh, and the spouse of my mother Mary, went away with his sons to his trade, practicing the art of a carpenter. 3. Now when righteous Joseph became a widower, my mother Mary, blessed, holy, and pure, was already twelve years old. For her parents offered her in the temple when she was three years of age, and she remained in the temple of the Lord nine years. Then when the priests saw that the virgin, holy and God-fearing, was growing up, they spoke to each other, saying: Let us search out a man, righteous and pious, to whom Mary may be entrusted until the time of her marriage; because if she remains in the temple, what happens to women will happen to her on that account we sin, and God be angry with us.

(Author's note: Mary was of age to begin her menstrual cycles, which would

have defiled the temple under the law.)

4. Therefore they immediately sent out, and assembled twelve old men of the tribe of Judah. And they wrote down the names of the twelve tribes of Israel. And the lot fell on the pious old man, righteous Joseph. Then the priests answered, and said to my blessed mother: Go with Joseph, and be with him till the time of your marriage. Righteous Joseph therefore received my mother, and led her away to his own house. And Mary found James the Less in his father's house, broken-hearted and sad on account of the loss of his mother, and she brought him up. Then Mary was called the mother of James. Thereafter Joseph left her at home, and went away to the shop where he wrought at his trade of a carpenter. And after the holy virgin had spent two years in his house her age was exactly fourteen years, including the time at which he received her. 5. And I chose her of my own will, with the concurrence of my Father, and the counsel of the Holy Spirit. And I was made flesh of her, by a mystery which transcends the grasp of created reason. And three months after her conception the righteous man Joseph returned from the place where he worked at his trade; and when he found my virgin mother pregnant, he was greatly perplexed, and thought of sending her away secretly. But from fear, and sorrow, and the anguish of his heart, he could endure neither to eat nor drink that day.
6. But at mid-day there appeared to him in a dream the prince of the angels, the holy Gabriel, furnished with a command from my Father; and he said to him: Joseph, son of David, fear not to take Mary as your wife: for she has conceived of the Holy Spirit; and she will bring forth a son, whose name shall be called Jesus. He it is who shall rule all nations with a rod of iron. Having thus spoken, the angel departed from him. And Joseph rose from his sleep, and did as the angel of the Lord had said to him; and Mary abode with him.
7. Some time after that, there came forth an order from Augustus Caesar the king, that all the habitable world should be enrolled, each man in his own city. The old man, righteous Joseph, rose up and took the virgin Mary and came to Bethlehem, because the time of her bringing forth was at hand. Joseph then inscribed his name in the list; for Joseph the son of David and whose spouse was Mary was of the tribe of Judah. And indeed Mary, my mother, brought me forth in Bethlehem, in a cave near the tomb of Rachel the wife of the patriarch Jacob, the mother of Joseph and Benjamin.

8. But Satan went and told this to Herod the Great, the father of Archelaus. And it was this same Herod who ordered my friend and relative John to be beheaded. Accordingly he searched for me diligently, thinking that my kingdom was to be of this world. But Joseph, that pious old man, was warned of this by a dream. Therefore he rose and took Mary my mother, and I lay in her bosom. Salome also was their fellow-traveler. Having therefore set out from home, he retired into Egypt, and remained there the space of one whole year, until the hatred of Herod passed away.

9. Now Herod died by the worst form of death, atoning for the shedding of the blood of the children whom he wickedly cut off, though there was no sin in them. And with that impious tyrant Herod being dead, they returned into the land of Israel, and lived in a city of Galilee which is called Nazareth. And Joseph, going back to his trade of a carpenter, earned his living by the work of his hands; for, as the Law of Moses had commanded, he never sought to live for nothing by another's labor. At length, by increasing years, the old man arrived at a very advanced age. He did not, however, labor under any bodily weakness, nor had his sight failed, nor had any tooth perished from his mouth. For the whole time of his life, his mind never wandered; but like a boy he always in his business displayed youthful vigor, and his limbs remained unimpaired, and free from all pain. His life, then, in all, amounted to one hundred and eleven years, his old age being prolonged to the utmost limit.

11. Now Justus and Simeon, the elder sons of Joseph, were married, and had families of their own. Both the daughters were likewise married, and lived in their own houses. So there remained in Joseph's house, Judas and James the Less, and my virgin mother. I moreover dwelt along with them, as if I had been one of his sons. But I passed all my life without fault. Mary I called my mother, and Joseph father, and I obeyed them in all that they said; nor did I ever contend against them, but complied with their commands, as other men whom earth produces are accustomed to do; nor did I at any time arouse their anger, or give any word or answer in opposition to them. On the contrary, I cherished them with great love, like the pupil of my eye. 12. It came to pass, after these things, that the death of that old man, the pious Joseph, and his departure from this world, were approaching, as happens to other men who owe their origin to this earth. And as his body was verging on dissolution, an angel of the Lord informed him that his death was now close at hand.

Therefore fear and great perplexity came upon him. So he rose up and went to Jerusalem; and going into the temple of the Lord, he poured out his prayers there before the sanctuary, and said:

13. O God, author of all consolation, God of all compassion, and Lord of the whole human race; God of my soul, body, and spirit; with supplications I reverence you, O Lord and my God. If now my days are ended, and the time draws near when I must leave this world, send me, I beg You, the great Michael, the prince of Your holy angels: let him remain with me, that my wretched soul may depart from this afflicted body without trouble, without terror and impatience. For great fear and intense sadness take hold of all bodies on the day of their death, whether it be man or woman, beast wild or tame, or whatever creeps on the ground or flies in the air. At the last all creatures under heaven in whom is the breath of life are struck with horror, and their souls depart from their bodies with strong fear and great depression. Now therefore, O Lord and my God, let Your holy angel be present with his help to my soul and body, until they shall be dissevered from each other. And let not the face of the angel, appointed my guardian from the day of my birth, be turned away from me; but may he be the companion of my journey even until he bring me to You: let his countenance be pleasant and gladsome to me, and let him accompany me in peace. And let not demons of frightful aspect come near me in the way in which I am to go, until I come to You in bliss. And let not the doorkeepers hinder my soul from entering paradise. And do not uncover my sins, and expose me to condemnation before Your terrible tribunal. Let not the lions rush in upon me; nor let the waves of the sea of fire overwhelm my soul--for this must every soul pass through before I have seen the glory of Your Godhead. O God, most righteous Judge, who in justice and equity will judge mankind, and will render to each one according to his works, O Lord and my God, I beg You, be present to me in Your compassion, and enlighten my path that I may come to You; for You are a fountain overflowing with all good things, and with glory for evermore.
Amen.

(Author's note: The ideas of doorkeepers, demons that challenge the dead, and escorted passage to paradise seem to indicate a Roman religious influence.)

14. It came to pass thereafter, when he returned to his own house in the city of Nazareth, that he was seized by disease, and had to keep his bed. And it was at this time that he died, according to the destiny of all mankind. For this disease was very heavy upon him, and he had never been ill, as he now was, from the day of his birth. And thus assuredly it pleased Christ (the anointed one) to order the destiny of righteous Joseph. He lived forty years unmarried; thereafter his wife remained under his care forty-nine years, and then died. And a year after her death, my mother, the blessed Mary, was entrusted to him by the priests, that he should keep her until the time of her marriage. She spent two years in his house; and in the third year of her stay with Joseph, in the fifteenth year of her age, she brought me forth on earth by a mystery which no creature can penetrate or understand, except myself, and my Father and the Holy Spirit, constituting one essence with myself. 15. The whole age of my father, therefore, that righteous old man, was one hundred and eleven years, my Father in heaven having so decreed. And the day on which his soul left his body was the twenty-sixth of the month Abib. For now the fine gold began to lose its splendor, and the silver to be worn down by use. I mean his understanding and his wisdom. He also loathed food and drink, and lost all his skill in his trade of carpentry, and he paid no more attention to it. It came to pass, then, in the early dawn of the twenty-sixth day of Abib that Joseph, that righteous old man, lying in his bed, was giving up his unquiet soul. Then he opened his mouth with many sighs, and struck his hands one against the other, and with a loud voice cried out, and spoke after the following manner:

16. Woe to the day on which I was born into the world! Woe to the womb which bare me! Woe to the bowels which admitted me! Woe to the breasts which suckled me! Woe to the feet upon which I sat and rested! Woe to the hands which carried me and reared me until I grew up! For I was conceived in iniquity, and in sins did my mother desire me. Woe to my tongue and my lips, which have brought forth and spoken vanity, detraction, falsehood, ignorance, derision, idle tales, craft, and hypocrisy! Woe to my eyes, which have looked upon scandalous things! Woe to my ears, which have delighted in the words of slanderers! Woe to my hands, which have seized that which did not of right belong to them! Woe to my belly and my bowels, which have lusted after food unlawful to be eaten! Woe to my throat, which like a fire has consumed all that it found! Woe to my feet,

which have too often walked in ways displeasing to God! Woe to my body; and woe to my miserable soul, which has already turned aside from God its Maker! What shall I do when I arrive at that place where I must stand before the most righteous Judge, and when He shall call me to account for the works which I have heaped up in my youth? Woe to every man dying in his sins! Assuredly that same dreadful hour, which came upon my father Jacob, when his soul was flying forth from his body, is now near at hand for me. Behold. Oh! how wretched I am this day, and worthy of lamentation! But God alone is the disposer of my soul and body; He also will deal with them after His own good pleasure.

17. These are the words spoken by Joseph, that righteous old man. And I, going in beside him, found his soul exceedingly troubled, for he was placed in great perplexity. And I said to him: Hail! my father Joseph, you righteous man; how is it with you? And he answered me: All hail! my well-beloved son. Indeed, the agony and fear of death have already surrounded me; but as soon as I heard Your voice, my soul was at rest. O Jesus of Nazareth! Jesus, my Savior! Jesus, the deliverer of my soul! Jesus, my protector! Jesus! O sweetest name in my mouth, and in the mouth of all those that love it! O eyes which see, and ears which hear, hear me! I am Your servant; this day I most humbly reverence You, and before Your face I pour out my tears. You are altogether my God; You are my Lord, as the angel has told me times without number, and especially on that day when my soul was driven about with perverse thoughts about the pure and blessed Mary, who was carrying You in her womb, and whom I was thinking of secretly sending away. And while I was thus meditating, behold, there appeared to me in my rest angels of the Lord, saying to me in a wonderful mystery: O Joseph, you son of David, fear not to take Mary as your wife; and do not grieve your soul, nor speak unbecoming words of her conception, because she is with child of the Holy Spirit, and shall bring forth a son, whose name shall be called Jesus, for He shall save His people from their sins. Do not for this cause wish me evil, O Lord, for I was ignorant of the mystery of Your birth. I call to mind also, my Lord, that day when the boy died of the bite of the serpent. And his relations wished to deliver You to Herod, saying that You had killed him; but You did raise him from the dead, and restore him to them.

(Author's note: This refers back to one of the Infancy Gospels, and is an

indication of the earliest date of this book, since it could not have been written earlier than the Infancy Gospel or at least the oral tradition it drew from.)

Then I went up to You, and took hold of Your hand, saying: My son, take care of yourself. But You did say to me in reply: Are you not my father after the flesh? I shall teach you who I am. Now therefore, O Lord and my God, do not be angry with me, or condemn me on account of that hour. I am Your servant, and the son of Your handmaiden; but You are my Lord, my God and Savior, most surely the Son of God.

18. When my father Joseph had thus spoken, he was unable to weep more. And I saw that death now had dominion over him. And my mother, virgin undefiled, rose and came to me, saying: O my beloved son, this pious old man Joseph is now dying. And I answered: Oh my dearest mother, assuredly upon all creatures produced in this world the same necessity of death lies; for death holds sway over the whole human race. Even you, O my virgin mother, must look for the same end of life as other mortals. And yet your death, as also the death of this pious man, is not death, but life enduring to eternity. Nay more, even I must die, as concerns the body which I have received from you. But rise, O my venerable mother, and go in to Joseph, that blessed old man, in order that you may see what will happen as his soul ascends from his body.

(Author's note: This passage stands in opposition to the Catholic doctrine of the assumption of Mary.)

19. My undefiled mother Mary, therefore, went and entered the place where Joseph was. And I was sitting at his feet looking at him, for the signs of death already appeared in his countenance. And that blessed old man raised his head, and kept his eyes fixed on my face; but he had no power of speaking to me, on account of the agonies of death, which held him in their grasp. But he kept fetching many sighs. And I held his hands for a whole hour; and he turned his face to me, and made signs for me not to leave him. Thereafter I put my hand on his breast, and perceived his soul now near his throat, preparing to depart from its receptacle.
20. And when my virgin mother saw me touching his body, she also touched his feet. And finding them already dead and destitute of

heat, she said to me: O my beloved son, assuredly his feet are already beginning to stiffen, and they are as cold as snow. Accordingly she summoned his sons and daughters, and said to them: Come, as many as there are of you, and go to your father; for assuredly he is now at the very point of death. And Assia, his daughter, answered and said: Woe is me, O my brothers, this is certainly the same disease that my beloved mother died of. And she lamented and shed tears; and all Joseph's other children mourned along with her. And my mother Mary, and I also, wept along with them.

21. And turning my eyes towards the region of the south, I saw Death already approaching, and all Gehenna with him, closely attended by his army and his satellites; and their clothes, their faces, and their mouths poured forth flames. And when my father Joseph saw them coming straight to him, his eyes dissolved in tears, and at the same time he groaned after a strange manner. Accordingly, when I saw the vehemence of his sighs, I drove back Death and all the host of servants which accompanied him. And I called on my good Father, saying:

22. O Father of all mercy, eye which sees, and ear which hears, listen to my prayers and supplications in behalf of the old man Joseph; and send Michael, the prince of your angels, and Gabriel, the herald of light, and all the light of your angels, and let their whole array walk with the soul of my father Joseph, until they shall have conducted it to You. This is the hour in which my father has need of compassion. And I say to you, that all the saints, yea, as many men as are born in the world, whether they be just or whether they be perverse, must of necessity taste of death.

23. Therefore Michael and Gabriel came to the soul of my father Joseph, and took it, and wrapped it in a shining wrapper. Thus he committed his spirit into the hands of my good Father, and He bestowed on him peace. But as yet none of his children knew that he had fallen asleep. And the angels preserved his soul from the demons of darkness which were in the way, and praised God even until they conducted it into the dwelling-place of the pious.

24. Now his body was lying prostrate and bloodless; wherefore I reached forth my hand, and put right his eyes and shut his mouth, and said to the virgin Mary: O my mother, where is the skill which he showed in all the time that he lived in this world? Lo, it has perished, as if it had never existed. And when his children heard me speaking with my mother, the pure virgin, they knew that he had

already breathed his last, and they shed tears, and lamented. But I said to them: Assuredly the death of your father is not death, but life everlasting: for he has been freed from the troubles of this life, and has passed to perpetual and everlasting rest. When they heard these words, they rent their clothes, and wept.

25. And, indeed, the inhabitants of Nazareth and of Galilee, having heard of their lamentation, flocked to them, and wept from the third hour even to the ninth. And at the ninth hour they all went together to Joseph's bed. And they lifted his body, after they had anointed it with costly ointments. But I entreated my Father in the prayer of the celestials (heavens)--that same prayer which with my own hand I made before I was carried in the womb of the Virgin Mary, my mother. And as soon as I had finished it, and pronounced the amen, a great multitude of angels came up; and I ordered two of them to stretch out their shining garments, and to wrap in them the body of Joseph, the blessed old man.

26. And I spoke to Joseph, and said: The smell or corruption of death shall not have dominion over you, nor shall a worm ever come forth from your body. Not a single limb of it shall be broken, nor shall any hair on your head be changed. Nothing of your body shall perish, O my father Joseph, but it will remain entire and uncorrupted even until the banquet of the thousand years. And whoever shall make an offering on the day of your remembrance, him will I bless and recompense in the congregation of the virgins; and whoever shall give food to the wretched, the poor, the widows, and orphans from the work of his hands, on the day on which your memory shall be celebrated, and in your name, shall not be in want of good things all the days of his life. And whoever shall have given a cup of water, or of wine, to drink to the widow or orphan in your name, I will give him to you, that you may go in with him to the banquet of the thousand years. And every man who shall present an offering on the day of your commemoration will I bless and recompense in the church of the virgins: for one I will render to him thirty, sixty, and a hundred. And whosoever shall write the history of your life, of your labor, and your departure from this world, and this narrative that has issued from my mouth, him shall I commit to your keeping as long as he shall have to do with this life. And when his soul departs from the body, and when he must leave this world, I will burn the book of his sins, nor will I torment him with any punishment in the day of judgment; but he shall cross the sea of flames, and shall go through it

without trouble or pain. And on every poor man who can give none of those things which I have mentioned this is incumbent: that if a son is born to him, he shall call his name Joseph. So there shall not take place in that house either poverty or any sudden death forever.
27. Thereafter the chief men of the city came together to the place where the body of the blessed old man Joseph had been laid, bringing with them burial-clothes; and they wished to wrap it up in them after the manner in which the Jews are wont to arrange their dead bodies. And they perceived that he kept his shroud fast; for it adhered to the body in such a way, that when they wished to take it off, it was found to be like iron--impossible to be moved or loosened. Nor could they find any ends in that piece of linen, which struck them with the greatest astonishment. At length they carried him out to a place where there was a cave, and opened the gate, that they might bury his body beside the bodies of his fathers. Then there came into my mind the day on which he walked with me into Egypt, and that extreme trouble which he endured on my account. Accordingly, I bewailed his death for a long time; and lying on his body, I said:
28. O Death! who make all knowledge to vanish away, and raise so many tears and lamentations, surely it is God my Father Himself who has granted you this power. For men die for the transgression of Adam and his wife Eve, and Death spares not so much as one. Nevertheless, nothing happens to any one, or is brought upon him, without the command of my Father. There have certainly been men who have prolonged their life even to nine hundred years; but they died. Yea, though some of them have lived longer, they have, notwithstanding, succumbed to the same fate; nor has any one of them ever said: I have not tasted death. For the Lord never sends the same punishment more than once, since it has pleased my Father to bring it upon men. And at the very moment when it, going forth, beholds the command descending to it from heaven, it says: I will go forth against that man, and will greatly move him. Then, without delay, it makes an onset on the soul, and obtains the mastery of it, doing with it whatever it will. For, because Adam did not do the will of my Father, but transgressed His commandment, the wrath of my Father was kindled against him, and He doomed him to death; and thus it was that death came into the world. But if Adam had observed my Father's precepts, death would never have fallen to his lot. Think you that I can ask my good Father to send me a chariot of fire, which may take up the body of my father Joseph, and convey it

to the place of rest, in order that it may dwell with the spirits? But on account of the transgression of Adam, that trouble and violence of death has descended upon all the human race. And it is for this cause that I must die according to the flesh, for my work which I have created, that they may obtain grace.

29. Having thus spoken, I embraced the body of my father Joseph, and wept over it; and they opened the door of the tomb, and placed his body in it, near the body of his father Jacob. And at the time when he fell asleep he had fulfilled a hundred and eleven years. Never did a tooth in his mouth hurt him, nor was his eyesight rendered less sharp, nor his body bent, nor his strength impaired; but he worked at his trade of a carpenter to the very last day of his life; and that was the six-and-twentieth of the month Abib.

30. And we apostles, when we heard these things from our Savior, rose up joyfully, and prostrated ourselves in honor of Him, and said: O our Savior, show us Your grace. Now indeed we have heard the word of life: nevertheless we wonder, O our Savior, at the fate of Enoch and Elias, inasmuch as they had not to undergo death. For truly they dwell in the habitation of the righteous even to the present day, nor have their bodies seen corruption. Yet that old man Joseph the carpenter was, nevertheless, Your father after the flesh. And You have ordered us to go into all the world and preach the holy Gospel; and You have said: Relate to them the death of my father Joseph, and celebrate to him with annual solemnity a festival and sacred day. And whoever shall take anything away from this narrative, or add anything to it, commits sin. We wonder especially that Joseph, even from that day on which You were born in Bethlehem, called You his son after the flesh. Then, did You not make him immortal as well as them, and You say that he was righteous and chosen?

31. And our Savior answered and said: Indeed, the prophecy of my Father upon Adam, for his disobedience, has now been fulfilled. And all things are arranged according to the will and pleasure of my Father. For if a man rejects the commandment of God, and follows the works of the devil by committing sin, his life is prolonged; for be is preserved in order that he may perhaps repent, and reflect that he must be delivered into the hands of death. But if any one has been zealous of good works, his life also is prolonged, that, as the fame of his old age increases, upright men may imitate him. But when you see a man whose mind is prone to anger, assuredly his days are shortened; for it is these that are taken away in the flower of their

age. Every prophecy, therefore, which my Father has pronounced concerning the sons of men, must be fulfilled in every particular. But with reference to Enoch and Elias, and how they remain alive to this day, keeping the same bodies with which they were born; and as to what concerns my father Joseph, who has not been allowed as well as they to remain in the body: indeed, though a man live in the world many myriads of years, nevertheless at some time or other he is compelled to exchange life for death.

(See "The Lost Book of Enoch," published by Fifth Estate.)

And I say to you, O my brethren, that they also, Enoch and Elias, must towards the end of time return into the world and die--in the day, namely, of commotion, of terror, of perplexity, and affliction. For Antichrist will slay four bodies, and will pour out their blood like water, because of the ridicule to which they shall expose him, and the ignominy with which they, in their lifetime, shall brand him when they reveal his impiety.

(Author's note: This may refer to the two witnesses found in the book of Revelation, who were sent from heaven and are murdered on the streets for preaching the word of God.)

32. And we said: O our Lord, our God and Savior, who are those four whom You have said Antichrist will cut off from the ridicule they bring upon him? The Lord answered: They are Enoch, Elias, Schila, and Tabitha. When we heard this from our Savior, we rejoiced and exulted; and we offered all glory and thanksgiving to the Lord God, and our Savior Jesus Christ. He it is to whom is due glory, honor, dignity, dominion, power, and praise, as well as to the good Father with Him, and to the Holy Spirit that gives life, now on and in all time for evermore. Amen.

(Author's note: Tabitha and Schila were raised from death by Jesus.)

(This ends the story told by Jesus to his disciples when they were together on the Mount of Olives.)

Gospel of Luke from the Holy Bible

Luke 22

[1] Now the feast of unleavened bread drew near, which is called the Passover.
[2] And the chief priests and scribes sought how they might kill him; for they feared the people.
[3] Then entered Satan into Judas surnamed Iscariot, being of the number of the twelve.
[4] And he went his way, and communed with the chief priests and captains, how he might betray him to them.
[5] And they were glad, and covenanted to give him money.
[6] And he promised, and sought opportunity to betray him to them in the absence of the multitude.
[7] Then came the day of unleavened bread, when the Passover must be killed.
[8] And he sent Peter and John, saying, Go and prepare us the Passover, that we may eat.
[9] And they said to him, Where will you that we prepare?
[10] And he said to them, Behold, when you are entered into the city, there shall a man meet you, bearing a pitcher of water; follow him into the house where he enters in.
[11] And you shall say to the goodman of the house, The Master said to you, Where is the guest chamber, where I shall eat the Passover with my disciples?
[12] And he shall show you a large upper room furnished: there make ready.
[13] And they went, and found as he had said to them: and they made ready the Passover.
[14] And when the hour was come, he sat down, and the twelve apostles with him.
[15] And he said to them, With desire I have desired to eat this Passover with you before I suffer:
[16] For I say to you, I will not any more eat thereof, until it be

fulfilled in the kingdom of God.
[17] And he took the cup, and gave thanks, and said, Take this, and divide it among yourselves:
[18] For I say to you, I will not drink of the fruit of the vine, until the kingdom of God shall come.
[19] And he took bread, and gave thanks, and brake it, and gave to them, saying, This is my body which is given for you: this do in remembrance of me.
[20] Likewise also the cup after supper, saying, This cup is the new testament in my blood, which is shed for you.
[21] But, behold, the hand of him that betrayed me is with me on the table.
[22] And truly the Son of man goes, as it was determined: but woe to that man by whom he is betrayed!
[23] And they began to inquire among themselves, which of them it was that should do this thing.
[24] And there was also a strife among them, which of them should be accounted the greatest.
[25] And he said to them, The kings of the Gentiles exercise lordship over them; and they that exercise authority upon them are called benefactors.
[26] But you shall not be so: but he that is greatest among you, let him be as the younger; and he that is chief, as he that does serve.
[27] For whether is greater, he that sits at meat, or he that serves? is not he that sits at meat? but I am among you as he that serves.
[28] You are they which have continued with me in my temptations.
[29] And I appoint to you a kingdom, as my Father has appointed to me;
[30] That you may eat and drink at my table in my kingdom, and sit on thrones judging the twelve tribes of Israel.
[31] And the Lord said, Simon, Simon, behold, Satan has desired to have you, that he may sift you as wheat:
[32] But I have prayed for you, that your faith fail not: and when you are converted, strengthen your brethren.
[33] And he said to him, Lord, I am ready to go with you, both into prison, and to death.
[34] And he said, I tell you, Peter, the cock shall not crow this day, before that you shall three times deny that you know me.
[35] And he said to them, When I sent you without purse, and scrip (purse-bag), and shoes, lacked you any thing? And they said,

nothing.

[36] Then said he to them, But now, he that has a purse, let him take it, and likewise his scrip (purse-bag): and he that has no sword, let him sell his garment, and buy one.

[37] For I say to you, that this that is written must yet be accomplished in me, And he was reckoned among the transgressors: for the things concerning me have an end.

[38] And they said, Lord, behold, here are two swords. And he said to them, It is enough.

[39] And he came out, and went, as he was wont, to the mount of Olives; and his disciples also followed him.

[40] And when he was at the place, he said to them, Pray that you enter not into temptation.

[41] And he was withdrawn from them about a stone's cast, and kneeled down, and prayed,

[42] Saying, Father, if you be willing, remove this cup from me: nevertheless not my will, but yours, be done.

[43] And there appeared an angel to him from heaven, strengthening him.

[44] And being in an agony he prayed more earnestly: and his sweat was as it were great drops of blood falling down to the ground.

[45] And when he rose up from prayer, and was come to his disciples, he found them sleeping for sorrow,

[46] And said to them, Why sleep you? rise and pray, lest you enter into temptation.

[47] And while he yet spoke, behold a multitude, and he that was called Judas, one of the twelve, went before them, and drew near to Jesus to kiss him.

[48] But Jesus said to him, Judas, betray you the Son of man with a kiss?

[49] When they which were about him saw what would follow, they said to him, Lord, shall we strike with the sword?

[50] And one of them smote the servant of the high priest, and cut off his right ear.

[51] And Jesus answered and said, Suffer you thus far. And he touched his ear, and healed him.

[52] Then Jesus said to the chief priests, and captains of the temple, and the elders, which were come to him, Be you come out, as against a thief, with swords and staves?

[53] When I was daily with you in the temple, you stretched forth no

hands against me: but this is your hour, and the power of darkness.
[54] Then took they him, and led him, and brought him into the high priest's house. And Peter followed afar off.
[55] And when they had kindled a fire in the midst of the hall, and were set down together, Peter sat down among them.
[56] But a certain maid beheld him as he sat by the fire, and earnestly looked upon him, and said, This man was also with him.
[57] And he denied him, saying, Woman, I know him not.
[58] And after a little while another saw him, and said, You are also of them. And Peter said, Man, I am not.
[59] And about the space of one hour after another confidently affirmed, saying, Of a truth this fellow also was with him: for he is a Galilaean.
[60] And Peter said, Man, I know not what you say. And immediately, while he yet spoke, the cock crew.
[61] And the Lord turned, and looked upon Peter. And Peter remembered the word of the Lord, how he had said to him, Before the cock crow, you shall deny me thrice.
[62] And Peter went out, and wept bitterly.
[63] And the men that held Jesus mocked him, and smote him.
[64] And when they had blindfolded him, they struck him on the face, and asked him, saying, Prophesy, who is it that smote you?
[65] And many other things blasphemously spoke they against him.
[66] And as soon as it was day, the elders of the people and the chief priests and the scribes came together, and led him into their council, saying,
[67] Are you the Christ? tell us. And he said to them, If I tell you, you will not believe:
[68] And if I also ask you, you will not answer me, nor let me go.
[69] Hereafter shall the Son of man sit on the right hand of the power of God.
[70] Then said they all, Are you then the Son of God? And he said to them, You say that I am.
[71] And they said, What need we any further witness? for we ourselves have heard of his own mouth.

Luke 23

[1] And the whole multitude of them arose, and led him to Pilate.

[2] And they began to accuse him, saying, We found this fellow perverting the nation, and forbidding to give tribute to Caesar, saying that he himself is Christ a King.
[3] And Pilate asked him, saying, Are you the King of the Jews? And he answered him and said, You say it.
[4] Then said Pilate to the chief priests and to the people, I find no fault in this man.
[5] And they were the more fierce, saying, He stirs up the people, teaching throughout all Jewry, beginning from Galilee to this place.
[6] When Pilate heard of Galilee, he asked whether the man were a Galilaean.
[7] And as soon as he knew that he belonged to Herod's jurisdiction, he sent him to Herod, who himself also was at Jerusalem at that time.
[8] And when Herod saw Jesus, he was exceeding glad: for he was desirous to see him of a long season, because he had heard many things of him; and he hoped to have seen some miracle done by him.
[9] Then he questioned with him in many words; but he answered him nothing.
[10] And the chief priests and scribes stood and vehemently accused him.
[11] And Herod with his men of war set him at nought, and mocked him, and arrayed him in a gorgeous robe, and sent him again to Pilate.

Author's note: Here we break from the Bible to read letters written between Pilate and his friend, Seneca. These letters are provided as a historical background leading up to Pilate's station and his decision regarding Jesus. They tell of his thoughts and feeling toward the Jews. The letters also add much insight into the political and social environment surrounding Jesus from the time of the beheading of John the Baptist until the time of the arrest and crucifixion of Jesus. Conversations with the High Priest are recorded, and the political relationship between Rome and the ruling priests are illuminated. In light of these things, Jesus' world comes to life and decisions of Pilate and the Jews regarding Jesus are explained.

LETTERS OF PONTIUS PILATE

Written during his Governorship of Judaea to his friend Seneca in Rome

ON THE WAY TO JUDAEA

Shipboard off Alexandria

We are at last within sight of Alexandria, my dear Seneca, and tomorrow we land. I shall spend a week meeting my staff, interviewing applicants for jobs (shoals of Greeks, of course), receiving deputations of loyal Jews, and talking to every one who can be useful to me. Then on to Caesarea, which, as you know, is my headquarters.

Here at Alexandria I am to meet Valerius Gratus, my predecessor as Procurator of Judaea, and if anyone can tell me how to solve the riddle of getting along with the Jews, he ought to be the man. Not that I shall not get along with them; I intend to, and I believe I shall. Valerius has stood them, or they have stood him, would you say? - for over ten years, so it can be done, though no one else has done it.

(Valerius Gratus was Procurator of Judaea from A.D. 15 to A.D. 26.)

By the way, I have been lucky in engaging two of Valerius's staff for myself.

One is Marcius Rufus, his chief military officer and now mine, who has been on leave and is travelling back with me. The other is even more important. He is his Secretary Alexander. He is a Jew, but one of those Jews that are half-Greek: Greek on the surface, and Jew at the bottom. You cannot do without them. It seems that you cannot get a real Jewish Jew to put himself at the service of a mere Roman governor, and if you could you would be little better off because he would not have the languages. And languages are needed, I assure you. There is one sort of Hebrew for their sacred writing, there is the Aramaic that they commonly talk, there is Greek for non-Jews and for all educated people, whether Jews or not, and there is Latin for the Roman Procurator and his staff if they don't choose to use Greek. Alexander speaks them all, Alexander knows everything. I am told that the only person in this part of the world who is sharper than a Greek is a Greek-educated Jew. Congratulate me, therefore, on my Alexander. I rely on him to tell me what I do not know about my province of Judaea - which is almost everything. There are two persons I must not at any price offend, you see: Caesar Imperator (whom the gods preserve) and my Jew Alexander.

(The Emperor Tiberius, who reigned A.D. 14 to A.D. 36.)

Marcius, on the other hand, is a Roman of the Romans. He despises all foreigners, especially Jews. He knows how inferior they are to Romans, and he has never got over the shock of discovering that the Jews are equally satisfied that the Romans are immeasurably inferior to themselves. I was telling him that I had promised to receive the addresses of loyal Jews in Alexandria. 'Impossible!' he said. 'There aren't any.' The other day, when the sea was rough, a wave came over and struck me in the back, knocking me down. When I could get my breath, I said, 'A treacherous blow!' 'We are on our way to Judaea,' said Marcius.

Procula (Pilates wife) is worried that we are to have only a week in Alexandria. She says that she will not have time to do the necessary shopping. My own opinion is that from that point of view a week is much too long. But it really is ridiculous that the Treasury should not make a special 'furnishing grant' or something of that kind to a man in my position. You know I shall have to keep up the palace of Herod at Caesarea and another that he built for himself at Jerusalem and probably there's a third of the same kind at Samaria. How in the world is a poor man going to maintain these enormous places? It was all very well for Herod. He was one of the richest men in the world and Judaea was only a small part of his kingdom. Valerius will be waiting for me here with an inventory of his private 'fixtures' in these palaces and there will be a pretty bill for me to pay. Besides, he is sure to take a great many things away with him, and I shall have to replace them. So you may imagine Procula spending a happy week among what she declares are the finest shops in the Empire - much better, she says, than those of Rome.

You can see yourself how the whole affair has been mismanaged by Rome. When we decided that we must take over the government of Judaea because of the unruliness of the Jews, we should have annexed the whole country that Herod ruled from near Damascus to the Dead Sea and not have left his two sons in possession of large parts of it.

(Note: When Herod the Great died in 4 B.C., the Romans divided his territory between his sons Archelaus, Antipas and Philip, Judaea falling to Archelaus. In A.D. 6, however, they deposed Archelaus and placed Judaea in the hands of a Roman Procurator, but left the other territories still in the hands of Antipas and Philip.)

It's an unfair tax on the Procurator of Judaea, who has to keep up the state of Herod on a fraction of his income. Well, some one will have to find the money, and there's no one for it but the Jews. A Roman Procurator must not be worse housed than a semi-barbarous king like their Herod, must he? I tell Procula that if she wants rugs and tapestries, she should wait till she goes on a visit to Damascus or Antioch, but she only smiles at that; a rug in the hand is worth two in the desert to a woman any day. I say again, the Jews will have to pay. After all, it is a reasonable charge to impose on them and they can afford it. The Jews all over the world - and they are all over the world, you can't get away from them anywhere - are sending money to Jerusalem all the time.

(Note: Pilate is speaking of the Temple-tribute' which all Jews sent to Jerusalem each year. The Roman Governors in the provinces resented these contributions, but the central government at Rome upheld the Jews in sending them.)

You would be astonished at the sight before me as I write - a perfect forest of masts. I did not think there were so many ships afloat. No wonder the Alexandrines says their city is the greatest commercial center in the world.

The Captain has just pointed out to me a whole fleet of big ships on one side of the harbor - the fleet that carries grain to our people in Italy. He tells me the grain traffic is in the hands of - whom do you think? - of course, the Jews. He also confided to me that he liked the Jews better outside Judaea than in it. I shall see. At all events I rejoice that, though I might easily have had a more important province, when I am in Judaea I shall be governor, chief tax collector and commander-in-chief all in one.

I will write again before we leave for Caesarea.

POLICY TOWARDS THE JEWS

Alexandria

I found your letter waiting for me when I landed and I hasten to thank you for it. I count myself happy that you who are so busy and making for yourself so brilliant a name in the courts should have had the inclination and the time to write me a long letter of good wishes and advice. It was shrewd of you, too, my friend. 'Pilate,' you said to yourself, 'the impulsive, headstrong Pilate, will not be able to argue with me; he will have to take my warnings on with him from Alexandria and chew upon them all the way to Caesarea.' I will do that, I promise you, and whenever I do so I shall wonder again that one so young as you should be so wise.

(Note: Seneca was about thirty years of age at this time.)

The State is fortunate which can boast not only of Caesars but of Senecas to serve them, and I shall watch your progress with affectionate eagerness from my exile among the savages.

'What,' you will say, 'savages! So that is all that my letter has accomplished, so that is the spirit in which you take up your task? The Jews are not savages.' No, they are not; I seek but to provoke you. The Jews are highly civilized. They are intelligent and subtle, industrious and tenacious; they can split a hair with the most learned and steal a march with the most cunning. You need not be afraid; I shall not under-rate them.

But, you say, beware of their religion, for on that subject they are the most sensitive, the most prone to take offence, the most indomitable in resistance, of any people on this earth. And, you add, holding up a warning finger, 'You know what Caesar wishes!' I know. No commotions, no rebellions, taxes duly paid: that is what Caesar wishes. Yet you will not pretend that Caesar loves the Jews, at least in Rome. Precisely, says the wise Seneca: in Rome Caesar does not love the Jews any more than he does the Egyptians. They will not mix, they are a race apart, they will not do sacrifice to the Gods or to Caesar, and they claim all sorts of privileges. Caesar does not want such people in Rome, though they flock there more and more. They should stop in their own Judaea, then, and in their own Judaea - let them alone! Is not that the instruction? Have I not laid your letter well to heart? Believe me, I shall not interfere with their religion, their priests or their Temple. But I have heard - and have you, who know so much, not also heard? - that with a Jew religion comes very near to politics? What, pray, is a Roman Governor to do when religion becomes politics? I have heard that some of them will acknowledge no ruler except their God, not even Caesar. Not even Caesar, mark you! Let them beware. I think that Caesar will be highly displeased with servants who are not concerned to secure respect for his authority. In religion the Jews may go their own way. In politics they shall go my way, the Roman way, or I will know the reason why.

Tomorrow I meet Valerius in the morning, and in the afternoon a deputation of Alexandrine Jews, who wish to pay me their dutiful respects and (so their letter says) make representations to me about lightening of the burdens on their countrymen in Judaea. I shall be expected, I suppose, to show how much finer a fellow than Valerius I am by reducing the taxes.

The shopping campaign is already in full swing.

MEETING WITH HIS PREDECESSOR VALERIUS

Alexandria

My time has been so fully occupied that I am only now able to write to you, and we sail for Caesarea in a few hours. Every few minutes there is some interruption; but I will write this letter though I miss the ship.

There is one thing of great importance, which I must say at once lest I forget it; the Jews can wait. You told me, you may remember, of a new wash which you had devised for your vine-plants - more efficacious against pests than any known to you, and you attributed to it the generous crop that you had last year. I have told my freedman Leon who manages my farm at Laurentum to write and ask you for the particulars, and I shall be grateful if you will give them to him. He is ingenious in all such experiments and omits no details; you may be sure that you will not have the annoyance of finding that those who have not the wit or the will to make the best of it have sought your advice.

I have seen Valerius - a ruddy complexioned, jolly fellow, delighted at the prospect of going home. I wanted to ask about Judaea but he would scarcely talk of anything but Rome and chariot racing, for which he has a passion. However, he told me enough about the furnishing of Herod's palaces to make it clear that my worst fears are true. He says that when Caesar deposed him Archelaus, sold the contents of the palaces as being his private property, and that consequently every governor since then has had to furnish anew or buy the 'fixtures' of his predecessor. 'How can I pay so much,' I said, 'at the beginning of my term of office?' 'Borrow the money from the Jews,' said Valerius, 'and then increase their taxes in order to pay it back.' 'But,' I replied, 'I am just going to inform a Jewish deputation that out of respect and admiration for their race I intend graciously to remit a tenth part of the taxes.' 'Why not?' said Valerius, 'I did the same myself. But in six months you must restore the ten per cent, and in twelve months put another tenth on that.' He told me also that I should by all means encourage the Jews who throng to Jerusalem from Asia and Africa at the time of the great festivals, especially the Passover. So long as Caesar maintains peace in the provinces, the Jews flourish. They travel in tens of thousands to Judaea, carrying their money with them. 'Then is your chance,' said he. 'Make them pay a visitors' tax when they enter, raise the customs duties on everything that is bought and sold while they are there, and put a specially heavy tax on all the mementoes that they carry away when they go back. They will grumble, but since they are departing to other provinces, that need not trouble you, and the Jews in Judaea, having helped to suck them dry, will take no further interest in them.' I like Valerius. He knows what is helpful, and is practical.

I had meant to describe the Jewish deputation to you but that must wait. I shall have more leisure time to do it adequately on the way to Caesarea. You may think of me, during the voyage, taking lessons on Judaea from

Alexander. What kind of man is he, you ask. You know the sort of Jew that is aggressive, insistent, loud? He is the other sort. He is quiet, deferential, often obsequious - and, unless I am mistaken, as deeply disdainful of you, and me and of Rome, and Caesar as the noisiest of them all.

At present Alexander is engaged in a brisk flirtation with Acme, Procula's Greek slave, a pretty girl. He has succeeded Marcius. Jew does not marry non-Jew, I believe, but outside marriage they are not particular.

INSTRUCTION FROM VALERIUS

Shipboard: On the way to Caesarea

The sea is only choppy and I must not grumble, but I am glad that it is a short voyage compared with that from Italy.

I had meant to tell you what Valerius said to me about Galilee. As you know, both Galilee and Peraea , which is east of Jerusalem on the far side of the river Jordan, are both possessions of Antipas, son of the Herod who, by turning his coat skillfully during our civil wars, not only kept his kingdom but continued adding to it. I complained to Valerius that these territories ought to be under the Governor of Judaea, especially Galilee. Common sense demands it. Galilee is Jewish, it is flourishing and rich, and Jerusalem is its national and historic capital. Its inhabitants look to Jerusalem as their sacred city and are always travelling to it. Would anyone in his senses dream of carving up a country into strips in such a way, and why should we tolerate it just because Herod had three sons for whom he wanted to provide? Valerius agreed with me at once. 'There is more in it than that, too,' he said, 'as you may soon find out. The Galileans, like all the Jews, hate the Romans, and they are as independent and stiff-necked as can be. But when they want to make trouble, they come out of Galilee, where they can change nothing and achieve nothing, and make it in Judaea, which means Jerusalem. The last serious uprising was about twenty years ago, when we took over the country. The trouble was raised by a rascal called Judas who belonged to Galilee. That was a real rebellion. The unfortunate Procurator of Judaea is not allowed by Caesar to have any rebellions, while at the same time he is prevented from dealing with the beginnings of seditions in Galilee even if he knows of them, because it is the kingdom of Antipas and he must not interfere.' 'Then we ought,' I said, 'to get rid of Antipas.' Valerius smiled.

'I have been waiting for ten years,' he said, 'and he has never given me a handle.

(Note: Judas of Gamala led a revolt at the time Herod died in 4 B.C. He tried again in A.D. 6-7, when the Romans imposed taxation. It was from the party of Judas and Zaddok, a Pharisee, that the 'Zealots' arose. The Zealots were so named because of the fire and fervent hate they felt toward Rome. It was this uncontrolled hatred that led to the fatal revolt against the Romans.)

You may take it that Antipas will not allow sedition to start in Galilee if he can help it, because he knows the Romans might seize the chance to absorb his kingdom into Judaea. He keeps on good terms with the Roman Governor of Syria and he has friends in Rome. Like his villainous old father, he flatters the Jews by observing their customs and he keeps himself in power by paying court to the Romans. All the Herods are the same. They know that if it were not for the Romans the Jews would have them out in no time, for the Jews love them little though they love the Romans less.'

I asked Valerius if all the Jews detest the Romans equally how had he managed to keep things quiet for ten years. 'It's quite true,' he said, 'that they all hate us. There is scarcely one of them that would speak to us, let alone eat with us, if he could help it, but they do not all hate us in the same degree. There are some of them at Jerusalem who would sooner put up with the Romans than lose the power and position that they hold. Their noble priestly families - as arrogant a crew as can be found in Asia - ruled the whole country before the time of Herod. Herod destroyed their power and almost destroyed them. Now they have raised their heads again. We have given them back much of their authority, especially in regard to their religion, and, in order to keep it, they are ready to tolerate us. They do not want another Herod to sweep them aside and send them to the executioner. Nor do they like sedition, unless it were likely to be successful, because they know the power of Rome. They have no use for a Judas, whether from Galilee or anywhere else, who by raising a popular revolt may bring them into conflict with Rome and end their privileges. They make a bargain with Rome. "We hate you and despise you," they say, "but on terms we can help you. Leave us alone and we will keep the country quiet for you."'

You see, my friend, how quickly I am learning. I am to work with these priests at Jerusalem and look out for an opportunity, which I am not likely to get, of tripping up Antipas. Between you and Valerius and Secretary Alexander I shall soon be a statesman. All the same, I shall press for an increase in the garrison of Judaea. Four thousand men are not enough. When I get the chance I shall say that I need more troops to watch the frontiers of Galilee and Peraea.

I have not told you about the deputation after all, but I will write again before we land at Caesarea.

A JEWISH DEPUTATION AT ALEXANDRIA

Shipboard, near to Caesarea

Now at last I can describe the Jewish deputation. It was a bigger affair than I had expected, but then the Jews in Alexandria are much more important than I had supposed. There is a Jewish settlement which they say occupies nearly half the city; I know that on the day before the deputation came I drove and drove and always the people and the placards and the shop-signs were Jewish. Everywhere children and everywhere aged greybeards, grave or talking with animation in the street. I have never seen so many old men. Do they ever die, I wonder? Or is it only that one notices them more because they are so different?

It had become known that I intended to receive some of their leading men and there was a great crowd in the square before the palace of the City Prefect, Junius Macrinus, with whom I was staying. You should have heard the uproar when the deputation appeared. The Jews, who were there in force, gave their countrymen an excited welcome, I suppose because they were going to admonish the prospective oppressor of Judaea. This provoked the mob, who were mostly Greeks and they began to hoot and then to hustle the Jews and finally to throw stones. The Jews resisted and I thought that there would be a riot. However, Junius, who is used to this sort of thing and was amused at my taking it so seriously, had a company of troops in readiness and they soon hurried the deputation indoors and cleared the square. Everything went like clockwork. Two men, whom I believe to be Greeks were killed.

You would scarcely believe how much the Jews are disliked in this part of the world. The crowd called them 'swine,' 'robbers' and 'blood-drinkers.' Partly it is because they are arrogant and exclusive, but the Greeks cannot forgive them for beating them in trade. There is a saying in Alexandria that 'an Egyptian could make money from a pyramid, a Greek from a stone, and a Jew from a grain of sand.'

(Note: Apparently "blood drinkers" is allusion to rumors of Jewish ritual murder and sacrifice of infants spread by their enemies from very ancient times.)

Alexander, the secretary, had prepared me for the deputation. He hinted that he could write my speech, but I intend to make my own speeches. 'The deputation,' he said, 'will be important: as a sign of respect to the new Procurator it will be headed by Philo and Alexander.' He seemed to expect me to say something. 'Oh yes,' I said, 'Philo and Alexander. I must remember their names.' Junius was delighted. 'I do not believe you have ever heard of either of them,' he said. The secretary went on unmoved. 'Philo has a certain reputation as a philosopher.' 'Why,' said Junius, 'he is the greatest living Jew. He is called "The Jewish Plato," which infuriates the Greeks. I have never read a word of him, but I believe he has set out to prove that the Hebrew Scriptures contain the whole of Greek philosophy.' 'Alexander,' added the secretary, 'is Philo's brother, and is the leader of the Jews in commerce and finance as Philo is in letters.' Junius added that Alexander was the recognized head of the Jewish community, enormously wealthy and ready to lend money on good security. I thought myself that I must take note of Alexander. Philo and Alexander were, in fact, the spokesmen of the party. I was brief and soldierly. 'You have, I hear, a petition to make to me,' was all I said when Junius presented them. Each of the pair had something to ask of me. They spoke quietly but, I need scarcely say, with complete assurance, as though equals to equals.

Philo spoke first, since he was to deal with religion. He began with compliments to Rome, to Caesar, and to me. He said that the Jews had always fought hard for their independence, but had never for long been able to preserve it. Always some great Power from the north or from the south had overcome them: Egypt, Assyria, the Greeks, the Syrian kings, and finally Rome. Nowadays they not only recognized that they could not hope to prevail against the might of Caesar, but they no longer desired to, for Caesar gave them peace and good government. I interrupted to say that there were constant complaints of some fellow springing up in Judaea - an itinerant preacher or a so-called patriot or a mere bandit - and he always ended by inciting the people against Rome. Philo rejoined that these were in any event ignorant, illiterate men who counted for little, and that the rulers at Jerusalem, supported by all that was best and most educated among the Jews, were satisfied to have things as they were, provided that they were left undisturbed in the exercise of their religion, and in this every Jew throughout the world was on their side. He went on to warn me, with professions of respect, that in Judaea the Jews would not abate one jot or tittle of their religious convictions. They had, he said, endured the extreme of persecution before, and, if need be, they would do so again. Antiochus of Syria had tortured and slain them by the thousand in his determination to force heathen customs upon them and to make them Greeks rather than Jews, but at the end they had defeated him.

Herod had sought to bribe them by the impressiveness and opulence of his gifts and bribes and by building them a Temple, which was said to be the wonder of the world, but when he set a golden eagle over the Temple Gate they had pulled it down, for neither the cross nor the stake had terrors for the God-fearing Jew

(Note: Antiochus Epiphanes (175-164 B.C.) endeavored to destroy Jewish religion and 'Hellenize' the Jews. The successful revolt led by Judas Maccabaeus marked the failure of his policy. Antiochus dedicated the Temple at Jerusalem to the Olympic Zeus and erected in it the pagan altar which is the 'abomination of desolation' spoken of in the Book of Daniel. The eagle placed over the entrance was a symbol of the Roman nation and its ownership of the temple.)

Although he said he thought it not necessary, he reminded me that the Jews, worshipping an invisible God, would accept no statue or image of living beings, and that even Herod had not placed his head on his own coins in Judaea.

(Note: The policy of Herod the Great toward the Jews was one of lenience mixed with suspicion and contempt. He did not seek, like Antiochus, to 'Hellenize' them. At the same time to gratify them he restored the Temple on the grandest scale but he also established an amphitheatre at Jerusalem whose pagan character was a constant offence to them.)

I asked him bluntly whether he proposed that Caesar's head should not be placed on his own coins within his own dominions; but he was too shrewd to be trapped by the question; he only hoped, he said, that I would respect the feelings of the Jews in the ancient home of their race and their religion even as Caesar himself desired that they should be respected.

I asked him whether he was aware that in Rome Caesar had ordered that the Jews should abandon their special forms of worship on pain of being expelled from Italy or forced into the labor battalions of the army.

(Note: Emperor Tiberius had enforced this measure seven years earlier - in A.D. 19.)

He replied that he knew this was so, but that whereas Caesar would not tolerate a distinctive race with special exclusive privileges in Rome, he was equally firm in allowing them the undisturbed enjoyment of their religious customs in their own home. He added pointedly that everybody knew this was the policy laid down by Caesar for his governors, and they were grateful for it both to him and to them. He ended with a petition: the instructions given me at Rome before I left. Valerius had also stressed this. He informed me that at Jerusalem the Roman Governor keeps the vestments of the High Priest in his custody. He only hands them over to the High Priest on the eve of the great festivals and he receives them back again when the festival is finished. It is a sign of authority to which Rome attaches great importance. The Jews, of course, resent it. Philo proposed that, since Judaea had behaved so well during Valerius's term of office, I should restore the vestments to the High Priest. I answered coldly that the Jews must earn any concession by good behavior shown to me, that I knew Caesar's mind and should carry it out, and that I had every intention of allowing the Jews the full exercise of their religion, provided that they recognized in every proper manner the authority of Caesar. The question of the vestments, I said, was one which only Caesar could decide.

(Note: Herod the Great had kept the vestments in his own custody and the Romans continued the practice. When, Pilate was summoned to Rome in A.D. 36 to answer to the accusations of misgovernment that were made against him, the vestments were restored to the charge of the priests in the Temple.)

I hope you will approve of this mild and cautious utterance. Religion is one thing; by all means let them have their religion. But when they say that their religious scruples forbid them to tolerate the symbols of the authority of Rome - a statue or an image or even an inscription - that is another matter altogether. I shall see about it. I do not think that Caesar will blame me for enforcing his authority.

I thought Philo would never stop. His brother, Alexander, I am glad to say, was briefer. He was full of the poverty of the Jews. He said there was an impression about that all Jews were rich, but it was a great mistake. Judaea was a poor country, a large part of it mountainous and barren. The really rich territory was Galilee. I know it, but people thought Judaea was wealthy because of the contributions which Jews everywhere sent up to Jerusalem. This, however, was 'Temple-money' designed to maintain the services and the priests, and it could no more be touched than the jewels, given by pious benefactors. He himself, by the way, is one of these which adorn the Temple itself! He urged me to create peace and contentment at the beginning of my governorship by a large remission of taxation. He spoke of my reference to troublesome agitators in Judaea and said that his own experience as a collector of taxes in Egypt was that the less people were taxed the less likely they were to listen to sedition. I said I would consider it. I could not tell him the truth, could I? The truth is that a Governor never needs money so urgently as in his first year of office and that every Governor has an endless string of creditors at Rome. If it were not for his creditors, would any man consent to govern Jews? You may say that this is a most unrefined sentiment. So it is, but I cannot always be a Seneca. To think of the untold wealth that flows from every city of Asia and Africa and almost of Europe to Jerusalem, and I cannot so much as touch it! Nor, I assure you, will I attempt to.

Soon we shall be within sight of Caesarea. Procula is full of excitement about it: but then, she does not realize for how many years she may have to live in it.

ARRIVAL AT CAESAREA

In harbor, Caesarea

Congratulate me, my friend, for I have reached my 'province.' Wish me a quiet and uneventful term, without rebellion, droughts or tumults, so that I *may earn promotion and in some higher post than this help to make history.*

I have left Procula on deck. She is wildly excited. She expected, I believe, to find tents and savages, and here is a city which looks, she says, almost as good as Naples. Certainly there is nothing Jewish about its appearance. The first thing we saw, from many miles out, was a temple of white, gleaming marble high up on a hill. Then the outline of a great amphitheatre, also white. Next, as we came nearer, a tall, dark tower standing straight up, as it seemed, out of the water. We found that it was established on the end of a gigantic pier (harbor) made of enormous blocks of stone. I have seen nothing so striking as this pier harbor) in Italy. It runs out crescent-shaped, from the southern end of the city towards the north; it is several times as broad as any of our roads, with towers upon it and arches where seamen may lodge. It projects so far towards the northern shore that it leaves only a narrow entrance from the open sea and within it is the haven of calm waters in which we now lie. The size of the stones is almost beyond belief, and how Herod contrived to get them here and have them hewn and plant them in position is more than I can understand. He must have searched all Asia and Africa for skilled engineers.

Before Herod built the harbor and called it after Caesar, the place was a mere roadstead, open and dangerous. Now the commerce of the whole country can flow through it and much comes here that used to go to Tyre, farther north. I hope still more will come that I may get the benefit of the customs duties!

As we approached the entrance, Marcius pointed out to me first one building and then another, and always he added, 'Herod built it - Herod built them all.' Truly he was a wonderful man, for this is only one of the cities that he created out of nothing, and wherever he built he never forgot to build to the glory of Caesar and of Rome. (The temple that I first saw is dedicated to Caesar.)

As I watched and listened to Marcius I exclaimed, 'A great king, no wonder Caesar praised him!'

(Note: It was reported that the Emperor Augustus and his minister Agrippa had said that 'the dominions of Herod were too little for the greatness of his soul.')

I was astonished to hear a harsh voice near me saying, 'A great murderer!' and there, if you please, was my humble Alexander, with a scowl on his face and a snarl in his voice, looking as though he hated (as I am sure he does) even the stones that Herod had set up.

'He was a Jew himself,' I said, in order to tease Alexander. I knew that Herod was only a half-Jew, being of the race of Idumaeans, and I suppose that if there are any persons whom the Jews hate more than pure Romans and Greeks, it is people who are part-Jew like Idumaeans and Samaritans.

(Note: The Idumaeans, whose country lay south of Judaea, had been defeated in war and forcibly 'Judaized' by the Jewish ruler, John Hyrcanus I (135-105 B.C.).)

'He was no Jew,' said Alexander curtly. 'And he was the vilest murderer that ever came even from Idumaea.'

'Whom did he murder?' I asked. 'I know he executed rebels somewhat freely, but I expect that most of them deserved no less. You mean the executions in his own family?'

'Murders!' said Alexander. (He is rather pertinacious.) 'He put to death Hyrcanus, the aged grandfather of his wife Mariamne, and then her brother. He put to death her mother Alexandra. He put to death Mariamne herself and for that, by the justice of God, for he had a deep passion for her, he suffered the tortures of the damned. He put to death his own two sons by Mariamne and another son by another wife, who had set his mind against those two. He put to death -' and then he rolled off a long list. I cannot remember all of them - I have so much to think of - but I know there were two successive husbands of Herod's own sister Salome among them. I asked Alexander what motive Herod had. Was it merely pleasure in killing?

'No,' he said, 'the family of Hyrcanus was of the princely Jewish stock and Herod exterminated every member of it lest it should produce a rival to himself.'

'At Rome they call that statesmanship,' I said, I hope not indiscreetly.

(Note: Apparently a dangerous allusion to the jealousy and suspicion with which the Emperor Tiberius regarded all possible claimants to the Imperial power.)

I asked Marcius what was his view of Herod. He was thoughtful. 'A great prince,' he said. 'He had large ideas about everything. Caesar Augustus was right when he said that Herod was big enough to rule both Syria and Egypt. He was the shrewdest man that Rome has had to deal with in these parts. He knew how to be useful to Rome and also how to use her. But at home he was a wild beast; he lived on blood.' It is true enough. (Killing) his own wife and his own sons, that takes some tolerance (for blood.)

The streets are decorated in our honor, and we can hear the noise of the crowds assembling to greet our procession.

MEETING WITH CAIAPHAS

In the Palace of Herod, Caesarea

We are duly installed and I am hard at work. I sit from morning to night, studying reports from every quarter of Judaea, going into accounts, listening to petitions. I really believe that for the last twelve months Valerius must have saved up every difficult and disagreeable question for me to settle. There is no end to the disputes between Greeks and Jews, Samaritans and Jews, Idumaens and Jews, and Jews and Jews. All of them are described as important; there is a fine crop of trouble for me, however I decide them. I suppose that I shall do the same by my successor when my turn comes. My reception was fairly good, but the non-Jews were much more cordial than the Jews. The Jews in the streets were cool and unresponsive. Marcius says that Valerius has ruled them so gently that they see no reason to hope for much from me. 'They will be more enthusiastic,' he added, 'about your successor.'

When I reached the palace I found the high officials gathered to welcome me: my own staff, representatives of the two Herods, and the High Priest from Jerusalem. The High Priest is one Joseph Caiaphas. He is a tall man, imposing in appearance, suave in manner and, I should say, of supple mind. I observed that his mere presence made a great impression on every one. There had been great discussion whether he would come to Caesarea or wait at Jerusalem until I paid my first visit there. Had he not come, I should certainly have taken it in a negative light, for it would have been a plain sign of hostility.

On the other hand, he came alone. There are several living ex-High Priest, and none came with him. Especially, neither Annas nor any of his sons were there. This Annas and his sons, I should tell you, are the most powerful of the priestly families at Jerusalem. For years they have either held the highest offices or made it difficult for anyone else to hold them. Old Annas himself was High Priest when Valerius came here and Valerius found him impossible; he merely wants the protection of Rome so that he can go his own way in everything. Valerius transferred the office to a member of another family, but the experiment was a failure: then he appointed one of Annas's sons, but that was like having the old man back again. Once more he appointed a rival priest and once more the rival was not strong enough. So he chose Caiaphas, who is Annas's son-in-law, hoping that the ambitious crew would regard this as enough of prestige and influence for the family and that Caiphas would be willing and able to hold his own against them. It is not a bad arrangement, do you think?. Caiaphas keeps the peace with us and the office in the family; Annas and his sons stand a little farther off and hold the support of those who think Caiaphas is too subservient. At heart, all of them are alike and office-holders and office-speakers, accept the Romans for the present. The last thing that any of them want is a clash with Rome that would destroy their own power.

Caiaphas, at the public ceremony, merely said, 'The Jews greet the representative of Caesar.' A chilly welcome, but afterwards, in private, he was more communicative. He told me that he regarded it as his duty to work with the Romans. He said that his people, as he hoped I knew, were passionately attached to their independence, but that he and the great Jewish families recognized that they could not struggle against Rome. He said that the thing that he always feared was a popular uprising, which he and his friends could not check in time. 'This country,' he said, 'is very difficult to control. It is full of mountainous and desolate tracts in which evil-disposed or ambitious persons cannot be prevented from gathering together and from which they can venture out to make trouble in the towns.' There had, after the death of Herod, been several instances of adventurers who gathered a band of people about them and actually set themselves up for King. One of them might be a mere bandit; another might be a political rebel against any sort of foreign rule; a third might presume to lay down the law about religion. In any event there was danger. The common people were extremely ignorant - I was amused to see the contempt with which he spoke of them - and any sort of leader with a gift of action or of speech meant to them some one who might restore the liberties, which they had once enjoyed. Then, he said quietly and with a smile, 'Besides,' he said, speaking very quietly, 'you have to remember that all Jews believe that on some distant day a deliverer will arise who will restore the ancient glories of our people.' I do not pretend to understand their religion, but I gathered that the coming of this deliverer (Messiah he called him) would be incompatible with government by Rome, or by any other power. I must ask Alexander about this. The voice of Caiaphas was equable, almost casual, as he talked to me. I take it that he and his friends will support no rivals, be they Kings or Messiahs, who endanger their authority under Caesar's governor.

I thanked Caiaphas and asked him where Annas was. He replied that Annas had a cold, and in any event seldom left home. He would present himself to me at Jerusalem. I said that Annas had several sons, one of whom had been High Priest. He answered that it would not be seemly for them to come in the absence of their father. I imagine that the old man completely overshadows them.

(Note: Eleazar was appointed by Valerius Gratus. In all, five sons of Annas at one time or another held the office of High Priest. Annas himself was High Priest for nine years and Caiaphas for eleven.)

Caiaphas and I understand each other, I think, but I shall need to watch him.

The position is extraordinary; I wish that you were here to study it. As I look out from the palace, I see below me this town, which, apart from Jews, is full of Greeks, Egyptians and the rest. Away to the south is a strip of plain along the sea. Behind it are foothills and then, rising behind them, a barrier of mountains, bare and rugged, among which dwell the real Jews, stiff-necked and obstinate. They are surrounded by enemies - Samaritans to the north, Idumaeans to the south, Romans at the points of military vantage and Greeks everywhere, and they do not desire to have them other than enemies. The very troops, the auxiliaries, by which we hold them down, are recruited from these enemies on their own soil, for they themselves will not serve in the army and we - wrongly, as I think - exempt them. They shut themselves up in their Jerusalem and, still more, in their Temple, unchanging and, at heart, unyielding.

I have had no letter from you, my friend, since I came here. Take heed; I shall not write again until I hear from you.

A GOVERNOR'S PROBLEMS

Caesarea

Your letter has come and I am grateful to you for it and for your offer of services. I shall venture to make use of you at once and you yourself have given me the hint. You say that things are not only quiet at Rome but too quiet for some people; that the mob grumbles as 'stingy Caesar' for not giving them largesse and games and hopes that he will treat them more generously when he comes back to Rome. You approve of Caesar's policy, and so do I; let them go without their Games and do some honest work for a change. But I am not Caesar and I cannot afford to have my people grumbling. Therefore I must exhibit Games, and that is why I ask for your assistance.

(Note: In this year Tiberius retired to the island of Capreae, in the Bay of Naples. He never returned to Rome.)

First of all, I shall have some fighting with wild beasts. I would have liked to have the sort of contest that I saw in Alexandria - some bulls against an elephant, but elephants cost too much for Procurators. The chief display will be half a dozen lions against a dozen Idumaean prisoners armed with darts. You can see at once that it will be an affair of tactics; if they can separate the lions, but there - I know you have a mind above such things. (They have six light darts each, so the odds are on the lions.) Some other prisoners - these are criminals - will fight on horseback against the bulls. These prisoners are chosen because they cannot ride. Later, the gladiators. Here you can assist me. I want to give the people a novelty. I find that they have rarely seen a Gaul and scarcely ever a Briton. Now I design a chariot-fight between Parthians on the one side and Gauls and Britons on the other. The chariots are here. I shall have six on each side. I am getting the Governor of Syria to send me some Parthian prisoners. There will be six to drive and six to do the fighting. Can you get me the Gauls and Britons, especially the Britons? They must be used to chariot-fighting, and I want to buy them outright, so that those who survive can be used at other Games by me or loaned to friends. I should be very willing to have none but Britons if so many are available. There is much interest here in that island, and every one is asking why Caesar does not go in and add it definitely to our possessions. We shall never be really safe in Gaul until we do so. But, I know, caution is nowadays the word.

(Note: Tiberius, following the maxims of Augustus, was reluctant to extend the boundaries of the Empire and the conquest of Britain was not seriously undertaken until A.D. 43, under the Emperor Claudius.)

I have asked Alexander what the High Priest meant with his talk about a Jewish deliverer or Messiah, and I know that you, of all people, will want to hear his answer. Like everything in this strange country, it is a mixed question of religion and politics. Apparently the Jews are led by their sacred writings to believe that some day or other their God, who has chosen them out from all the peoples of the world (a funny notion), will re-establish them in the position which they held hundreds of years ago, when neither Romans nor Greeks had come upon them. But, says Alexander, their educated men and their rulers, like Caiaphas, are much too sensible to think that it can be done in these times of ours, and so they postpone the coming of a deliverer to the indefinite future, or even say that it applies not to this world at all but to another life succeeding this is a very sensible view to take, you will say, and so do I. But the ordinary Jew, who buys and sells or farms or fishes, sees the future differently. The more he is oppressed by barbarians, as he would say, like Greeks or Syrians, Egyptians or Romans, the more does he look forward to the coming of a deliverer, a sort of God, sent from his heaven to liberate the Jews; some of them even think that this deliverer will not only free Judaea but will conquer all the world. That is why Caiaphas spoke meaningfully to me; there's never a rascal sets himself up anywhere in these parts but a horde will gather round him and believe his story that he is sent to be their King. 'What would Caiaphas and Annas make of that?' I said to Alexander. He never stirred a muscle. 'It is doubtful,' he said, 'how far the deliverer would require the services of a High Priest any more than of a Roman Governor. Annas and Caiaphas undoubtedly believe that the deliverer will come some day. They must believe no less, but they will be very slow to admit that he has actually come; the common people believe that he may come now and they may decide at any moment that he has arrived.'

Is it not a comic idea that this paltry little race, that has been overrun by half a dozen conquerors, carried into slavery, and scattered about the earth, believes that it is chosen out of all others and that its God, who has never been able to prevent its misfortunes, will send some one to overthrow Caesar and Rome? You would think that when they see we only keep 4,000 soldiers here they would know how weak and contemptible they really are, but I suspect that, though Caiaphas knows better, many of them think that those 4,000 are all that Rome has got. In any case, if you can rely on a God to perform all sorts of miracles, it does not matter how many soldiers are on the other side. I fear that some day they will require a lesson.

If you have the chance I beg you to commend me to Lucius Aelius Sejanus. Pray tell him that I am contemplating making some new roads in this country and that I shall ask permission to call the first of them by his name. I shall write to him myself later. I had hoped to send him a present of the wine of the country, but oh, my dear friend, it is like vinegar. No wonder the Greeks here do a roaring trade in noble Chian and our warm Falernian.

DECISION TO VISIT JERUSALEM

Caesarea

I have decided to go up to Jerusalem shortly. Here I see next to nothing of my Jews. Caesarea is full of Greeks, Syrians, Phoenicians, Egyptians, and all that sort of rabble. There are many Jews, it is true, but they are of the common sort, such as traders, moneylenders and the like. The men who count are at Jerusalem, and it might be thousands of miles away, though it is just up in the hills. Caiaphas is careful to keep in touch with me, but so far as most of them are concerned I might not exist at all. I am going up, therefore, to make the acquaintance of Annas and his friends.

Besides, I want to see their head-quarters: the nest in which they harbour their seditions, if any there be; the stronghold which, according to Marcius, will give even Rome no little trouble if ever they should defy us. I must take a look at the defenses and consider how my little garrison will be situated if there should be a rising. The roads, too, and the water-supply and such are things which are always bad until the Romans take them in hand. Also I am curious to see their Temple, though I suppose they will hardly let me take a look at it, and I must find out where they keep the Temple-money, if only to protect it against robbers. You need not suspect me; I shall not emulate Crassus or Sabinus,(both plundered the Temple treasury) but you know that if anyone raided their treasury I would get the blame. I assure you I am ready to get on with them, but I must find out what sort of people they are and what they are doing. Here in Caesarea I feel that I am cut off from my own province, and I remain uneasy, though the chief of my intelligence section reports that all is quiet and no sign of trouble brewing. He, by the way, is a Graecized Samaritan, Joseph by name. Most of his family lost lands and life at the hands of Herod. He hates Herod's sons and he hates the Jews, so he is a useful servant to us. I hope to go to Jerusalem in three weeks' time.

The Games went off very well. The Gauls and Britons fought magnificently. The crowd were so delighted that they insisted on them fighting again and again with new antagonists until almost all were killed. The contest between the lions and the Idumaeans was not so successful; the lions separated the Idumaeans, so it was soon over. One of the Idumaeans fought splendidly and I would have liked to save him, but the lions were too quick.

There was one curious episode which illustrates the obstinacy of these Jews. There were four of them in prison here condemned to death for highway robbery. I offered to let them fight against a tiger, the conditions being that they should be armed with any sort of wooden weapons that they liked to choose or make, but that they should first do public homage to the bust of Caesar in the arena. They were quite willing to fight and they were fine strong men, all of them, but they refused to sacrifice to Caesar. I told them they would be thrown to the tiger as they were, and they laughed at me. So thrown they were, and now Alexander, with a glum face, warns me that the Jews have some religious objection (apart from the personal one) to having their bodies torn by animals. They have so many religious objections.

Postscriptum.

I have opened this letter to inform you that Alexander, supported by Marcius, Joseph and every one else, now tells me that I cannot go up to Jerusalem on the day which I had fixed, because it is the Sabbath of the Jews. It would give deep offence, they say; it would be taken as a deliberate provocation; there would be mourning and protests and perhaps rioting.

'Rioting on the Sabbath!' I said. 'Surely not!' But I suppose they might make an exception to do a little rioting. Of course, I had to give way; I could tell that at once from Marcius's face. The Sabbath is incredible sacred to them, he says; they will neither do nor tolerate labor of any kind; you must not do this, you must not do the other; it seems to me there is scarcely anything you can do. I wonder, does their sacred river Jordan flow on the Sabbath or does it take a rest? I asked Marcius the question. 'There are some of them,' he replied, 'who will not eat an egg if it is laid on the Sabbath.' 'If you have a wooden leg,' I asked, 'can you walk it out with you upon the Sabbath?' Nothing disturbs my Marcius. 'I believe,' he answered, 'that their learned men are divided on that subject.' I could hardly contain myself. 'Of course,' I said, 'on the Sabbath they do not perform the functions of Nature?' Alexander intervened. 'You are quite right,' he said, looking at me with admiration. 'Some of them do not.' (The ascetics of the Essene sect.) I was a little puzzled. 'But supposing... ' I said, and then we were interrupted and the subject dropped.

You had better write me another of your admirable essays on the virtue of toleration and the equality of man, for I assure you I am at present in great need of it.

DIFFICULTIES IN VISITING JERUSALEM

Caesarea

I could burst with indignation. Everything is ready for the journey to Jerusalem and this morning I have discussed with Marcius the last touches. 'Anything else that you can think of?' I inquired. I felt brisk, full of a lively expectation about Jerusalem, and almost amiable towards my Jews. 'Of course,' he said, 'we do not take the images on the standards.'

(Note: The standards of the Roman soldiers frequently had fixed to them medallions bearing images of the Emperors.)

I protest that I showed no astonishment; I am learning not to be astonished in this country. Then, 'Why not?' I said. 'When we take the standards to Jerusalem,' he repeated, 'we always leave the images behind.' 'Not on this occasion, I think,' said I, 'whatever Valerius Gratus may have been weak enough to do.' He did not turn a hair. 'Every Procurator since Caesar took

Joseph Lumpkin

over the country has left the images behind,' he asserted, 'otherwise the Jews would be deeply offended.'

I assure you, my blood boiled. 'Do you mean to tell me,' I asked, 'that when the Roman Governor makes his formal entry into the chief city of the Jews, he is to omit from the standards of his troops the images of the Imperator Tiberius Caesar, whom may the gods preserve, and of Augustus Caesar Imperator, his great predecessor?' 'I do,' he said. 'It is the accepted policy and I beg you to follow it. The Jews will not tolerate the image of any god or emperor in Jerusalem: neither statues nor medallions on the standards nor images on coins. You know yourself that although the silver coins minted in Italy that reach this country bear Caesar's image. That cannot be avoided. The copper coins that are minted in Judaea itself have not his image on them. So, too, with the standards.' He looked me in the face. 'It is Caesar's will that their religion not be offended. They have no image of their god. In the depths of their Temple in Jerusalem is a little chamber which is inhabited by their god, but it is empty; there is nothing in it.'

'Caesar would not object,' I said, 'if I took his image into Jerusalem, and nothing happened. He would be pleased to think that I was breaking down the hostility of these Jews to him and Rome and all the outside world.'

'If there is a tumult,' Marcius said, 'and an attack on the troops in the narrow streets of Jerusalem, I cannot answer for the consequences. Would Caesar be pleased then?'

Straight talking, as you see. Alexander was there and I looked at him from time to time, but the little Jew had the good sense to keep his mouth shut. At the finish, I have had to give way. What else could I do? I cannot risk a tumult and a rising so early in my term of office, with so few troops available and the certainty that I should be condemned for failure, though if I were successful all Rome would praise my 'firmness.'

But it goes against the grain. To enter Jerusalem before the eyes of these arrogant priests and their surly people, as though we were on sufferance! It is the same everywhere. What do the Britons think when they see that we stop short at their island? What do these Jews think when they see that we choose rather to humiliate Caesar than offend them? They will take toleration for weakness and caution for timidity. And it will do no good.

Evil will come of it. Mark me, we shall have our work to do over again and in the end we shall have to do it thoroughly. At present I must yield. I would offend the Jews cheerfully, but I cannot afford to cross Caesar or Sejanus.

Procula goes with me. She has long ago exhausted Caesarea; she insists that it is time she saw something truly Jewish. I tell her that at all events, when we go up without the images, she will be seeing something that is truly un-Roman.

RECEPTION AT JERUSALEM

Jerusalem

We have been here a week and it seems like a year. It is as though we were in a different country. I felt it immediately as we came up from the coast. Caesarea, after all, is bustling and cheerful, with a friendly face towards one. Here, as we marched up and up into these bleak hills, which stretch away north and south as far as the eye can see, I felt like an invader entering for the first time a hostile land. All the way along we saw groups of people from the farms and scattered hamlets watching us silently. It was the same when we entered Jerusalem. There was no welcome at the gates nor in the street. Not a shout nor a salute; no sign even of Caiaphas nor of any of the high-priestly caste. Crowds enough in the streets, for the place is like a rabbit-warren, but all of them glum and silent, as though they had been given the order, or sneering at us if they thought that they had caught our eye. The place is a volcano, and if I had more troops, and Caesar permitted, I would not mind if the explosion came. Marcius says that it will not come, at least, not yet. The high priests, he asserts - and by that he means the little ring of families from whom the high priest is always chosen - will have as little to do with me as possible, but they have things well in hand. And I will have them well in hand before I finish, and so I have told Marcius. He warns me to expect no friendliness from the priests or people. To all of them alike we are aliens and usurpers, to be regarded with coldness and suspicion until their god thinks fit to remove us from their necks.

This is a wretched city. Except for the great Herod's works there is scarcely a single building worth a glance. Whatever pride and taste they possess they have put into their Temple. The streets are narrow and ill-paved. Their drains and water-supply are disgraceful even for Asia; it is no wonder that they suffer from all kinds of disease. I shall have to see about this.

The hand of Herod is evident everywhere. How that man must have despised and laughed at the Jews! On one day he would humor them and on the next strike them in the face - or, more likely, do both things almost together. He built them a Temple which is one of the wonders of the world and they are proud of it, as well they may be, and at the same time he built a theatre in the City and an amphitheatre outside it. And of what use was that, you say, since they so much resent the introduction of such wicked spectacles? I think that is just what must have delighted Herod. Their priests and all their stricter folk denounced him and his evil works, but many of the common people flocked to the spectacles. What people could resist the temptation? So Herod, in the eyes of the good Jew, was a corrupter of the people, more subtle and more dangerous than the mere persecutor.

It goes without saying that Herod built a palace too. It was an enormous affair which is also a fortress. It gave him an additional grip on the City. Whatever else he did, he never forgot the necessity of securing himself against his people. The whole country is dotted with his fortresses. I do not live in the palace; something more modest is enough for my pretensions. Besides, I like to have my soldiers near me. I live in the Antonia, the citadel which is close to and overlooks the Temple. I have the troops there and can keep a keen eye on the Temple, for if there is trouble afoot, especially at the time of the great Festivals, it is in the Temple that sooner or later it will show itself. You cannot imagine the eagerness of the Jews to fight each other. They are as full of factions as the Greeks, and you know what that means. A few of them favor the family of Herod; the chief priests, as I have told you, think it well to make the best of us Romans; the fanatics and agitators of the common people look askance at them both. Then the country people are always coming up from over Jordan or from Galilee and the inhabitants of the City are quick to make trouble with them, not to mention the Samaritans, with whom any good Jew is ready to pick a quarrel.

The Temple is astonishing. There cannot be its like in the world. It is a city in itself, and the priests and servants attached to it must number thousands. There are enormous colonnades and courts, one after another. Foreigners may go into the outer court, and then there is a barrier, and if any foreigner *goes through and is detected, he suffers the death penalty. Even our own soldiers are executed by us if they transgress the barrier. Then there is another court which marks the limit for women and another for men, and so on to the priests' courts and the great altar of sacrifice and the inmost chamber of all - the empty one - which no one enters but the High Priest, and he only once a year. The quantity of sacrifices made by private persons is amazing, and the part of the outer court where the offerings are bought and sold is just like a great fair. The priests get part of all the offerings, and, to make sure of their income, they insist that no one shall offer sacrifice except in Jerusalem and in the Temple itself. And then there are the presents from rich Jews and the tribute-money from rich and poor alike. The Treasury is concealed somewhere in the depths of the Temple, but I don't know where precisely.*

You will ask me how I have been received since I first entered the City. Not well. They ask for trouble. I had invited all their chief men to meet me at the Antonia on the morning after my arrival. There was no reply, but they came. I had been told by Alexander that I had better receive them in the outer court, as some of them would have scruples about entering the actual building. I even offered to give them food and wine - not wine of the country, but real wine - before they left, but, of course, Alexander replied that that was impossible; they would not accept it; besides, it was the day before or the day after some festival or other, and that made them stricter than ever about meeting those whom they call the heathen. In this, as in everything, I gave way. You cannot say that I am not patient with them.

There was a great crowd when they came. I expect that most of them were as curious to see me as I to see them. All the Sanhedrim were there, some seventy of them. This is the body that rules the Jews, under our authority; their chief priests, officials and most distinguished lawyers and philosophers compose it. I greeted Caiaphas and he presented the leaders to me; among them Annas and one or two who had held the office of High Priest, the Captain of the Temple Guard, the chief of the Treasury and a few more. Annas had his sons there, a whole row of them. One of them has already been High Priest, and no doubt the others expect to be. The old man, I should say, is worth the lot of them.

(Note: Five sons of Annas held the office. Eleazar had been High Priest about A.D. 16-17. Jonathan became High Priest in A.D. 36-37 and was later assassinated at the instance of the Procurator Felix. Theophilos was

High Priest after Jonathan, and Matthias a few years later. Annas the younger became High Priest for a few months in A.D. 62, and was murdered by the populace.)

He has a hawk's face, with thin lips (for a Jew), and every now and then, when he is moved, a spark of fire in his eyes. I do not know whether it is cunning or inclination that decides his policy, but, although he is one of the heads of the priestly nobles who work with us and are almost all of the faction called Sadducees, he seeks the support and applause of the other faction, the Pharisees, who are all for the utmost observance of the Jewish law and for as much opposition as is practicable to Greeks and Romans and any other foreigners.

Now observe what happened. The leading Sadducees have seats on the Sanhedrim, but the majority of its members are Pharisees, who regard the Sadducees with suspicion and disapproval as temporizers in religion and (therefore) in politics. All were listening to hear what I would say and what the noble Sadducees would say to me. After the presentations, I began by saying to Caiaphas that I was sorry that they had not thought fit to greet me at my entry into the City. I spoke in Greek because that, as you know, is the language of the educated throughout the East. Before Caiaphas could reply Annas said something sharply in a foreign tongue and there was a little movement of applause among some of them. Caiaphas said hurriedly that it was a matter of custom and that the Roman Governor had never, so far, demanded a formal welcome on entering Jerusalem.

I am becoming, I really think, a miracle of self-control. I did not ask what Annas had said, but I discovered afterwards that he had said in Aramaic, which they use among themselves, that it was surely enough that they should consent to come to me at all. I turned to them, however, and said - again in Greek - that I hoped the indisposition was better which had prevented him from coming to welcome me at Caesarea. He smiled slightly and replied, again in Aramaic - an insulting thing to do - and there was a general laugh. I made Alexander translate for me this time. It appeared that the insolent fellow had said that his indisposition was better but might return at any moment. However, I know how to deal with such gentry and I addressed them in Latin, to teach them their place, and ordered Alexander to translate into Greek. I told them roundly that I was displeased with my reception in Caesarea, and, still more, in Jerusalem, but that they should have no reason to complain of me so long as their conduct was sincerely loyal. They listened sourly and then Caiaphas said hastily that they knew their duty to Caesar and to Rome. I asked if they had any request to make of me, and he replied that it would make for good feeling and contentment if I would restore the High Priest's vestments to their keeping. That, I replied, as at Alexandria, was a matter for Caesar, and it would depend entirely on their conduct whether I could make any recommendation. Then I went on to say that I had greatly admired what I had seen of the Temple and I desired to inspect it; perhaps some of them would show me its wonders on the following day. Caiaphas assented. I suggested that those who had been High Priests should accompany us. They all looked at Annas. He bowed gravely. 'To the outer court!' he said, this time in Greek. Really, the man is intolerable. 'I know that,' I said. 'Have we not set up inscriptions both in Greek and in Latin forbidding strangers to pass beyond the outer court?' Then I could not resist temptation. 'Yet I have heard,' I added, 'that one of my predecessors visited even the inmost chamber.' You remember that when Cneius Pompeius took Jerusalem in the course of his Eastern conquests he penetrated to the most sacred chamber - an act of desecration which they have never forgiven. You should have seen their faces. A murmur of horror and anger broke from them; some of them spat upon the floor; some of them took a step towards me. Annas stepped forward, but I did not give him time to speak. 'I have no intention myself,' I said, 'to go beyond the outer court, just as I have confidence that you will continue to perform the daily sacrifice in honor of Caesar and of Rome.' That quieted them, for it was a reminder that, tolerant as we are, we do exact from them a daily symbol of submission.

(Note: Pompeius the Great, who entered the Holy of Holies in 63 B.C.)

Finally, I told them that I would expect them to report to me promptly any agitator among the common people who might threaten trouble. I need not, I said, particularize the kind of trouble that I meant; they knew well enough what happened when some robber or fanatic, half crazy about religion or the liberty of his country, began to set up himself as a leader and collect a following. I relied on them for loyal support. With this I dismissed them.

I shall spend a fortnight here and then make a round of inspection before I return to Caesarea. I must see the country-people. I believe they have not the slightest understanding of the power and importance of Rome - a most dangerous form of ignorance. I shall be glad to get away, but Procula will be sorry to leave Jerusalem. She finds everything picturesque, and, besides, their religion and their Temple-worship attract her. It is curious how these

Eastern religions fascinate the women. If it is not Egyptian, it is the Jewish brand; the greater the mystery and hocus-pocus, the readier they are to submit themselves to the priests. Procula visits the outer court and questions Alexander about their wonderful inmost empty chamber. I tell her that some day she will forget and pass through the barrier. Then it will be my unpleasant duty to have her executed.

By the way, I have two questions for you. How many synagogues are there in Jerusalem? Fifty, do you say? There are nearly five hundred. And who discovered the alphabet? The ancient Egyptians or the Assyrians, you reply. No, it was Abraham, the ancestor of the Jews. You do not believe it? What presumption! Neither do I, but the Jews do, or pretend to. Everything good must have come out of the Jews. I do not know, but I expect they claim the discovery of fire and the cartwheel. It is a consolation that at least we have the credit for the good Roman sword.

Your equable and tolerant mind will not, I fear, approve the tone of this letter. I freely confess that Jerusalem does not improve my temper.

FIRST MENTION OF JOHN THE BAPTIST

Caesarea

I thank you for your letters and especially for your zeal in defending my interests against Pomponius Rufus. I warned him long ago that his new house, if built to that height, would interfere with my rights of light. The sly rascal has waited long enough to carry out his plans. Let him discover in the courts, my friend, how staunch a champion and how eloquent a counsel I possess in you.

I heard last week that an itinerant preacher had turned up in the hill-country south of Jerusalem. His name is John. As it appeared that he was causing a certain amount of excitement, and might cause more, I sent Joseph to Jerusalem on a mission of inquiry. I have given him authority, if he thinks it necessary, to seek out personally the source of the ferment and report what it amounts to. It may be nothing, but I ought to know.

FURTHER NEWS OF JOHN

Caesarea

I have heard from Joseph. He says that the matter may be serious, and after gathering such information as is available in Jerusalem, he has gone off into the mountains to hear for himself what the preacher John is saying. I wish him joy of the expedition. It is about as disagreeable a region as there is in the whole of my dominion - bleak and barren mountains, seamed with deep ravines and watercourses, which lead down steeply to the valley of the Jordan and the Dead Sea. It is chiefly inhabited, so far as I can ascertain, by ill-omened birds, wild beasts, lepers and half-mad hermits such as this John seems to be. In Joseph's absence, I have been examining the reports of our spies in other parts of the country. It appears that John's fame is spreading and the common people are beginning to talk about him. Some of them are setting off in high expectation for the scene of the preaching. I shall be glad to have Joseph's report. This is my first experience of this sort of agitation and I shall deal firmly with it.

One more word about Pomponius. Spare no expense. What is important is not so much that my rights of light should be protected as that Pomponius should be shown to be a rascal.

EYE-WITNESS'S REPORT ON JOHN

Caesarea

What I hear from Rome makes me almost glad to be a mere Procurator. A mutual friend of ours - I had better not mention names - writes to me that Sejanus not only is ambitious of marrying into the family of Caesar, but that at the same time he speaks slightingly of Caesar himself. 'Monarch of an islet,' he called him the other day - had you heard that? I scarcely dare write the words. If these things get to Caesar's ears, I shall be glad that I did not owe my appointment to the favor of Sejanus.

Joseph is back at last and I have been in consultation with him and Alexander. He had some difficulty tracking the preacher down. He had to go up-hill and down-dale in all sorts of weather, and was regarded with an unfriendly eye by the Jews who were also on the road. There are many of them on the road, too: most of them from Judaea, but a good many from Antipas's territory on the other side of Jordan, and some from Samaria and even Galilee. When he did discover John - the fellow moves from village to village all the time - do you know what he found? One of Antipas's officers, who was watching John on behalf of his master. The talk was that John would soon be leaving my territory and crossing over Jordan to that of Antipas. I don't know whether I shall give him the chance.

This may be a very serious matter. John is just one of those people of whom I have been warned. According to Joseph's report he is 'half-clad, half-starved and half-crazy,' but that does not matter with these Jews. It is what he says that counts, or rather, perhaps, what they choose to think he means. He is telling them that the great time, the new era, which they all expect, is coming, and for them that only means one thing: no more Herods, no more Romans, no more Governors, troops or taxes. The idea of liberty, of independence, of the revival of the glorious days which they enjoyed under their old kings - it's that which draws them from all over the country. Joseph declares that John has only to announce that he is the expected leader and the whole countryside will be on fire. He makes no pretence, so Joseph says, that he is himself a leader, but he is doing what is almost as bad: he tells them that a leader is coming, and that soon, which is just what they are looking for. I have questioned Alexander about this and he is wise and mysterious. I asked him whether this leader was the same as the deliverer or Messiah that Caiaphas had spoken of. He says no; that before the deliverer there must come, according to their sacred writings, an advance-guard or messenger or prophet - whatever you like to call him - and that when this person arrives then all the people will know that the deliverer himself is to come next.

You will see that from the standpoint of the Roman Governor it is all the same thing. John predicts the imminence of a new prophet; the appearance of the prophet will be followed by that of the deliverer, and then Caesar and Rome will make way for the new age. It is, you will agree, impossible that such fantastic but pernicious ideas should be allowed to spread among the people. You cannot imagine the expectancy that there is everywhere in the air here. Every one is waiting, waiting, for things that are to happen. I have the conviction that the best place for people like John is prison, and that is where I propose shortly to put him.

I have written to Caiaphas asking what he and the Sanhedrim have to say about it and informing him of what I intend. They ought to have reported to me before now.

I must not forget to tell you an amusing thing about John. He is telling the Jews that, in order to make themselves worthy of the great days that are coming, they must humble themselves for the wicked lives which they have led. This tickles me, as it would do you if you knew the Jews. Most of them do not relish this part of the doctrine at all. In their own opinion they have nothing to be humble about; nor ever have had. The new age is all very well, but its business is to set the Jews above all other peoples. Humiliation is proper to Greeks, Romans and such-like. I would like to know what my friend Annas thinks about humbling himself at the bidding of a ragged preacher escaped out of a cave! But I know already. The priests are used to the like of John. There is a whole sect of fanatics of his breed in this country - a good many of them in the very region that he comes from - who live severe lives and despise the easy-going priesthood at Jerusalem. Annas and Caiaphas would give him short shrift (confession / absolution), I am sure, especially if he showed signs of becoming really popular. It is all very well for their God to produce a new age, but the High Priests certainly expect to be consulted first.

This seems to me an opportunity to assert myself. I shall wait for a letter from Caiaphas, but whatever he says, I now intend to strengthen the garrison at Jerusalem. I hope for your approval.

THE IMAGES OF THE CAESARS

Caesarea

I have heard from Caiaphas about John. He sends me an official answer which is most discreetly framed. You might like the text of it. It says:

'The Sanhedrim, having sent representatives to question John the son of Zacharias and having satisfied itself that he does not claim to be either the Messiah of the Jews or one of the Prophets, is of the opinion that he has committed no offence under the Law which would justify it in putting him on his trial. At the same time it recognizes that the civil power may reasonably take a wider view of the consequences which might follow an extension of his teaching.' Caiaphas sent a private note by the messenger.

He has no objection to my taking measures if I think them necessary. I am sure that at heart he and his friends hope I will. You see the game. John may easily become an embarrassment to them, even if he is not so already. They would like him out of the way, but it would suit them better for me to remove him than that they should bear the odium themselves. Upon my word, I would not oblige them but that I have thought of a new measure for teaching both them, and the common people, who is their master here. I told you that I had decided to send up more troops to Jerusalem in case this affair of John should cause disturbances. I have made up my mind that the new troops shall this time carry the Imperial images on the standards when they enter Jerusalem. 'What madness!' I hear you say, and at once you conjure up visions of riot, tumult and open war. But listen. You do not give your Pilate sufficient credit for sagacity. Do you think that only Jews are cunning? My troops will enter Jerusalem in the dead of night. In the morning, when the Jews awake, go about their business, throng into the Temple, they will see the standards, with the images prominently displayed upon them, already established on the ramparts of the Antonia. They will storm the Antonia, you say? Tell that to the Marines. But, if they did attempt it, what a story I should have to send to Rome! The tiresome, treacherous Jews making a direct attack upon Caesar's images and the standards of the legions after I had so far respected their scruples as to send the troops in under cover of the dark! What would our patriotic Roman mob say to that story? Why, I should be a hero for a day and have the Syrian legions placed at my disposal. But do not fear. When Jerusalem hears that the talker John is to be arrested and sees the Roman eagles in its midst, it will think twice before openly resisting. Caiaphas will be shocked at my imprudence, but it is time they understood that they are part of the Roman State, and I have given Marcius his orders.

I am sending you some Syrian pottery. I hope your slaves are more careful than mine. I have told mine that the next one who damages a valuable vase or statue will figure at the Games, and not as a spectator.

THE ROMAN'S BURDEN

Caesarea

Commend me, my friend, for a good Roman. I too am carrying the blessings of Italy to the benighted East. I have brought two surveyors, one from

Alexandria and one from Antioch. I have instructed them to present plans to me for remaking certain roads, for constructing baths at Samaria, and for leading a good supply of water to Jerusalem from the springs south of the City. I shall get no thanks for this, but where or when does the Roman receive gratitude for the benefits which he brings to the Eastern peoples? They live like pigs and when he raises them from their filthy state they only complain that he sweats money out of them to pay for public works which he wants and not they. Was it not Caesar Augustus - or was it the great Julius - who called this the Roman's burden, which, whatever his inclinations, he cannot avoid?

Would you believe that at Samaria there are no baths, although our officers, both military and civil, go up there in the hot weather for their health? As to the roads, I propose to reconstruct that which runs along the coast and the two which run into Jerusalem from the north and the east. Our troops will move much more quickly, and so of course will trade and the pilgrim traffic, which will help my revenues. As to the water-supply, it will be a pure benefaction to Jerusalem for which they ought to set me up a statue. Yet, do you know, the only question that interests them at all is, who is to pay for it. How in the world they survive at all under present conditions at the time of their great festivals I cannot understand. Normally, perhaps, Jerusalem has some 50,000 inhabitants, and there are only a few wells of water to supply them all. But at the time of the Passover the pilgrims arrive by tens of thousands. No one knows the exact total, but some say that there are half a million people crowded into Jerusalem and the surrounding villages. Jerusalem itself is packed out; they sleep on the roofs and even in the streets, and they flock in droves each morning from the surrounding country. Where do they all get their water from for drinking and for their ceremonial washings? I cannot tell you, unless perhaps their god Yahweh provides it by a miracle or the festival counts as a continuous Sabbath and they must not drink at all. However, water they shall have, both clean and plentiful, whether they like it or not, and pay for it they must according to the custom of the Roman provinces.

The troops have gone, with Marcius in command. They carry the images of three Caesars - Tiberius himself, Augustus and Julius. They will be in the Antonia before dawn tomorrow. I addressed the men personally. I told them that the name of Rome and the Caesars was in their charge and that they must protect it, but that on their side there must be no provocation.

I have told Marcius to send a troop, arrest John and dispatch him to me at Caesarea. I must do this in any case, since if Antipas knows, as he does, that disaffection is being stirred up on my side of the border, he will make the most of it.

CONFLICT WITH THE JEWS

Caesarea

Now I have news for you. I have had the most exciting week of my life. Truly I have put the fat in the fire. Jerusalem is in an uproar, the hubbub spread throughout the country, and here in Caesarea I am beset by a multitude of angry Jews.

At the first all went well. The troops reached the Antonia while it was still dark and the standards were erected on the battlements. They could be seen from some parts of the Temple. I must tell you that with the earliest dawn the priests begin their preparations for the morning sacrifice and soon the crowd of worshippers assembles. (A good custom, since it makes the people get up early.) It was barely daylight when some one discovered the images on the standard-poles. They have the eyes of hawks where we are concerned. At once there was an outcry. Some of them rushed to the Antonia, others to the priests, others back into the town to spread the news. Caiaphas was round at the Antonia in no time and begged Marcius at any rate to remove the standards from the public view. Marcius politely said no and referred him to me. Caiaphas said he would have to take a strong line; he had already summoned the Sanhedrim; they would complain not only to me but to Rome and would tell the people so, but that he was doubtful whether the mob could be restrained from an actual attack upon the citadel. Marcius did not budge and Caiaphas was at his wits' end what to do. Meanwhile, all Jerusalem gathered in the Temple, and round the Antonia. They threatened not only us but the Sanhedrim as well. Many of them carried clubs and stones, and when Caiaphas emerged from the offices of the Sanhedrim to address them they menaced him violently, accusing the Sanhedrim of having brought this 'insult' on their religion by its tolerance of us and demanding that it should at once secure its removal. Caiaphas replied that the Sanhedrim would do its utmost, but there must be no violence; they would at once send a powerful deputation to me at Caesarea and, if I did not yield, they would forthwith appeal to Caesar and ask for my removal. He added that if any of the crowd chose to accompany the deputation they could do so; they could help to prove to me how deeply moved they were by this act of sacrilege, but they would only do serious injury to their religion and their country by an uproar in Jerusalem. Caiaphas is a shrewd man. He provided them with an outlet for their anger and himself with the means (as he hoped) of intimidating me.

Taking him at his word, they have come to Caesarea. Yes, my dear Seneca, they left their work and their religion and set off to walk, thousands and thousands of them, to me at Caesarea. They came not only from Jerusalem but from a hundred towns and villages; everywhere, as the news spread, they set off for Caesarea. When I heard what was happening I went up on the roof of the palace - this was four days ago - and the roads were black with them as far as the eye could see. They were marching steadily like men with a purpose, as people do in Rome when they are going to the Games. All ages were there, from greybeards down to boys. Their most learned Rabbis came, each with a following of pupils and admirers. A crowd of priests from the Temple escorted the deputation, which was led by Caiaphas and Annas. When the deputation entered the palace there was a tremendous scene of enthusiasm among them. The rest of the population looks on sourly. With a little more provocation, there would be a massacre.

I rather enjoyed the conversation with the priests. Caiaphas was dignified, Annas truculent, and his son Eleazar (formerly High Priest) noisy. But one and all they are anxious to get out of a hole. They are afraid of the mob and still more afraid of their enemies in Jerusalem who are busy undermining their position, calling them pro-Romans, 'abettors of idolatry' (the crime of crimes in the eyes of a good Jew), traitors and the like. You can readily imagine the arguments. On their side, no Procurator had ever done such a thing before; Caesar would disapprove of it; Caesar had always been considerate; neither I, nor Caesar - especially Caesar - could desire riot and open revolt, which were to be expected if I did not cancel my order. On my part, the presence of the images was an ordinary sign of the Roman authority; it was much less offensive than the daily sacrifice which already they performed to Caesar and to Rome; I had gone out of my way to spare their feelings by sending the troops in under cover of the night; to withdraw the images now would be an unprecedented humiliation of Caesar and to withdraw them in the face of threats would be a signal proof of weakness.

Since this meeting they have been here several times, both publicly and privately, and at intervals they harangue the crowd. I have told Caiaphas that he must order his people to go back home, but he says that the most he can do is to keep them quiet by promising to give me no peace until he has persuaded me. Their numbers, so far from diminishing, increase steadily. A great many people come in from curiosity, but all kinds of wild fanatics are arriving from distant parts and making violent speeches. I don't know how they all subsist, but I suppose a good quarrel over religion is meat and drink to them.

The situation cannot last, but I confess I find it a little difficult to deal with. I could disperse them by force, but I do not want bloodshed; all the people at Rome who are for peace and quietness (and who don't in the least understand the difficulties of provincial governors) would be up in arms against me. On the other hand, I ought not to yield. I dearly want to teach these Jews a lesson. Besides, it is really important, as a matter of policy, to break down their exclusiveness, and I have made a beginning. So far from Roman rule being genuinely accepted here, there is a slow but steady movement against it and against the priests who tolerate it. Unless we begin to break their obstinacy we shall, before long, have to re-conquer Judaea. If I could only rely on proper support at home, but there – I know that when I talk with hand on sword-hilt I must not expect too much sympathy from you.

I wish you had the job yourself for a few months.

I will let you know the upshot.

DEFEAT OF PILATE

Caesarea

I thank Jove that the place is clear of Jews again. The last of their rag-tag-and-bobtail is disappearing into the mountains, and I write to you, my dear Seneca, in haste to tell you what has happened. I shall be quite frank with you, for the truth is that I may need the help of you and of my other friends. I am glad that Caesar himself is not in Rome, for I cannot conceal from myself that the facts might be misrepresented to him. No, I said I would be frank with you; I should be afraid that the facts might be reported to him *truly.*

After four days the Jews showed no signs of weakening. They stood and sat and slept and said their prayers all round the Palace and in the adjoining streets and squares. Especially they said their prayers. Marcius wrote to me that everything in Jerusalem was at a standstill and that he was passively besieged in the Antonia. Joseph reported that the Sanhedrim had sent envoys to Herod Antipas, his brother and the Governor of Syria begging them to intervene with me on the ground that a serious outbreak in Judaea would have an unpleasant repercussion in their territories. The priests had also chosen the mission which they would, if need be, send to Rome. I determined to use a direct threat of military force. I announced that on the next day - the sixth day of these proceedings - the Jews were to assemble in the market-place early in the morning and I would address them personally. At the same time I ordered all the available troops to be concealed in the surrounding buildings. At the conclusion of my speech they were to pour out and advance upon the Jews.

The market-place is an open space which will hold twenty thousand people, and it was packed. The din, when I arrived, was indescribable. For ten minutes they shouted at me and at one another. They behaved like madmen. I do not know what they were saying; I doubt whether many of them knew themselves. The priests, who had made a line (to protect me, I believe) in front of the raised platform on which I sat, could not obtain silence. At last I rose, gave a signal to my officials and made as though to leave. That quieted them for a second and Caiaphas, mounting the platform, told them that the Sanhedrim had asked me to address them personally (this was not true) and that it was their duty to listen quietly. They became silent for the time.

I was polite, I was conciliatory. I told them that Caesar had always been anxious not to interfere with their religion and that I was no less disposed than other Governors to respect their scruples. But this was not religion, it was purely an administrative act to which they ought not to take exception. They could not expect to be exempt from the symbols of Roman dominion, I might almost say of Roman citizenship, which were common to the whole civilized world. At this murmurs arose. I was willing, I said, to consider any reasonable request that they might make, but first of all they must return quietly to their homes. Until that, nothing could be done. Or did they desire to enter on a conflict with the power of Rome? I ceased abruptly and gave the signal. Immediately the troops appeared on every side and, with all their weapons ready for immediate use, hemmed in the crowd.

What do you suppose they did, wisest of the wise men of Rome? Fall into panic, tremble before the Roman sword, seek to escape? They showed no signs of it. Assail the troops, plunge into the conflict with which I threatened them? Not for a moment. At first they were taken aback and made no sound or movement. Then one of their leaders in front of me cried out loudly in Aramaic and, baring his neck to the sword, knelt down before the soldier nearest to him. He had said, so I was told, that sooner would they suffer death than yield. In a flash they followed his example. Everywhere, priests and people alike, they did the same thing. They struggled among themselves to get to the front in order to present their necks to the Roman executioner and behind the lucky ones they knelt down with bared necks, row after row, thousands upon thousands, to await their turn. The position was ludicrous. I could not very well order a wholesale butchery. I had never intended to. Even had they had but one head I could not have cut it off, though it would have given me the greatest pleasure. I had failed and knew it. It took but a few seconds for me to make up my mind. I signaled to the chief priests to follow me and withdrew for consultation. Let me cut short the story of my humiliation. I announced that I was deeply impressed by their devotion to their religion (and that was true enough), but that what impressed me most was the order and calm resolution which they exhibited. Had it been otherwise, had they sought to intimidate me by violence - but you see the argument and, though you may smile, I assure you that the priests did not. They thanked me gravely and Caiaphas went out and announced my decision in almost my own words, adding that they must have confidence in me and in their priests and return quietly to their homes. Thereafter jubilation, thanksgiving and, of course, more prayers. Yahweh gets the credit for it. All day long they have been departing, singing their psalms. Let them sing while they may. But if some day they get a different sort of governor from me, if Caesar abandons his policy of patient toleration, if their wild fanatics overthrow these politic and cunning priests, if the Roman armies march - will Yahweh save them then?

I look to you and to my other friends to put the best face on it when this story reaches Rome. After all, I have but sought to compel respect for Caesar and his images have lorded it above their Temple for a week. It is a beginning, even if at the finish I have lost the throw.

Now I await the preacher John. Marcius should by now have laid him by the heels. When he is safely here in Gaul, the sword shall deal with him. If their victory over me makes them think that the new age has begun, I will at least take care that the prophet does not live to see it.

So you have been reading one of your tragedies to an admiring audience in Rome? I am sure it will be full of fine sentiments. Would I were there to listen to them. Would you were here that you might apply them to these incorrigible Jews, with me to watch the fun.

ARREST OF JOHN BY HEROD ANTIPAS

Caesarea

Marcius has returned to Caesarea bringing two pieces of information. The first is that I have become popular in Jericho, the border-city down by the river Jordan. It is a most important place, for the commerce of the lower Jordan valley passes through it and the customs-revenue is large. Some time ago complaints of gross extortion against the customs-staff were made to me. The chief collector is - was, I should say - a low-class Jew. He was robbing the merchants right and left and the proceeds were not reaching my treasury. One of his underlings, another Jew, who thought he was not getting a fair share of the spoils, betrayed him and two subordinates. It was a bad case; they had kept back some of our moneys as well as the profits of their own extortions. I tried them here in Caesarea and then sent them back to Jericho, the leader to be crucified and the other two to be scourged to death. The Jews were delighted, not only because the chief collector had robbed them but because he was a Jew whom they hated for entering our service. Now they can hate his successor, for I am going to appoint the informer to his place. I ought to be able to rely on his loyalty if he is not murdered by his countrymen. The other news is that John has escaped me. He went on one of his preaching expeditions into Antipas's country. The result was the same as with us: crowds of wretched peasants working themselves up into frenzy and wanting to know whether they could not follow his leadership. Antipas can do with talk of a new Kingdom even less than we can. If there is any trouble in his country, Roman troops will be sent in to help him, and once they are there it will be good-bye to his ridiculous little monarchy. He knows that and he was waiting for John. The preacher is safely put away now in the dungeons of Machaerus, an unpleasant, gloomy fortress in the hills east of the Dead Sea. I should say that he has seen the last of his Judaea. If Antipas has any sense he will make an end of him. It is the only safe method, believe me, with people who mix up their religion and their politics.

I am not sorry, on reflection, that Antipas has taken this business on himself. A certain amount of odium will attach to him, for John has many followers. But sometimes, when I lie awake at night, I wish that I had had the handling of John. The Jericho tax-collector is a poor substitute.

THE PROBLEM OF THE AQUEDUCT

Caesarea

I was not surprised to hear that the two Herods had lodged a complaint against me at Rome when they heard about the images. The dogs! They have the morals of the mongrel tribes from which they spring. But - thanks no doubt to you and my other friends - I have defeated them. I have received an official letter in Caesar's name (written by one of Sejanus's freedmen) commending me for getting out of a difficult situation without bloodshed and at the same time censuring my action in getting into it. The moral is that one must not fail; one should indeed think long before taking action but then go through despite all opposition.

Antipas is too busy with his schemes against me. It is many weeks now since he imprisoned John and he has just sent me a letter, a suave piece of hypocrisy, saying that a certain John, a dangerous fanatic, had been arrested on his side of the frontier, but since the man belonged to my province and had preached disaffection for a considerable time within my border, he presumed that I would wish to deal with him myself and he was therefore ready to hand him over to me. I have replied that my officers would several times have arrested John had he not been able to take refuge in Antipas's territory and that Antipas had therefore better handle the incidents that arose on his own ground. I may have yet to face difficulties of my own, for I hear that some of John's followers are going up and down, following his example and, needless to say, declaring that their master will come back.

It is a relief to turn to the making of roads and aqueducts. I am really happy when I see the gangs of laborers at work on the hill-roads up to Jerusalem: 'roads,' mark you, my good Seneca, not 'road,' for I am remaking both that which runs up from the coast and that which leads up from the Jordan and Jericho. 'Why bother?' you say. 'Is that not an extravagance?' No, because by those roads the materials come up for my Jerusalem aqueduct. I shall be proud of the aqueduct, I can assure you. I shall rely on it to perpetuate my name in history. I have spent more time in the hills south of Jerusalem during the last few weeks than I have spent in Caesarea. There are twenty-four miles of the roughest country imaginable to be subdued and I ride from point to point watching the men cutting through the hills, breaking up rocks, bridging ravines, laying the foundations for my reservoirs. I have drawn laborers from all the surrounding regions, from Galilee and Samaria, Trans-Jordan, Idumaea, and even from Syria, but comparatively few from Jerusalem, the place which is to benefit. The people of Jerusalem will have nothing to do with us even when we seek to help them. They have nothing but scorn for Samaritans and Galileans who take our part to bring them a good supply of water. They would sooner go without water, or have it foul, than take a Roman wage. Let me tell you a story. There is a Rabbi at Jerusalem who said that probably there were only two really good Jews in the whole world - himself and his son. Or perhaps, he added, there was but one - himself.

I am anxious over the cost of the aqueduct. The men are paid regularly, but large sums will soon be due to the contractors. They cannot come out of the ordinary taxes nor, so far as I can see, can I make a special levy which would produce the necessary amount. I have asked the Sanhedrim to make suggestions to me, but they are unhelpful. They talk and talk but they make no proposals. They say the contractors are extravagant or they admit the necessity of the aqueduct but say the work should have been postponed or they declare outright that Rome should pay for it. I will make them sing a different tune, when I have finished with them.

FIRST MENTION OF JESUS

Caesarea

The Sanhedrim are obstinate. I have told them that they must find ways and *means within three months of paying for the aqueduct and roads. I have had endless conferences with their chief men. I repeat until I am weary - 'For the first time in its history Jerusalem will have good drinking-water. It is essential for the health of your great city.' They remain unmoved. One of them said loftily - 'Water for drinking is not of real importance. That is only an affair of the unclean body. What matters is provision for the soul - water for the ablutions that are ordained by our Law.' (They are always at their ceremonial washings; I have never been able to understand how people who wash so much can look so dirty.) This argument gave me a chance. 'Precisely,' I retorted, 'you require great quantities of water for your ablutions and for the temple sacrifices.' (They have, you must know, a huge bowl of water in the Temple for swilling away the blood from sacrifices.) 'The aqueduct is therefore a matter of religion as much as of health and decency and I should expect you to be prepared both to support me and to pay for the service which I am doing you.'*

Then a brilliant idea came into my head. 'Since,' I added, 'the aqueduct, on your own showing, will be a great assistance to your religious exercises, why not pay for it with the Temple-money?' You would hardly believe with what fury they received this reasonable suggestion. 'Robbery' and 'sacrilege' were the weakest words they used. I protested to them that they might regard it as a loan and by imposing a levy on the population of Jerusalem and spreading it over twelve months (or longer if they chose) repay the Temple funds. They were almost beside themselves, but I stood firm and ordered them to bring the proposal before a formal meeting of the full Sanhedrim. The more I think over it, the more agreeable does this project look to me. It solves the difficulties with such simplicity.

The news in your last letter makes entertaining reading. I thought we had fallen low enough when sprigs of our ancient noble houses drove their own chariots at the Games, but I never expected to hear that a Claudius was fighting as a common gladiator before the lousy mob or a Domitius fawning as an actor on the stage. I have, I fear, no such exciting scraps of gossip for you. One of the Rabbis who was suspected of looking with favor on my aqueduct was murdered yesterday as he left his house for the Sanhedrim. Five ruffians fell on him with knives; he had over twenty wounds. There is not the smallest chance of catching the murderers, although their hiding-place will be known to many people. Reports from the frontier state that another wandering preacher, one Jesus, has turned up in Galilee; I have told Joseph to keep an eye on him. The only daughter of one of the chief priests of

The Life and Times of Jesus: From Child to God

Jerusalem has run off with a Greek merchant. They wanted me to arrest the pair and declared that she has taken some of her father's money. He can spare it. Alas! the soldiers did not arrive at the quay till the ship was safely gone, and today I am very much in Procula's good graces.

I cannot get over my astonishment at your letter. What will Tiberius Caesar say when he hears that a Claudius has become a gladiator!

(Note: The Emperor Tiberius belonged to the Claudian line, which was notorious for its arrogance. 'The pride of the Claudian family,' says Tacitus, 'was inveterate in his nature.')

DEATH OF JOHN AND QUESTIONS ABOUT JESUS

Jerusalem

I have come up to Jerusalem to settle my quarrel with the Sanhedrim and this time I mean business. They formally refuse to make any contribution from the Temple-tribute, even for a few months. They have sent me a tiresome screed (tedious writing) arguing that an aqueduct is an Imperial affair and that Caesar's treasury should pay for it. At the most they will only admit that it should be paid for out of the ordinary taxation of the province, and that, they say, is already heavier than the province can bear. They are insolent enough to assert that the supply of water for the ceremonial ablutions demanded by their Law has always been sufficient and that their other needs do not justify so lavish an expenditure. I have informed them that the money must be found without delay and that I shall, if necessary, take steps to find it for them.

I have no patience with their precious Law, which hedges them (and us) at every turn with minute regulations. Some of it comes from their Sacred books but the most tedious part, so far as I can learn, is of their own creation. Their learned men have spent their lives for generations in devising the most elaborate and ridiculous religious rules. Can you believe that they have whole volumes written about their rules for washing and that there is a tome or two devoted solely to the subject of washing before meals? Have you ever heard of the Rabbi who died of thirst? He was shut up in a besieged town and had a few spoonfuls of water assigned to him each day. He used it all for ceremonial washings and died in agonies of thirst. I would like to put old Annas to that test. Or do you know the story of the pious mule? It belonged to a priest who would touch no food on which, at purchase, tithe had not been paid to the Temple. For days the mule refused its feed. Was it sick? Was it lame? Was it merely mulish? No, my dear Seneca, believe me they discovered that when its food was bought tithe had not been paid to the Temple. It would not break the Law. They are all mules in Jerusalem.

By the way, I shall not be troubled any more by John, the preacher, son of Zacharias. He is dead. I have received a formal intimation from the Governor of the castle of Machaerus. He received orders from his master Herod Antipas - dispatched from his capital, Tiberias in Galilee - to execute John as a fomenter of rebellion and to inform me of the fact. There was, I hear, a special reason for Antipas's action. You remember I told you that another agitator called Jesus had turned up in Galilee. Alexander, who knows a great deal of what is going on - and tells me because he is jealous of the worthy Joseph - says that this Jesus originally came from Galilee to visit John. He was actually in Judaea when the news spread that John had been arrested, whereupon he fled to his own country. There he is playing exactly the same game as his master. He is exhorting his fellow-countrymen to be humble (I like him for that) and talking large about the coming kingdom. Also he has set up as a wonder-worker, curing people who are sick and various madmen (they are numerous in Galilee) and of course this draws the superstitious mob. Antipas would not like it in any case, but what really disturbed him was the discovery that communications have been passing between Jesus and the followers of John. So, very wisely, he has made an end of John and is already - Joseph confirms this - inquiring about Jesus. I shall have good ground of complaint if he lets this business grow.

There is one side of it which amuses and delights me. Jesus is quarrelling with the lawyers and the priests. Anything that touches the Law or threatens their authority rouses their instant jealousy. Just as I have told the Sanhedrim that I expect them to report to me any agitation that they hear of, so I make it a point to let them know pretty briskly of any negligence I can impute to them. I informed Caiaphas of the reports concerning Jesus that were reaching me and told him that since the Sanhedrim claimed authority even in Galilee, he had better see to it. He replied at once with emphasis, saying that from what they had heard of Jesus, though it was little as yet, *they disapproved of him heartily and that they were sending a deputation of learned men to Galilee to summon him for examination. In himself the man is a person of no consequence: the son of a common workman. But then, Simon, one of the rascals who gave trouble some years ago, was a slave, and Athronges, another mischief-maker, was a shepherd. It is the worst of these Jews that rank means nothing to them. They will follow any son of the soil if he can fight well, rob well, or talk well - especially if he work a few wonders into the bargain - and, before you know where you are, they will set him up for king. However, with Antipas and the Sanhedrim watching him, and with me waiting for him in Judaea, it is a poor prospect for Jesus.*

In any case I cannot feel excited about anything at present except my aqueduct. It is a noble work, worthy to rank with that of Herod himself at Caesarea. Can you suggest to me how I am to get the money? My ears are wide open. But wait in patience. I have a secret; I rub my hands over it but I dare not tell it even to you. I hope, when I write next, to inform you that I have the money in my hands, and get it I will, though the Jews smart for it.

SEIZURE OF THE TEMPLE-TRIBUTE

Jerusalem

Three days ago, early in the morning, I seized the Temple-tribute. Not all of it - admire my moderation. I did not raid the treasury in the Temple itself, for that would have meant a pitched battle and casualties which I could not afford. You will excuse my diffidence, I think, when you remember the circumstances of my more fortunate exemplars: Crassus had occupied Jerusalem with a great army when on his way to Parthia, while Sabinus actually took the Temple by storm. Both my pretensions and my methods were more modest.

The Temple-tribute is brought to Jerusalem from the foreign Jewish communities about this time every year (in early spring). Egypt, Asia Minor and the Euphrates region are the largest contributors. Most of it comes in coin, but there are also the rich gifts of the pious: plate for the

Joseph Lumpkin

Temple service, jewels and ornaments, gold to be melted down. Egypt's contribution, alas! reached the Temple safely a week ago, but that from the Asiatic cities was waiting at Caesarea for an escort and that from the Euphrates (it is included a fine bar of solid gold, the gift of Ctesiphon) was under escort a few miles from Jerusalem. The Jews, I should explain, send guards of their own, but within the province the governor provides a military escort. The chest which had arrived at Caesarea I confiscated without more ado. The Jews could not resist; they went off, howling, to Jerusalem, and found on arrival that the same fate had befallen the Euphrates caravan. That required some arranging. We doubled the escort on the last night and when the caravan arrived at the neighborhood of the Temple in the early morning Marcius sallied out from the Antonia with a full cohort and literally ran the whole procession into the citadel. The sight was really comic. Our men enjoyed it thoroughly. It was all done so quickly that the Jewish guards, who included some highly dignified officials, could hardly believe their eyes when they saw the gates of the Antonia shut behind them and my men methodically counting and carrying off the chests. One or two were foolish enough to offer resistance but we soon cured that. No bloodshed, but they had some bruises to show their countrymen.

The uproar over the images in my first year - you remember that regrettable incident? - was nothing compared with what happened now. All Jerusalem turned out within an hour. They shouted and screamed, they threatened to tear down the aqueduct, they beat on the walls of the Antonia with their fists. The priests packed themselves in a dense mass round the Temple-treasury lest that also should be attacked by me. The loss of money touches them on the raw. I was not minded, this time, to let them demonstrate for days. I had dressed up a large part of my soldiers in ordinary clothes, beneath which their arms were hidden. Some I slipped out of the Antonia before daybreak. Another large contingent was concealed in Herod's palace. They were all Samaritans and Idumaeans, so that they could disguise themselves easily without fear of recognition. There were about a thousand of them. They gathered on the outskirts of the crowd and took part in the shouting. From what I know of some of them I should say that they did all they could to stimulate the mob. In the afternoon I came out on the tower above the gateway. I announced that the money would be used by me for their benefit in the way that I thought fit. I then ordered them to disperse. Redoubled tumult; threats against the sacrilegious governor, curses, and even stones. A trumpet blew, and my fine fellows, disclosing their weapons, fell upon the mob. The cry of rage and terror that went up might have been heard at Rome. The crowd fled pell-mell, but the crush was so great that many could not escape into the narrow streets and the arms of the soldiers were weary with striking. I have no idea how many were killed, for the dead were carried off quickly by their friends, but the number is large. Everything has been quiet since. I ought to tell you that I strictly forbade my men to pursue the crowd into the Temple and the order was obeyed. I have seen nothing of Annas and Caiaphas, not because they did not come but because I refused to have anything to say to them. They are sending the usual deputation to Rome, but I am not nervous about the result. The principal contractors, whom I have already paid with the Temple-money, are good friends of Sejanus and they have no doubt that with a judicious expenditure among his freed-men all will be well.

So I am satisfied. The aqueduct will shortly be finished and there is money and to spare to pay for it. I have settled some of my accounts with the Jews and especially with their religion-mongering priests. They have had a sharp lesson - let us hope that they will profit by it. Yet I fear that the tone of this letter will not be pleasing to you, my dear Seneca. I will therefore make a suggestion. You complained bitterly of Rome in your last letter to me: of the noise, the exorbitant rents, the dearness and badness of the food. Visit me, then, in Judaea, and revive your wearied spirit. Do you say, with the admirable Horace, that those who cross the sea change only their climate and not their mind? Ah, but cross to Judaea and see whether your liberal-minded tolerance does not undergo a striking change. I know I am disposed to prepare against the Jews; it is a just ridicule. But then I live among them, you only see their shops and synagogues from a safe distance as you hurry past in your litter to a cause such as a party or a gathering of the wits.

A LESSON TO GALILEANS

Jerusalem

I felt that I must write to you again before I set out on one of my periodical inspections of the province. Marcius and Joseph both warn me that I shall have a bad reception because of the seizure of the sacred money. I am not so sure. It is sacrilege, of course, to all of them, but the country-people do not love the greedy, grasping priesthood at Jerusalem, who fatten on their *offerings and, besides, only Jerusalem benefits from my gift of good water; why did not Jerusalem pay for its water and so save the Temple-tribute from spoliation? Perhaps I shall not be so unpopular after all. I shall let the people know that their Sanhedrim wanted to pay for the aqueduct out of the people's taxes.*

It is a month now since the coup, on which I have received many congratulations from my friends. Except for one serious episode, everybody has been fairly peaceful. I did not weaken in my determination. I forbade all demonstrations, public-meetings and even gatherings in the streets. That put a stop to their street-corner oratory. The worst of the offenders were not the priests and lawyers themselves, but the young know-alls who attend their lectures, and supply the wits that the common people lack. There was one man in particular, a pertinacious fellow, a loud-mouthed logic-chopping Jew from Tarsus, who had much to say, when arrested, about being a Roman citizen. It turned out that he was, so he was released, but I bade the centurion whisper to him not to come into our hands again since even a Roman citizen might be killed in attempting to escape. There were seditious placards too, during the first few days, defaming me and Caesar. The city broke out into a perfect rash of them, until we caught a party of three at work on the walls of the Antonia in the night. There was something else on the wall of the Antonia, besides placards, in the morning.

As I told you, there was one serious incident. It was produced by a part of Galileans who came up to the Temple. These people are never very popular in Jerusalem. They are regarded as a mixed race, as a little inferior to the pure Judean Jew, and so I daresay they are, being so close to Phoenicians and Greeks and various sorts of Syrians. The Galileans think themselves as good as any Jew alive; they are all the more defiant of us Romans because they are themselves ruled by a semi-Jew, like Antipas, and in any case a visit to Jerusalem is to them an excursion on which they enter with boisterous high spirits. This party, which arrived a fortnight ago, had heard of my seizure of the Temple-money but had not heard that demonstrations were prohibited. When the noisy rabble reached the Antonia I sent to warn them, but in vain. They abused us angrily and declared that on entering the Temple they would protest against the customary sacrifice to Caesar and to Rome. I had them followed into the outer court of the Temple by a troop of soldiers who fell upon them with swords while they were buying the animals for their own sacrifices. The other Jews looked on. I think this proof that I would not stop short even at entering the Temple has made a good impression. The remnant of the Galilean party set off again for their own country the same day and when they spread the news it should teach their fellow-countrymen not to take liberties with me. I have sent a report to Antipas and begged him to restrain his subjects better.

I do not like what you tell me about the prevalence of 'informers' at Rome. If a man sides with or against Sejanus, he takes the risk and ought not to complain of the result, but this system is exposing even the most innocent to private spite and vengeance. Surely a Roman ought to be safe from denunciation by his freedman. I pay no attention to anonymous informers here, though there are many of them at work. Those who hate us most are always seeking to ruin the priests and nobles who work with us, but unless the accuser is prepared to stand forward I do not listen to him. In that I know I shall have your support. For rebellion, no mercy! But our Roman justice must not be used for settling private grudges. 'Admirable,' says L. Annaeus Seneca, 'and under which heading comes the appropriation of the sacred Temple-money!'

ANTIPAS'S INQUIRIES AT NAZARETH

Caesarea

I have spent nearly a month going round the northern districts of my province. I have inspected frontier posts, conferred with my revenue officers, heard innumerable grievances and redressed not a few. I wanted to find out for myself whether this part of the country was suffering as much from the effects of drought and bad harvests as I had been told. I found that it was. In many places the condition of the people was truly miserable. I discovered that every synagogue had been used as a centre of ill-will against me, but I summoned the village elders, heard their stories of distress, and announced remissions of taxation. In certain cases I promised to send them relief as soon as I got back to Caesarea, and that I am now doing. On the whole, I am not dissatisfied.

It was a pleasure to be among the Samaritans. They have a most likeable hatred of the priesthood at Jerusalem, who treat them like dogs and keep them out of the Temple. They think themselves every bit as good as the real

Jews and certainly they have the same general characteristics: one day they are peasants and the next they are robbers; this week it is the plough and the next it is the knife or the pitchfork against Caesar or Herod or whoever the 'tyrant' of the day may be. Still, I have been governor for three years now without many grave troubles, which is as much as any of my predecessors except Valerius has done. If I were withdrawn now, I should leave the province better than I found it. I am not discontented.

At the beginning of my tour I took Procula up to the border of Galilee. She is paying a visit to the wife of the Governor of Syria, an old school-fellow of hers, and I set her on the high road to Damascus. I sent Alexander with her into Galilee and told him to find out something for me about the latest agitator. He accompanied her to Damascus. He paid a flying visit to Nazareth, to which Jesus belongs, and visited his family. He found them in a state of fright. Antipas's agents have been in Nazareth cross-examining them about Jesus and they fear that they will be involved in any punishment that befalls him. The whole town shares their nervousness. It seems that the family and their friends actually pursued Jesus, who moves about rapidly from place to place, as all these preachers do, and would like to have carried him off and shut him up to keep him - or rather themselves - out of trouble. They told Antipas's people that Jesus was not wholly responsible for his actions; he had always been a little queer and caused his family trouble, and they had never been able to control him. Certainly they cannot now, for he not only repudiates them brusquely, but the crowds who follow him increase every day and will not hear a word against him. So the wretched people are panic-stricken. I have written to Caiaphas pressing to be told whether the Sanhedrim have taken any action.

Do you remember the Greek merchant who ran off with a priest's daughter? While I was away he turned up again in Caesarea - alone. He told every one that the Jewess had left him, but the story goes that he abandoned her somewhere in Africa and the Jews have sent an account of it to her family in Jerusalem. Like a fool he persisted in going on his usual round of business in Judaea. He even talked of visiting Jerusalem. He was a cheery fellow with a mop of black hair, always making jests and laughing at himself. When warned not to go to Jerusalem he said that he had turned proselyte and being converted to Judaism he would be looked after by Yahweh. So he went laughing to Jerusalem and that is the end of him. He has vanished off the face of the earth. The young woman had several brothers and cousins who are among the strictest of the strict. In Rome the whole thing would have been a joke, but you soon learn not to smile over such things here. At least you ought to. The Greek would not learn, and now where is he?

ATTEMPT IN GALILEE TO MAKE JESUS KING

Caesarea

A budget from you has made me happy. Ships have been delayed by stormy weather so that several letters have arrived at once. Before I open them I think myself important, occupied with weighty affairs of State, a not inefficient part of Caesar's great machine. But when I read them, ah me! I wish that I were again at the centre of the world, in the Forum or the Senate-house, the theatre or Sejanus's ante-chamber, amid the noise and smoke of Rome, where after all a man does live. Here nothing happens - nothing, at least, that matters; from here nothing can arise; how much, I beg you to tell me, will Rome ever know or care about Judaea unless there is a war and comfortable appointments have to be found for our noble idlers on the Commander's staff? There, I have had my growl. Let me see whether, after all, I have any news to repay you for your letters.

Procula has seen and heard the Galilean Jesus. She writes to me that as soon as they had crossed into Galilee and started on the road which runs along the west side of the lake they began to hear of little else. Alexander, the ferret, was nosing here and there, collecting information. It seems that all Galilee is agog about Jesus; every one knows of someone who has heard of someone else who has been cured of some disease or other, and the interesting thing (to me) is that a number of my good subjects of Judaea are also in Galilee, following the preacher when they would be better employed following their jobs at home. Alexander had arranged, as it happened, for Procula to make a halt at a farm-house towards the northern end of the lake, and as she went along - but you shall have the story in her own words as she has sent it me:

'We came suddenly on a crowd of people who were hurrying along the road in front of us and over the slopes leading down to the sea and even along the beach. Others were joining them from the paths that came in from the hills. No one took any notice of us. They were Jews of all kinds - mostly hale and

hearty people, but there were sick and cripples too, who were dragging themselves along or being carried by their friends. The crowd was excited, gesticulating, pointing to a boat that was following the coast line, and shouting to those on board. I thought at first that they were angry but Alexander said that they were calling to Jesus, who was on board, to come to shore and speak to them. They kept on shouting the same words over and over again. I could not make it out because it was all in Aramaic and when I asked Alexander he only shook his head and muttered something about it being a bad business. He would not tell me what they meant, though he told me later. When we stopped at the farm-house the crowd rushed on and presently I could see them leaving the high road and hurrying down to the shore. Alexander asked permission to go after them and I said he could provided that he took me with him. So we went, with an escort - you need not be afraid - and after half an hour we found them all in a great mass, down near the sea, with Jesus standing on a knoll in the field, addressing them. There were thousands upon thousands of them, and at the back, quite close to us, some groups of better-dressed Jews, who were standing aloof, watching and listening. Alexander took a look at them and muttered again. "Spies from Jerusalem," he said and went off to talk to them.

'I saw the preacher clearly. He is a strange man, gaunt and rugged, as though he were burnt up by the fire of his passion. When you see his face and hear him speak, he is full of self-confidence, imperious, often fierce. The crowd was noisy at first because those at the back could not hear and there were interruptions. He put them down with a few words. He was like a general among the legions and they obeyed like common soldiers. He spoke always as though he thought no one could contradict him. He began quietly but then raised his voice and it became harsh and vehement. The Jews from Jerusalem were fidgeting and muttering to each other. Alexander said he was denouncing them and their friends. I have never heard anything that sounded so passionate and bitter. Then he became quieter again and went off in a rapt way as though he did not know the people were there. There was a murmuring and stirring all through the crowd then but not angrily, and they pressed forward to him. Alexander could not take his eyes off him. He would pay no attention to my questions. He kept on saying to himself "A better time coming!" and laughed in a queer, anxious sort of way. I thought he was quoting something that the preacher had been saying. He kept looking at the party from Jerusalem and said he must get a report to you at once.

'Then a curious thing happened. Jesus suddenly raised his arm and cried out something sternly. They stopped pushing towards him and sat down on the grass in a great circle round him - except the Jews from Jerusalem, who made no movement but went on watching. I am sure I have seen some of them going to the Sanhedrim. Then Jesus called some men who were standing close to him and they brought him bread. He broke this into little pieces - so small that from where I stood you could scarcely see them at all. He gave these to the men and they went along the ranks distributing them to the crowd, who ate them while the preacher went on talking. I wish I could have understood. All I could get out of Alexander was that the preacher was enrolling them as his followers but that it was not a military business at all but purely religious; the eating of the bread was a symbol that they enrolled themselves under him, to live as he lived and to do all the things that he had been telling them to do. Alexander added that it was dangerous, it might be misunderstood.

'The strangest thing was to follow. When the ceremony was finished everything was still for a few seconds and then the crowd began to stir and talk. Gradually they became more and more excited. Jesus said something to the men about him, and running down to the sea, they began to pull the boat close in so that he could embark again. When the crowd saw that he was going to leave them they broke all bounds. They ran forward, crying and shouting, and surrounded him. Some of them were brandishing sticks and clubs and knives. They were not threatening him; it was quite different. Others of them were weeping. Many of them fell down at his feet. All the time I could make out that they were shouting the same words that I had heard them using on the high-road when they were looking out to sea. I asked Alexander what they were saying. I had to shake him by the shoulder before I could get an answer out of him. He was impatient with me. "King!" he said, "that's what they are saying. King of Israel! King of the Jews! And Messiah!" I am not sure what the last means, but you will know.

'I could see that Jesus was repelling them. He would not listen to them. He almost drove them back with words and gestures. I am sure he was telling them that they had made a great mistake. He was almost beside himself. He made those who were kneeling rise and those who were brandishing weapons put them down. He was more stern and determined than he had been all the afternoon. At the same time he began to move down to the sea hurriedly as though he must escape. The crowd followed slowly in a dejected way. They seemed to be disappointed and bewildered. "He is angry with them for calling him King of the Jews," I said to Alexander. "He has cause to be," said Alexander. "He is a dead man from today."

'There was another incident. Before Jesus could get on the boat, the Jews from Jerusalem, who had been watching every movement of the crowd, walked rapidly down the hill and spoke to him. They met each other as enemies; I could see that though I could not hear the words. The talk only lasted a few moments. They said something to him and he looked at them with a face of stone. Then he answered curtly and turned his back on them. Some of his followers helped him into the boat. I thought they were puzzled too, and perhaps afraid. He was not afraid himself. He spoke and acted as though he was ready to fight the whole world.

'Whatever it was that was said to the Jews from Jerusalem they were pleased about it. They came away whispering and smiling and, when I left, they were going about among the crowd, as busy as bees. I knew they were denouncing Jesus, because they kept on looking out to sea and pointing to the boat. Alexander is now engaged in writing you a report upon the whole affair.'

'King of the Jews!' my dear friend - you mark the words! Yes, I know, it is only in Galilee and, likely enough, I shall not myself be worried. Trust Antipas to look to it! Would you like to hear the report of the sage Alexander? He says:

'Galilee would rise at a word but he does not say the word. He puzzles the people even while he attracts them. He has performed strange cures, though every one has a different story of his own about them and it is impossible to say how much of it is truth. The gatherings that he addresses have been like clay between his hands. In controversy no one can stand against him. He is at daggers-drawn with the priests, the lawyers and the Law. He is terrible in his attacks upon them: most fierce and unsparing. He would overthrow the whole system which the priests have imposed upon the Jewish nation, and the priests will never forgive him for it. At the first sign that the people are turning against him, the priests will make an end of him.

'There are signs that they are about to turn against him now. They have hailed him as the expected deliverer, the new king of the Jews. He refuses the titles. This afternoon he beat the crowd off almost by force when they acclaimed him. You never saw such a hang-dog look as they had when they drifted away. In his own mind he is no king or Messiah. I believe he dreads lest they should insist on treating him as either one or the other. Above all else the popular ferment has been caused by the cures, and I have found, by careful inquiry, that on every occasion he has tried to conceal what he has done and so to prevent the people from hailing him as the deliverer. He seeks to avert the danger that he fears. The war which he wages is against the Sanhedrim and the Judaic Law. If he persists they will surely take his life. Their delegates were on the watch today and some of them are remaining in Galilee. But I doubt whether they will be under the necessity, or have the chance, of taking him. Unless he takes to immediate flight, Herod Antipas will seize him.

'Antipas can do nothing else after today. I hear that Jesus has already sailed for the other side of the lake to take refuge in the territory of Herod Philip. If he stays there Philip will lay hands on him. If he returns to Galilee he is lost. May I suggest that it would be interesting to have a report from the High Priest on his view of the case?'

You see, then. Another popular hero rising to worry me and call himself King. No, you will say, he does not so; it is they who call him King. And what difference, pray, does that make to the Procurator? If Jesus values his life he will keep out of Judaea. If Antipas lets him slip through his fingers I will not. Only one thing grieves me. 'He is at daggers-drawn with the priests, the lawyers and the Law.' I could like him for that. But a king in Judaea, even one who would not (at present) be a king, a man imperious, fierce, burnt up by his own passion, the type of man to whom this restless and insurgent people willingly gives heed - no, no, that will not do! When he is dead, then they can call him king.

By the way, the Greek merchant has been found under a pile of stones in a ravine outside Jerusalem. There was scarcely a whole bone in his body. Apparently they used clubs. The story is that the Jewess has gone off to Rome with an Egyptian actor. You know how she will end.

FLIGHT OF JESUS INTO SYRIA

Joseph Lumpkin

Caesarea

What, my dear Seneca, all the Jews expelled from Rome! A clean sweep of tailors and milliners, money-lenders and red-nosed comedians! O most desirable of cities: would that I could be there! Yet it is unjust, as you say, that the whole community should be banished because some rascals turned Temple-gifts to their own private uses. Yes, yes, it is unjust, yet no one will sympathize. It must be their own fault that, all the world over, no one sympathizes with an ill-treated Jew - no one, that is to say, except my Seneca. A dreadful thought assails me. Where is Caesar going to send them? Pray Yahweh it be not to Judaea!

(Certain Jews had induced Fulvia, a Roman lady converted to Judaism, to make gifts to the Temple and had then appropriated the money. The Jewish community was thereupon expelled from Rome.)

(Alexander was right. Jesus of Nazareth has fled. Nothing has been heard of him for weeks. He is not in Galilee and he is not in Philip's territory. He must have gone north into Syria, where no one cares about him.)

Let me tell you first about Caiaphas. The wily Priest has sent me several of his unctuous statesman-like reports. I know his difficulties. He has to keep an eye on the Governor (who has the soldiers and Rome behind him); on his own Pharisees who think he is obsequious to us; on the people who might be led away by any wild man this day or tomorrow; and on the priests and lawyers who love their law and suspect that in its defense he and his kind are no better than they should be. He says it would be charitable to suppose that Jesus is a madman, and that this is indeed the opinion of his family, but whether mad or not, he is seducing ignorant people from their duty alike to their religion and to the recognized authorities. He adds that the delegates from the Sanhedrim have exposed him repeatedly, and the exposure is now rapidly having an effect. They will take the sternest measures against Jesus, should he come into their hands, as a false pretender and rebel against the Law and as for the political side of it - do you remember they said the same thing about John? - they realize that it may cause me a legitimate concern. Themselves, too, I should say, for in the long run with these ruling priests it all comes down to politics. It is their nature: all Jews are politicians - but so is their Procurator.

For the time being, then, the preacher has taken to his heels. I have other reports from Galilee. It seems that he paid some flying visits from Philip's territory, only to find that the tide had set against him. The events which Procula and Alexander saw were decisive with his followers. He would not be their King, he would not acknowledge that he was the promised deliverer. Maybe, as Alexander says, it is no part of his intention to be the one thing or the other. After his refusal, the Jerusalem Rabbis dogged him everywhere. They found it much easier to persuade the people that, after all, he was only a rebel, an enemy to their venerated Law. I believe that in his own town an attempt was made to murder him, though, of course, they have their special grievances against him there. Now he is without friends and has vanished into the far north.

This is a small matter, but still something of a relief to me. The country is fairly quiet - if those Jewish friends of yours don't come from Rome! - and I shall have, I suppose, to stop here for some years more. I am a poor man, in spite of the jesting threats against the Jews which I used to send to you over three years ago, and I would prefer to spend my remaining years of office quietly until Caesar transfers me. As this thing stands at present, I can handle it comfortably, but if a fanatic of this sort were to accept the popular demand - to 'give the word,' as Alexander said - I might be hard pressed with the miserable little force that is allowed me.

PILATE COMES TO JERUSALEM FOR THE PASSOVER

Jerusalem

I have come up as usual for their great festival the Passover. It amused me, when I received your letter just before leaving Caesarea, to find you complaining of the congestion in Rome. You should be here. Judaea has been filling up for weeks past. They come by tens of thousands, weeks in advance, and spread over the country, visiting their friends and relatives, searching out the villages their fathers came from, and making pilgrimages to the places where their history began. During the last week they have been concentrating on Jerusalem. Every ship that has reached Caesarea has been crowded inside and out. The conditions on board some of them must have been disgusting. You never saw such a medley as passes out from these ships. Some of them must have spent their last penny in paying the fare; not a few have got here without paying any fare at all. You know the sort of mixture that comes out from the Games in Rome - riff-raff from the slums and blue blood cheek by jowl. It is the same here and Jewish blue blood has no more liking for riff-raff than blue blood has in Rome. They smell abominably. You should see the aristocrats turning up their rich or learned noses.

The whole lot throng the roads. The stream is continuous from the coast, from Samaria and from Jericho. Many of them sleep in the open. Some of the wealthier bring tents and bedding with them. In Jerusalem and the neighborhood everybody who can takes in lodgers. They charge a pretty price. Foodstuffs are doubled and trebled in price. I believe the language that the foreign Jews use about their brethren in Judaea shocks even the Greeks. To-day, when I approached, there was a complete block for a good mile from the city, and had it not been for some stout work by my escort I should still be kicking my heels outside the walls.

I have half my total force in readiness - 2,000 men. There is no reason to anticipate anything beyond the usual brawls, but one must be prudent. You know how religion always excites the lowest passions. The Jerusalem Jew is at his worst at these times and the visitors resent his arrogance. They are most apt to brawl in the Temple, that being the heart and kernel of their worship! In the synagogues they are not so dangerous, because most of these foreign communities have each a synagogue of their own, where they can agree fairly well, but in the Temple they all meet together and can quarrel about priority in offering sacrifice, or about the inadequacy of the other people's gifts, or about being more Jewish than one another.

Having got through earlier Passovers without serious disturbance I have no reason to be anxious. The danger lies in the immense suppressed excitement that underlies the festival. They work themselves up to a state of ecstasy. With all these thousands gathered from the far ends of the earth, they imagine themselves a free and independent people, they live again in the old days, they think that their Yahweh has only to perform one of his preposterous wonders and we Romans would vanish in the wind. If the spark were handy, a fire might easily be lit.

Do you know that since I arrived today, the Jews have been complaining that I have not expedited the carriage of foodstuffs to the city? They block the roads and then complain that the foodcarts don't come through. But that is their way. They are intractable. If the place were full of pigs they would sooner starve than eat.

I will let you know how we go on.

REAPPEARANCE OF JESUS

Jerusalem

Do you remember the preacher Jesus, who fled to Syria some months ago to save his life from Antipas? He has appeared again. What is more - you may think it incredible, but it is true - he is on his way to Jerusalem. My spies report that having passed hurriedly through Galilee he has crossed the frontier. I have dispatched agents to keep in touch with him. According to present information he denounces the priests and Pharisees at every step and avows his intention to be in Jerusalem for the Passover. He brings a following with him. I suppose there are always people who are tired of life.

It was good of you to find me an expert on vine-culture so quickly. These Jews have wits - none sharper - and they are industrious, but they are sadly lacking in scientific knowledge. If they were not bled by their priests they would have much more money for modern knowledge and equipment, but what can you do when a bloated corporation of priests fattens on an impoverished people? Send your expert at once, I pray you, by way of Alexandria and he shall go straight out on a round of country visits.

JESUS IN JERUSALEM

Jerusalem

So far all goes well. I derive a modest amusement from what I hear of the divisions and jealousies among these different Jews. Remarkable enough at any time, they are much more so when the foreign Jews are here. To begin with, the extreme Pharisees despise even the Jews in their own country who do not belong to their special sect. To them a man is good, that is to say virtuous, if he observes the Law minutely, and not otherwise. I assure you that if they have a woman of the common folk to work in the house, they think the house and all the inmates are made unclean by it. You may imagine how much greater is their contempt for the Jews from Egypt or Syria who actually mix with heathen folk like you and me, or Sejanus and Caesar.

The foreign Jews resent this arrogance. Many of them are extremely rich, many of them (especially those from Egypt) are more learned than their Pharisaic critics, and, of course, they are civilized. Yet when they go into the Temple, mix with the Pharisees and listen to the lectures of the learned, they find themselves treated with sneers and insinuations that they are little better than the Greeks whose language they speak - and often enough, it is the only language that they do speak, since they have neither Hebrew nor Aramaic. On several occasions the rank and file have almost come to blows, but this is a harmless recreation and I do not interfere.

You will expect to hear more about the preacher Jesus. I am, for two reasons, proceeding cautiously. My first thought was to arrest him before he entered Jerusalem and came in contact with the crowds. But that course would have its dangers, at a time like this. Since he crossed the frontier he has done nothing openly to justify it, his followers would spread the report that I had seized a noble patriotic Jew, and so, figuring once more as the oppressor, I might have on my hands a sudden outburst of passion of the kind which I desire to avoid. Besides, Annas and Caiaphas have both been to see me. It was at once apparent that they, and especially Annas, were extremely desirous that I should remove what they consider a danger to themselves. They hate the man and no doubt with good reason. The Pharisees and lawyers are really disturbed about the attacks on the Law; the priesthood scents a danger to its livelihood; while Annas, Caiaphas and the other noble Sadducees are not only concerned for the maintenance of the whole priestly system (they are pretty indifferent themselves about the Law), but fear some sudden turn of affairs which might convert this Jesus into a national hero - and then what would become of them and their power? (I suggest to you, as a subject for one of your plays or meditations, that the greatest stimulant of all to a man's activities is the desire for Power.)

They suggested to me that, remembering what had happened in Galilee, it would be wise for me to seize Jesus quietly and put him out of the way. I am

The Life and Times of Jesus: From Child to God

not, however, so stupid as to pull the chestnuts out of the fire for them and bring on myself an unnecessary odium. I replied that the trouble was primarily their affair but undoubtedly it might concern me at any moment. I wished to avoid a tumult and presumed that was also their desire. They were emphatic that it was so. I said that I should hold my hand for the present, but that if there were any disturbances I would act at once and I expected their loyal co-operation. This they promised me. If nothing happens during the festival it is my intention, though I did not tell them this, to wait until the crowds disperse again and then make an end of Jesus. I cannot allow him to stir up Judaea as he stirred up Galilee. If he provokes trouble during the festival - whether by his own act or by the people losing their heads over him, even against his will - I shall strike at once. But the priests must co-operate and I am certain they will. Do you understand fully why they will? Not only because they hate this particular man, though they do, but because, if they stand out, the case may easily become one of the nation against the wicked Governor, which does not suit their plans, and because also there are some of them whose names I know - and they know that I know - who are tarred with the anti-Roman brush and had better show themselves zealous to assist me when the chance is offered them.

Jesus is in Jerusalem. He entered yesterday. His entry, if he had any intention of raising the populace, was a failure. Few of them knew about it. He came up by the road from Jericho. It was crowded with Jews from the Euphrates region and from Syria, who had never heard of him. If there were any Galileans who recognized him, they would only remember that he had failed them in Galilee last year. His own immediate followers are poor stuff. (I had Alexander following the group and Joseph mingling with the general crowd.) They are ignorant and superstitious men who are only dangerous because they share the usual delusion about leaders of his kind. They are always expecting Jesus to perform a 'wonder,' whether it is bringing to life a dead man or killing a live one, and they think about him just like the peasants and workmen of Galilee, expecting him at any moment to set about delivering the nation and bringing in a new age. I know by this time that a Jew in his own country can scarcely think in any other terms.

There was no evidence yesterday, any more than there has been before, that the preacher takes this view of himself. He entered with no more than the stir that there usually is when a party escorts some local notability. His followers shouted themselves hoarse and a few others, seeing them do it, shouted too. If six men throw their caps up for a reason, six others of the herd will follow suit. I had taken all precautions. I had some disguised soldiers walking with the crowd from Jericho and some more ready at the entrance to the city. Marcius had orders, if any attempt was made to rouse the mob, to cut down Jesus and his followers at once, but nothing happened. That is not to say that nothing will happen. Alexander wormed himself into the confidence of some of the preacher's followers. He says they have the most extraordinary ideas about the brilliant change that is going to come over their fortunes, but that all that their leader intends - Alexander is positive about this - is to pursue in Jerusalem his quarrel with the priesthood and the Law. It is enough.

I hope I am not mistaken in believing that you are interested in these long explanations. Were I writing to anyone else, I would say merely that I have cause to fear another pestilent agitation and that I mean to crush it while I may.

SCENE IN THE TEMPLE AND DECISION TO ARREST JESUS

Jerusalem

Both Herod Antipas and brother Philip are in Jerusalem. These princelings behave as though they owned the East. They have brought rich presents for the Temple, they pose, they cultivate the Jews. They go in procession to and from the Temple services and the mob, which has forgotten how many Jews old Herod tortured, burned or crucified, claps and cries out for them as though it would be a fine thing to have a Herod instead of me at the Antonia. I have not met the princes, but I have stationed a guard of Roman soldiers at their gates. It is a proper mark of respect; it is also a hint that we keep an eye on them. Some of the noble families who supported the father have sent representatives to wait on the sons and accompany them to the Temple, but the ruling coterie, those who have office and those who hope to have it, hold aloof. They know which side their bread is buttered.

The affair of Jesus is coming to a head. Yesterday, accompanied by his immediate followers, he visited the Temple. He stopped in the outer court, which is an enormous place like a fair-ground, full of the paraphernalia for Temple-gifts and sacrifices, and thronged by thousands of Jews chaffering and arguing at the top of their voices in a score of languages and dialects. You know that market of theirs in Rome which one takes visitors to see from curiosity. It is like that, with a hundred times the hubbub. Suddenly Jesus began to assail his enemies the priests and all their works in the most violent terms. So far as I can learn, he denounced the whole ritual-mongering business of the Temple. Very sensible, too, except for his own safety. Had he been understood or attracted wide attention he would have been murdered on the spot. If you remember that the life of these Jews, not only here but to the far ends of the earth, centers in the Temple-worship and that it is a highly organized business controlled by a powerful and jealous corporation, you will see that only a madman or a suicide would act like this. As it went, there was only a scuffle and the thing passed off. It was rather like his entry into the City. He himself speaks Aramaic and a large part of his hearers would have no idea of his meaning. Besides, the noise is appalling. You know the Jews; if you are not noisy they think that you are ill. Nothing whatever came of the affair and, if it was intended as a demonstration, it was another failure. Jesus soon left the Temple again together with his followers who, according to my reports, are getting nothing out of their visit to Jerusalem but chagrin and disappointment. This is not at all the sort of thing which they anticipated. Denunciations of the Temple-worship in the Temple are likely to have an unfortunate end for them, as they probably suspect.

This incident has played into my hands. The man is an avowed failure. Ignored at first, he has now offended beyond forgiveness. Few people may have heard and seen his outburst, but a great many will know about it before to-night. You may say that if he has failed so signally, he is also negligible. Possibly, but there is a risk, and I do not take risks. Consider the audacity of his action. To me, who know these people, it is almost inconceivable. To challenge the priesthood in their sacred citadel and at the Passover, backed by a handful of peasants more ignorant even than himself - I could laugh at the thought were it not that a man so rash and passionate, and at the same time so determined, might make another sort of appeal tomorrow which might have a different ending. I have determined to suppress him. Public opinion, thanks to his folly, will support me. Still, I shall have the arrest carried through as quietly as possible in conjunction with the Sanhedrim. His companions will give no trouble.

After the scene in the Temple the old fox Annas sent an envoy to me. More than anyone he has a vested interest in the maintenance of peace; as you know, he has several sons whom he intends for the highest offices. At the same time, he has his finger on the pulse of the Pharisees who are rebels at heart against us and would help any seditious movement if it had a serious foundation. His point is the same as my own, that Jesus is not an actual but a potential danger. He urges that we should strike while few people know of him, and while those who do - and they will increase hourly - are shocked by his gross impiety (Annas's words). He adds that, if necessary, they will produce one of Jesus' own followers who will give damning evidence about certain ambitions which his master has avowed in private conversations. That does not concern me. I don't doubt they will provide themselves with the evidence they want, but I have already all that I require. The top and the bottom of it is that the man is, or might be, a political danger to me, as Antipas thought he was in Galilee last year, and as Antipas recognized the preacher John to be, when he cut his head off at Machaerus and so saved me the trouble.

I am concerting with the priests. Jesus and his following spend their nights outside Jerusalem; we know the place. He will be arrested quietly and executed without undue delay.

I had not thought of it before, but I think I shall give my friend Antipas the opportunity of condemning Jesus. The trouble began within his jurisdiction, so that it is the correct and polite thing to do. Besides, it would be pleasant to show Antipas both that a mischief-maker has slipped through his hands but not through mine, and also, that when he has condemned his subject, he has to hand him over to the superior authority, the Roman Governor, for execution of sentence. Yes, I will send him to Antipas.

ARREST OF JESUS

Jerusalem

Your freedman Krito has arrived this morning bringing your letters and others which he had picked up for me at Caesarea. He starts back again at once, so that the letter I write you now must be a short one. I wish it had been only your letters he had brought me, for they gave me the pleasure which I always experience in hearing about you in Rome. But no sooner had I read them than I was thrown into ill-temper by the news from Caesarea. You know - I am sure I have told you this before - that when the Passover is finished and a large part of the foreign Jews troop back to the coast on their way home, I hold Games in Caesarea for several days. It is a relaxation for

The Life and Times of Jesus: From Child to God

me as well as for them, and it is good for trade. Do you ask whether they come to my Games? Of course they come. They are not Pharisees. They are Greek Jews, Cyrenaic Jews, Asiatic Jews, who were merrier and more human folk than their harsh Judaic brethren.

Could anything be more exasperating than the blow which has befallen me? In the first place a ship bringing six lions from Cyrenaica has foundered. The crew had not even the good grace to go down with the ship. Still, lions are cheap and I do not make too much of it. What is more serious is the loss of my gladiator Aduatucus, a Gaul. He was the best swordsman in the East. Since I came out here he had fought nearly fifty contests and had never been beaten. The women love him. The Governors of both Syria and Egypt had tried to buy him from me - once or twice I lent him as a great favor, but I always refused to sell - and I had told him that when he completed fifty contests I would give him his freedom and make him trainer of the troop. He might have become manager of the Games, he might have gone back with me and become first favorite of the crowd at Rome. Why, he might have caught Caesar's eye, entered his Household and controlled provincial governors. With this career before him, and knowing the value that I attached to him, he was inconsiderate enough to enter into a tavern brawl about a girl with two Thracians. They stabbed him to death and then took their own lives, so that I have not even the poor consolation of using them for the Games. By Jove, I am annoyed.

You were asking about the aqueduct. It works admirably and I have reason to know that the foreign Jews applaud me for it. They disapprove, as they are bound to do, of my use of the Temple-money, but they see that I am not behind the Governors of more important provinces in my care for the Roman name and the health of my people. The Jews here also use the water, even the Pharisees. The only difference is that they show no gratitude.

Jesus was arrested late last night. I provided a troop of soldiers who accompanied the officials of the Sanhedrim. The advantage is that as the news spread this morning - if it did spread - it would be known that Procurator and Sanhedrim had acted jointly. The Sanhedrim are not popular with the most zealous Jews, but the general impression would be that if all the authorities, Roman and Jewish, were acting together, this must be a troublesome fellow who was better out of the way. The arrest was made without disturbance. Jesus himself gave no trouble and his followers ran at once. I believe some of them are well on their way home.

The prisoner was taken to the High Priest's quarters until this morning when he was handed over to my people. I believe Caiaphas got a few of the leading priests together and they questioned him for themselves. The case is a perfectly simple one, from my point of view, and will give no difficulty. Since Antipas will not handle the matter - I am coming to that in a moment - I shall execute Jesus as a maker or a cause of sedition against Caesar. But these priests have always to remember that sedition against Caesar is usually a merit in the eyes of the populace (and of a good many Pharisees too), and they will want to make out a good case for themselves. They will insist, I suppose, on Jesus' defiance of the Law, attacks on the ritual and outbreak in the Temple. Probably they will say that he regarded himself as the expected Messiah (of which there is no evidence), and the people, with their mouths agape, have no use for a Messiah who cannot keep himself out of the hands of the despised Romans. That is not the kind of deliverer the Jews want any more than his own followers.

I have not seen the man myself, though I shall do presently. I gave orders for him to be taken to Antipas, as I said I would, with a polite statement that as the disturber of the peace was a Galilean, he would perhaps consider the matter came within his jurisdiction. I received a reply, equally polite, that Antipas recognized my courtesy but waived any right that he might have over an offender in my City of Jerusalem. A touching exchange of courtesies! I shall finish the matter off today.

Your freedman waits, but one word more. Is it true, as I hear from Lentulus Spinther, that Sejanus's nephew has been refused an audience by Caesar and that Sejanus has doubled the Praetorian Guard at Rome? What if Sejanus falls? What if he refuses to fall? Do not become famous too hastily, my friend. Obscurity, though inglorious, is safe. When the master walks through the fields with stick in hand, fortunate is the poppy with inconspicuous head.

(Note: Sejanus was summarily executed in the next year and his friends were involved in the catastrophe.)

TRIAL AND EXECUTION OF JESUS

Jerusalem

I must complete the letter which I began this morning. Immediately after dispatching Krito, I confirmed with Marcius the military arrangements for the Passover, which begins tomorrow. I heard reports from Joseph, who thinks that acts of violence against individuals amongst the ruling Sadducees will grow. In his opinion it does not much matter whether the province is as quiet as I contrive to keep it or whether there is constant friction between us and the Jews; his feeling is that the extreme men are tired of peace. Afterwards I tried and condemned the prisoner Jesus. He was crucified at once along with some other prisoners who were awaiting execution. It is not a bad thing to have an object lesson of this kind on the eve of the Passover because, in such a nondescript gathering as we have here, there must always be dangerous characters who have exceptional opportunities for their special qualities. By this time Jesus is buried. It is their custom to bury an executed offender the same day and, besides, the Sabbath begins at sunset - has, indeed, already begun. The Sanhedrim asked permission to bury the body this afternoon. It suits them, having got Jesus out of their way, to dispose of the whole matter before the Passover begins and so to dampen down any discussion which might arise, especially after the inscription that I ordered to be attached to the prisoner, about which more presently.

The trial was short but in due form and order. Jesus was accused of disturbing the peace, stirring up disaffection and claiming to be King of the Jews. There was evidence both from our side and from that of the Jews, both from Galilee and from this city. Caiaphas, Annas and the leading Sadducees were prominent and so were some but not all of the chief Pharisees; some of the Pharisees would lend no assistance in convicting a rebel against Caesar however much they desired his death as a rebel against themselves. However, that did not help him. The priests had much to say of his attacks on their religion, but I cut them short on that. They cannot have it both ways. If we are not allowed to interfere in their religion, they cannot appeal to us when their observances are attacked; as soon as the offence becomes political, directly or indirectly, then we take note of it. They may squabble about Yahweh, like the Egyptians about Isis, till they burst, but when a man brawls in the Temple he tends to provoke a general explosion and that concerns us closely. The charge against Jesus of disturbing the peace was proved to the hilt and he could not deny it.

I inquired of the prisoner, through Alexander, whether he admitted the more serious accusations. The Jews alleged that he regarded himself as the destined deliverer of the nation, which involves the end of both their authority and ours. This would constitute a much more direct offence than that for which Antipas put John to death. They cited both the public utterances in which Jesus had spoken of a new kingdom as being imminent and also certain admissions about himself which they said he had made to his own followers. This was, I suppose, the special evidence which Annas said that they intended to produce. I put the question to him. I asked him whether he considered himself to be the deliverer. 'So THEY say,' he answered, indicating the High Priest and his neighbors, with a curt gesture of contempt. I pointed out to him that he was accused also of representing himself as King of the Jews. I asked him whether he considered himself to be that. He made the same answer - 'So YOU say,' meaning, I suppose, that in neither case was there anything in his own conduct or motives to support the accusation, but that he knew well enough that we meant in any case to fix the charge upon him. He realized that he was trapped, and that there was no way of escape, but he was bold and resolute, defiant, almost insolent. They are all alike, these Jews, bitter and unyielding, whether to us or to each other. Standing alone he might be, forsaken and with enemies on every side who meant his death, with his own countrymen delivering him to the Roman executioner, but he was cool and determined, like the men who engineered an attempt on the life of the great Herod and suffered the extremes of torture sooner than yield an inch. A dangerous breed!

I condemned him to death. I could, of course, do nothing less. All roads lead to that conclusion. Alexander, who has a cool and detached way of regarding his countrymen, insists that this man, so far from posing as Messiah, or King, like most of the mischief-makers during the last thirty years, did all that he could to prevent the stupid people from fastening that part on him. Alexander thinks that there was nothing that Jesus sought to avoid so much as this, knowing that if such a conception of him spread abroad, it would deliver him into our hands and be fatal to his campaign - a hopeless campaign in any case - against the priesthood and its system. Alexander has talked to some of his followers and says that the preacher had unquestionably warned them often and in the severest terms that they were not to regard him or speak of him as the Deliverer whom all these Jews expect, and that it was only when he thought that the old conception of him had died away in Galilee that he decided to come up to Jerusalem. It may be. But I am sure that if he was not a dangerous rebel yesterday, he would have been tomorrow. For either he would have succeeded in his assault on the priesthood or he would not. If he had not, how long would a man of his temperament, so passionate, headstrong and bold, have abstained from making that appeal to the patriotic feelings of these Jews which always - always - meets with a quick response, even when made by men of much less powerful character than his? You remember Procula's and Alexander's description of the scene in Galilee? And supposing that he had conceivably made headway against the priests and all the mummery of the Temple ritual, how long would it have been before he turned upon Caesar and the sacrifices to Caesar and to Rome? Would he have respected the cult of Divus Augustus, do you suppose? But long before we had to consider that eventuality we should have had to intervene with force between their contending factions. Why, as it is, they are almost in a state of suppressed civil war, ready to fly at each other's throats. Give them a bad governor - a governor even half as bad as they say that I am - and the feud between those who tolerate us and those who despise the tolerators will break into open war. This is an unfruitful soil in all respects but one. The seeds of disorder will grow if you only scratch the soil. My policy is to destroy them the moment that they sprout.

But I had forgotten: allow me one word about the inscription announcing the offence of Jesus. It was 'King of the Jews,' set up over the cross. The Pharisees were indignant. They themselves want a King of the Jews. It would give them the greatest pleasure to see Caesar overthrown tomorrow and a Jewish King installed - not a half-Jew like Herod - who would rule the country through them and suppress their Sadducean rivals. But it angered them to see the precious title, 'King of the Jews,' held up to ridicule; it was too plain a reminder of their servitude. Besides, they thought it an insult that a crucified criminal, a presumptuous countryman who had defied them, should be labelled 'King.' I took a short way with them. 'What I have written I have written,' said I, and bade them begone. I know the breed. From the moment that this Jesus set up his individual judgement against theirs they meant to have his life. Scratch a priest and find an autocrat. All the world over, if a man says that he will use his own intelligence about things divine, the priests prick up their ears and feel their knives. If he goes further and tells his fellow-men that they also are entitled to use their own intelligence - off with his head and there's an end of it!

I run on so, my dear Seneca. The subject carries me away. I must apologize to you again; I am afraid that even you will find the subject tedious. For, after all, what does it matter? What does it matter - one Jew more or less?

I wish I could find a substitute for Aduatucus.

Gospel of Luke From the Holy Bible

Luke 22.
[12] And the same day Pilate and Herod were made friends together: for before they were at enmity between themselves.
[13] And Pilate, when he had called together the chief priests and the rulers and the people,
[14] Said to them, You have brought this man to me, as one that perverts the people: and, behold, I, having questioned him before you, have found no fault in this man touching those things whereof you accuse him:
[15] No, nor yet Herod: for I sent him to you; and, lo, nothing worthy of death is done to him.
[16] I will therefore chastise him, and release him.
[17] (For of necessity he must release one to them at the feast.)
[18] And they cried out all at once, saying, Away with this man, and release to us Barabbas:
[19] (Who for a certain sedition made in the city, and for murder, was cast into prison.)
[20] Pilate therefore, willing to release Jesus, spoke again to them.
[21] But they cried, saying, Crucify him, crucify him.
[22] And he said to them the third time, Why, what evil has he done? I have found no cause of death in him: I will therefore chastise him, and let him go.
[23] And they were instant with loud voices, requiring that he might be crucified. And the voices of them and of the chief priests prevailed.
[24] And Pilate gave sentence that it should be as they required.
[25] And he released to them him that for sedition and murder was cast into prison, whom they had desired; but he delivered Jesus to their will.

Joseph Lumpkin

Author's Note: These Letters are attributed to Pilate and Herod during the exchange of Jesus as prisoner.

LETTER OF HEROD TO PILATE THE GOVERNOR

Herod to Pontius Pilate the Governor of Jerusalem, Peace: 1. I am in great anxiety. I write these things to you, that when you have heard them you may be grieved for me. For as my daughter Herodias, who is dear to me, was playing upon a pool of water that had ice upon it, it broke under her and all her body went down, and her head was cut off and remained on the surface of the ice. And behold, her mother is holding her head upon her knees in her lap, and my whole house is in great sorrow. 2. For I, when I heard of the man Jesus, wished to come to you, that I might see him alone and hear his word, whether it was like that of the sons of men. 3. And it is certain that because of the many evil things which were done by me to John the Baptist, and because I mocked the Christ, behold I receive the reward of unrighteousness, for I have shed much blood of others' children upon the earth. Therefore the judgments of God are righteous, for every man receives according to his thought. But since you were worthy to see that God-man, therefore it is appropriate for you to pray for me.

(Note: The author of this epistle was not Herod the Great who caused the massacre of the children at Bethlehem (Matthew 2:16), but by his son Herod Antipas, also known as Herod the Tetrarch.)

4. My son Azbonius also is in the agony of the hour of death. 5. And I too am in affliction and great trial, because I have the dropsy and am in great distress, because I persecuted the introducer of baptism by water, which was John. Therefore, my brother, the judgments of God are righteous.

(For this Herod's imprisonment and beheading of John the Baptist, see Luke 3:1, 19; Matthew 14:1-10.)

6. And my wife, again, through all her grief for her daughter, is become blind in her left eye, because we desired to blind the Eye of righteousness. 7. There is no peace to the doers of evil, says the Lord. For already great affliction comes upon the priests and upon the writers of the law because they delivered to you the Just One. 8. For this is the consummation of the world, that they consented that the Gentiles should become heirs. For the children of light will be cast out, for they have not observed the things which were preached concerning the Lord and concerning his Son. 9. Therefore prepare up your loins, and receive righteousness, you with your wife remembering Jesus night and day; and the kingdom shall belong to you Gentiles, for we the chosen people have mocked the Righteous One.

10. Now if there is place for our request, O Pilate, because we were at one time in power, bury my household carefully, for it is right that we should be buried by you rather than by the priests, whom, after a little time, as the Scriptures say, at the coming of Jesus Christ, vengeance shall overtake. 11. Fare you well, with Procla your wife. 12. I send you the earrings of my daughter and my own ring, that they may be for you a memorial of my decease. For already do worms begin to issue from my body, and lo, I am receiving temporal judgment, and I am afraid of the judgment to come. For in both we stand before the works of the living God; but this judgment, which is temporal, is for a time, while that to come is judgment forever.

LETTER OF PILATE TO HEROD

Pilate to Herod the Tetrarch, Peace:
1. Know and see, that in the day when you delivered Jesus to me, I took pity on myself and testified by washing my hands that I was innocent concerning him who rose from the grave after three days, and had performed your pleasure in him, for you wanted me to be associated with you in his crucifixion. 2. But I now learn from the executioners and from the soldiers who watched his sepulcher that he rose from the dead. And I have especially confirmed what was told me: that he appeared bodily in Galilee, in the same form, and with the same voice, and with the same doctrine, and with the same disciples, not having changed in anything, but preaching with boldness his resurrection and an everlasting kingdom. 3. And behold, heaven and earth rejoice; and behold, Procla (Procula / Proculla) my wife is believing in the visions which appeared to her when you sent that I should deliver Jesus to the people of Israel, because of the ill-will they had. 4. Now when Procla, my wife, heard that Jesus was risen and had appeared in Galilee, she took with her Longinus the centurion and twelve soldiers, the same who had watched at the sepulcher, and went to greet the face of Christ,

as if to a great spectacle, and saw him with his disciples.

(The original manuscript says "his wife," a manifest error by a copyist. Nicodemus 7:8 mentions Longinus as the centurion who with a spear pierced the side of Jesus.)

5. Now while they were standing and wondering, and gazing at him, he looked at them and said to them, What is it? Do you believe in me? Procla, know that in the covenant God gave to the fathers, it is said that everybody who had perished should live by means of my death, which you have seen. And now you see that I live, whom you crucified. And I suffered many things, till I was laid in the sepulcher. But now, hear me and believe in my Father -- God who is in me. For I loosed the cords of death and broke the gates of Hades, and my coming shall be in the future. 6. And when Procla my wife and the Romans heard these things, they came and told me weeping, for they also were against him when they devised the evils they had done to him. So that I also was on the couch of my bed in affliction, and put on a garment of mourning, and took to me fifty Romans with my wife and went into Galilee. 7. And when I was going in the way I testified these things: that Herod did these things by me, that he took counsel with me, and constrained me to arm my hands against him, and to judge him that judges all, and to whip the Just One, Lord of the just. 8. And when we drew near to him, O Herod, a great voice was heard from heaven, and dreadful thunder, and the earth trembled and gave forth a sweet smell, like to which was never perceived even in the temple of Jerusalem. 9. Now while I stood in the way, our Lord saw me as he stood and talked with his disciples. But I prayed in my heart, for I knew that it was he whom you delivered to me, that he was Lord of created things and Creator of all. 10. But we, when we saw him, all of us fell upon our faces before his feet. And I said with a loud voice, I have sinned, O Lord, in that I sat and judged you, who avenges all in truth. And lo, I know that you are God, the Son of God, and I beheld your humanity but not your divinity. But Herod, with the children of Israel, constrained me to do evil to you. Have pity, therefore, on me, O God of Israel! 11. And my wife in great anguish, said, God of heaven and of earth, God of Israel, do not reward me according to the deeds of Pontius Pilate, nor according to the will of the children of Israel, nor according to the thought of the sons of the priests, but remember my husband in your glory! 12. Now our Lord drew near and raised up me and my wife, and the Romans. I looked at him and saw there were on him the scars of his cross. 13. And he said, That which all the righteous fathers hoped to receive, and saw not -- in your time the Lord

of Time, the Son of Man, the Son of the Most High, who is forever, arose from the dead and is glorified on high by all that he created, and established for ever and ever.

(Most commentators understand the Theodorus mentioned to be the Emperor Tiberius.)

As an aside, there is a story of a man named Justinus, one of the writers in the days of Augustus and Tiberius and Gaius. Justinus wrote in his third discourse: "Now Mary the Gailaean, who bore the Christ who was crucified in Jerusalem, had not been with a husband. And Joseph did not abandon her, but continued in sanctity without a wife, he and his five sons by a former wife; and Mary continued without a husband. 2. Theodorus wrote to Pilate the Governor: Who was the man against whom there was a complaint before you, that he was crucified by the men of Palestine? If many demanded this righteously, why did you not consent to their righteousness? And if they demanded this unrighteously, how did you transgress the law and command what was far from righteousness? Pilate sent to him: -- Because he wrought signs I did not wish to crucify him, but since his accusers said, He calls himself a king, I crucified him. 3. Josephus says: Agrippa the king was clothed in a robe woven with silver, and saw the spectacle in the theater of Caesarea. When the people saw that his raiment flashed, they said to him, Until now we feared you as a man; from now on you are exalted above the nature of mortals. And he saw an angel standing over him, and he smote him to death."

Joseph Lumpkin

Author's Note: After the crucifixion of Jesus, Pilate wrote a report of the incident to Tiberius, who was Caesar in Rome at the time.

THE REPORT OF PONTIUS PILATE, GOVERNOR OF JUDEA, WHICH WAS SENT TO TIBERIUS CAESAR IN ROME

1. To the most potent, august, dreadful, and divine Augustus, from Pontius Pilate, administrator of the Eastern Province: 2. Though possessed with much fear and trembling, I have undertaken to communicate to your goodness by this my writing, most excellent king, the present state of affairs, as the result has shown. 3. For as I administered this province, my lord, according to the command of your serenity, which is one of the eastern cities called Jerusalem, wherein the temple of the nation of the Jews is erected, all the multitude of the Jews assembled and delivered up to me a certain man called Jesus, bringing many endless accusations against him, but they could not convict him in anything. But they had one heresy against him, that he said the Sabbath was not their proper rest. 4. Now that man wrought many cures and good works: he caused the blind to see, he cleansed lepers, he raised the dead, he healed paralytics who could not move at all, but had only voice, and all their bones in their places; and he gave them strength to walk and run, enjoining it by his word alone. 5. And he did another yet more mighty work, which would have been strange even among our gods: he raised from the dead one Lazarus, who had been dead four days, commanding by a word alone that the dead man should be raised, when his body was already corrupted by worms which bred in his wounds. And he commanded the fetid body in the grave to run, and as a bridegroom from his chamber so he went forth from his grave, full of sweet perfume. 6. And some who were grievously afflicted by demons and had their dwellings in desert places and devoured the flesh of their own limbs, and went up and down among creeping things and wild beasts, he caused to dwell in cities in their own houses and by a word made them reasonable, and caused to become wise and honorable those who were vexed by unclean spirits, and the demons that were in them he sent out into a herd of swine into the sea and drowned them. 7. Again, another who had a withered hand and lived in suffering, and had not even the half of his body sound, he made whole by a word alone. 8.

And a woman who had an issue of blood for a long time, so that because of the discharge all the joints of her bones were seen and shone through like glass, for all the physicians had dismissed her without hope and had not cleansed her, for there was in her no hope of health at all; but once, as Jesus was passing by she touched from behind the hem of his garments, and in that very hour the strength of her body was restored, and she was made whole as if she had no affliction, and began to run fast towards her own city of Paneas. 9. And these things happened thus, but the Jews reported that Jesus did them on the Sabbath. And I saw that greater marvels had been wrought by him than by the gods whom we worship. 10. Then Herod and Archelaus and Philip, and Annas and Caiaphas, with all the people, delivered him up to me to put him on his trial. And because many raised a tumult against me, I commanded that he should be crucified. 11. Now when he was crucified, darkness came over all the world; the sun was altogether hidden, and the sky appeared dark while it was yet day, so that the stars were seen, though still they had their luster obscured. 12. I suppose your excellency is not unaware that in all the world they lighted their lamps from the sixth hour until evening. And the moon, which was like blood, did not shine all night long, although it was at the full, and the stars and Orion made lamentation over the Jews because of the transgression committed by them. 13. And on the first day of the week, about the third hour of the night, the sun appeared as it never shone before, and the whole heaven became bright. 14. And as lightnings come in a storm, so certain men of lofty stature, in beautiful array and of indescribable glory, appeared in the air, and a countless host of angels crying out and saying, Glory to God in the highest, and on earth peace, good will among men: Come up from Hades, you who are in bondage in the depths of Hades. 15. And at their voice all the mountains and hills were moved, and the rocks were rent, and great chasms were made in the earth so that the very places of the abyss were visible. 16. And amid the terror dead men were seen rising again, so that the Jews who saw it said, We beheld Abraham and Isaac, and Jacob, and the twelve patriarchs, who died some two thousand five hundred years before, and we beheld Noah clearly in the body. 17. And all the multitude walked about and sang hymns to God with a loud voice, saying, the Lord our God, who has risen from the dead, has made alive all the dead, and Hades he has spoiled and slain. 18. Therefore, my lord king, all that night the light did not cease. But many of the Jews died, sunk and swallowed up in the chasms that night, so that not even their bodies were to be seen. Now I mean, that those of the Jews suffered who spoke against Jesus. Only one synagogue remained in Jerusalem, for all the synagogues which had been against Jesus were overwhelmed. 19. Through that terror, therefore, being amazed and being seized with great trembling, in that very hour I ordered what had been done by them all to be written, and I have sent it to your mightiness.

THE EPISTLE OF PONTIUS PILATE

Which he wrote to the Roman Emperor concerning our Lord Jesus Christ.

Pontius Pilate to Tiberius Caesar the Emperor, Greeting:
1. About Jesus Christ, whom I fully made known to you in my last letter, a bitter punishment has at length been inflicted by the will of the people, although I was unwilling and apprehensive. In good truth, no age ever had or will have a man so good and upright. 2. But the people made an amazing effort, and all their scribes, chiefs and elders agreed to crucify this ambassador of truth, although their own prophets, like the Sibyls with us, advised to the contrary; and when he was hanged supernatural signs appeared, and in the judgment of philosophers menaced the whole world with ruin.

(Sibyls were women soothsayers, or fortune-tellers.)

3. His disciples flourish, and by their behavior and continence of life do not repudiate their master; on the contrary, in his name they are most beneficent. 4. Had I not feared a sedition might arise among the people, who were almost furious, perhaps this man would have yet been living with us.

5. Although, being rather compelled by fidelity to your dignity, then led by my own inclination, I did not strive with all my might to prevent the sale and suffering of righteous blood, guiltless of every accusation, unjustly indeed, through the maliciousness of men, and yet, as the Scriptures interpret, to their own destruction. 6. Farewell. The 5th of the Calends (month) of April.

Gospel of Luke from the Holy Bible

LUKE 23

[26] And as they led him away, they laid hold upon one Simon, a Cyrenian, coming out of the country, and on him they laid the cross, that he might bear it after Jesus.
[27] And there followed him a great company of people, and of women, which also bewailed and lamented him.
[28] But Jesus turning to them said, Daughters of Jerusalem, weep not for me, but weep for yourselves, and for your children.
[29] For, behold, the days are coming, in the which they shall say, Blessed are the barren, and the wombs that never bare, and the paps which never gave suck.
[30] Then shall they begin to say to the mountains, Fall on us; and to the hills, Cover us.
[31] For if they do these things in a green tree, what shall be done in the dry?
[32] And there were also two other, malefactors, led with him to be put to death.
[33] And when they were come to the place, which is called Calvary, there they crucified him, and the malefactors, one on the right hand, and the other on the left.
[34] Then said Jesus, Father, forgive them; for they know not what they do. And they parted his raiment, and cast lots.
[35] And the people stood beholding. And the rulers also with them derided him, saying, He saved others; let him save himself, if he be Christ, the chosen of God.
[36] And the soldiers also mocked him, coming to him, and offering him vinegar,
[37] And saying, If you be the king of the Jews, save yourself.
[38] And a superscription also was written over him in letters of Greek, and Latin, and Hebrew, THIS IS THE KING OF THE JEWS.
[39] And one of the malefactors which were hanged railed on him, saying, If you be Christ, save yourself and us.
[40] But the other answering rebuked him, saying, Do you not fear God, seeing you are in the same condemnation?
[41] And we indeed justly; for we receive the due reward of our deeds: but this man has done nothing amiss.
[42] And he said to Jesus, Lord, remember me when you come into

your kingdom.

[43] And Jesus said to him, Truly I say to you, To day shall you be with me in paradise.

[44] And it was about the sixth hour, and there was a darkness over all the earth until the ninth hour.

[45] And the sun was darkened, and the veil of the temple was rent in the midst.

[46] And when Jesus had cried with a loud voice, he said, Father, into your hands I commend my spirit: and having said thus, he gave up the ghost.

[47] Now when the centurion saw what was done, he glorified God, saying, Certainly this was a righteous man.

[48] And all the people that came together to that sight, beholding the things which were done, smote their breasts, and returned.

[49] And all his acquaintance, and the women that followed him from Galilee, stood afar off, beholding these things.

[50] And, behold, there was a man named Joseph, a counseller; and he was a good man, and a just:

[51] (The same had not consented to the counsel and deed of them;) he was of Arimathaea, a city of the Jews: who also himself waited for the kingdom of God.

[52] This man went to Pilate, and begged the body of Jesus.

[53] And he took it down, and wrapped it in linen, and laid it in a sepulcher that was hewn in stone, wherein never man before was laid.

[54] And that day was the preparation, and the Sabbath drew on.

[55] And the women also, which came with him from Galilee, followed after, and beheld the sepulcher, and how his body was laid.

[56] And they returned, and prepared spices and ointments; and rested the Sabbath day according to the commandment.

Luke 24

[1] Now upon the first day of the week, very early in the morning, they came to the sepulcher, bringing the spices which they had prepared, and certain others with them.

[2] And they found the stone rolled away from the sepulcher.

[3] And they entered in, and found not the body of the Lord Jesus.

[4] And it came to pass, as they were much perplexed thereabout,

behold, two men stood by them in shining garments:
[5] And as they were afraid, and bowed down their faces to the earth, they said to them, Why seek you the living among the dead?
[6] He is not here, but is risen: remember how he spoke to you when he was yet in Galilee,
[7] Saying, The Son of man must be delivered into the hands of sinful men, and be crucified, and the third day rise again.
[8] And they remembered his words,
[9] And returned from the sepulcher, and told all these things to the eleven, and to all the rest.
[10] It was Mary Magdalene, and Joanna, and Mary the mother of James, and other women that were with them, which told these things to the apostles.
[11] And their words seemed to them as idle tales, and they believed them not.
[12] Then arose Peter, and ran to the sepulcher; and stooping down, he beheld the linen clothes laid by themselves, and departed, wondering in himself at that which was come to pass.
[13] And, behold, two of them went that same day to a village called Emmaus, which was from Jerusalem about threescore furlongs.
[14] And they talked together of all these things which had happened.
[15] And it came to pass, that, while they communed together and reasoned, Jesus himself drew near, and went with them.
[16] But their eyes were holden that they should not know him.
[17] And he said to them, What manner of communications are these that you have one to another, as you walk, and are sad?
[18] And the one of them, whose name was Cleopas, answering said to him, Are you only a stranger in Jerusalem, and have not known the things which are come to pass therein these days?
[19] And he said to them, What things? And they said to him, Concerning Jesus of Nazareth, which was a prophet mighty in deed and word before God and all the people:
[20] And how the chief priests and our rulers delivered him to be condemned to death, and have crucified him.
[21] But we trusted that it had been he which should have redeemed Israel: and beside all this, to day is the third day since these things were done.
[22] Yea, and certain women also of our company made us astonished, which were early at the sepulcher;

[23] And when they found not his body, they came, saying, that they had also seen a vision of angels, which said that he was alive.
[24] And certain of them which were with us went to the sepulcher, and found it even so as the women had said: but him they saw not.
[25] Then he said to them, O fools, and slow of heart to believe all that the prophets have spoken:
[26] Ought not Christ to have suffered these things, and to enter into his glory?
[27] And beginning at Moses and all the prophets, he expounded to them in all the scriptures the things concerning himself.
[28] And they drew near to the village, where they went: and he made as though he would have gone further.
[29] But they constrained him, saying, Abide with us: for it is toward evening, and the day is far spent. And he went in to tarry with them.
[30] And it came to pass, as he sat at meat with them, he took bread, and blessed it, and brake, and gave to them.
[31] And their eyes were opened, and they knew him; and he vanished out of their sight.
[32] And they said one to another, Did not our heart burn within us, while he talked with us by the way, and while he opened to us the scriptures?
[33] And they rose up the same hour, and returned to Jerusalem, and found the eleven gathered together, and them that were with them,
[34] Saying, The Lord is risen indeed, and has appeared to Simon.
[35] And they told what things were done in the way, and how he was known of them in breaking of bread.
[36] And as they thus spoke, Jesus himself stood in the midst of them, and said to them, Peace be to you.
[37] But they were terrified and frightened, and supposed that they had seen a spirit.
[38] And he said to them, Why are you troubled? and why do thoughts arise in your hearts?
[39] Behold my hands and my feet, that it is I myself: handle me, and see; for a spirit has not flesh and bones, as you see me have.
[40] And when he had thus spoken, he showed them his hands and his feet.
[41] And while they yet believed not for joy, and wondered, he said to them, Have you here any meat?
[42] And they gave him a piece of a broiled fish, and of a honeycomb.
[43] And he took it, and did eat before them.

[44] And he said to them, These are the words which I spoke to you, while I was yet with you, that all things must be fulfilled, which were written in the law of Moses, and in the prophets, and in the psalms, concerning me.
[45] Then opened he their understanding, that they might understand the scriptures,
[46] And said to them, Thus it is written, and thus it behoved Christ to suffer, and to rise from the dead the third day:
[47] And that repentance and remission of sins should be preached in his name among all nations, beginning at Jerusalem.
[48] And you are witnesses of these things.
[49] And, behold, I send the promise of my Father upon you: but tarry you in the city of Jerusalem, until you be endued with power from on high.
[50] And he led them out as far as to Bethany, and he lifted up his hands, and blessed them.
[51] And it came to pass, while he blessed them, he was parted from them, and carried up into heaven.
[52] And they worshipped him, and returned to Jerusalem with great joy:
[53] And were continually in the temple, praising and blessing God. Amen.

Documents used in this Work

All books used or quoted is this work are believed to be in the public domain. Modifications to texts have been made to make them more understandable to the modern U.S. English reader.

Gospel of Luke

The oldest manuscript with the start of the gospel, Papyrus Bodmer XIV (ca. 200 CE), proclaims that it is the euangelion kata Loukan, the Gospel according to Luke. This Luke has traditionally been identified as the one named in Philemon 24 as a co-worker of Paul.

It is thought that the same author who produced Luke also produced the book of Acts. There are statements or wording in Luke-Acts that have always been thought to support the idea that the author knew Paul. The passages stating "we" and are found in 16:10-17, 20:5-15, 21:1-18, and 27:1-28:16. For example, Acts 16:10-17 reads, "We set sail from Troas, making a straight run for Samothrace, and on the next day to Neapolis, and from there to Philippi, a leading city in that district of Macedonia and a Roman colony. We spent some time in that city. ... As we were going to the place of prayer, we met a slave girl... She began to follow Paul and us, shouting… " Another verse reads, "On the first day of the week when we gathered to break bread, Paul spoke to them because he was going to leave on the next day, and he kept on speaking until midnight. ... "

The distinction between Paul and "us" is odd. If the author were trying to connect himself with Paul falsely it seems that he would choose a more direct way of doing so rather than hinting at it. The author would ensure that the reader could not miss the point by emphasizing the point. The most probable conclusion is that Luke had travelled with Paul from time to time and knew him, but was not his best friend.

Other arguments are made concerning the authorship of Acts. The argument that the final voyage to Rome is an especially accurate depiction of sea travel can be met with the reply that the author (not Luke) had sailed that way at a later time or appropriated a sailor's account of the same. The differences between the theology of Luke and Paul are simply a consequence of the student or acquaintance going in his own way or thinking for himself.

The author of Luke did not know the contents of Paul's letters. This could speak to the fact that they actually were not acquainted that well, or it could actually point to the fact that Luke dates before ca. 100, after which the letters of Paul began to be collected, published, and canonized. Even though there are "disharmonies" between Luke and some of Paul's letter, such as Galatians, the vast similarities allow a conclusion that Luke knew Paul and Luke's Gospel was written before 100 A.D.

The Arabic Infancy Gospel

is found in a body of collected books known as the New Testament apocrypha. As the name suggests, The Arabic Infancy Gospel concerns the infancy of Jesus, and the text was written in Arabic. It is was compiled in the sixth century, and was based on the Infancy Gospel of Thomas, and Protevangelium of James. It consists of three parts:
The birth of Jesus - based on the Protevangelium of James
Miracles during the Flight into Egypt - seemingly based on local oral traditions, The miracles of Jesus as a boy - based on the Infancy Gospel of Thomas.

It contains a number of embellishments on the earlier text, however, including a diaper of Jesus that heals people, sweat of Jesus that turns into a healing balm, Jesus curing leprosy, and Jesus dyeing cloth various colors using only indigo colored dye. The document also reports an odd encounter between Jesus and Judas Iscariot, along with the thieves with whom he is later crucified.

According to textual criticism, the text was originally written in Syriac, but was translated into Arabic around the time that Christianity began to spread into the Arabian Peninsula.

The translation used here: The Arabic Infancy Gospel, translated by Alexander Walker. From <u>Ante-Nicene Fathers</u>, Vol. 8. Edited by Alexander Roberts, James Donaldson, and A. Cleveland Coxe. (Buffalo, NY: Christian Literature Publishing Co., 1886.)

Infancy Gospel of Thomas

The Infancy Gospel of Thomas may have been written in eastern Syria, the location of the Thomas traditions, although attribution to Thomas may be a later development to gain respect for the manuscript. The original language of the document may have been Syriac.

The Infancy Gospel of Thomas purports to describe the activities and history of Jesus in his youth and relates the miraculous deeds of Jesus before he turned twelve. Jesus instructs his teachers in the mysteries of the Hebrew alphabet, which Jewish mystics believe holds the power of the spoken word of God (See The Third Book of Enoch). Jesus astounds his family and playmates with miracles. This document contains the tale of the twelve sparrows which Jesus, at the age of five, fashioned from clay on the Sabbath day. When Jesus brought the clay to life he was accused of unlawful deeds on the Sabbath. This begs the question, "If someone can bring clay birds to life, what makes one think the same person could not kill if angered?"

The earliest manuscript is a sixth century one in Syriac. There was another version found written in Greek. The longer Greek version may be more accurate to the original text.

There is nothing particularly Christian about the stories attributed to Jesus; rather, the stories elaborate on the missing years of Jesus with reference to Hellenistic legend and pious imagination.

There is no certainty as to when the stories of the Infancy Gospel of Thomas began to be written down. Thus, while our present Infancy Gospel of Thomas may have been expanded over time, the original stories may have been written as early as the middle of the second century.

The translation used here is "The Infancy Gospel of Thomas," the
 Latin Text
From "The Apocryphal New Testament"
M.R. James-Translation and Notes
Oxford: Clarendon Press, 1924

Book of James, or PROTEVANGELIUM

Origen mentions the Book of James (and the Gospel of Peter) as stating that the ' brethren of the Lord' were sons of Joseph by a former wife. This is the first mention of it, and shows us that the book is as old as the second century. The text shows additions or alterations. Difficulty is caused by the sudden introduction of Joseph as the narrator in ch. xviii. 2 sqq. We cannot be sure whether this means that a fragment of a 'Joseph-apocryphon' has been introduced at this point; or, if so, how far it extends. We are sure, from a sentence of Clement of Alexandria, that some story of a midwife being present at the Nativity was current in the second century.
We have the book in the original Greek and in several oriental versions, the oldest of which is the Syriac. We know there was a Latin version because a book identifiable with ours in Latin is condemned in the Gelasian Decree.
In the early chapters of the Protevangelium the Old Testament is extensively drawn upon and imitated. However, it is obvious that the author was not Jewish and not familiar with Jewish life or language.

Joseph Lumpkin

The translation used is "BOOK OF JAMES, OR PROTEVANGELIUM"
From "The Apocryphal New Testament"
M.R. James-Translation and Notes
Oxford: Clarendon Press, 1924

The History of Joseph the Carpenter

The History of Joseph the Carpenter is one of the texts within the New Testament apocrypha concerned with the period of Jesus' life before he was 12. The most interesting thing about the story is that it is narrated by Jesus himself in a narrative told to his disciples while they were on the Mount of olives.

The story in one concerning the life of Joseph, his stepfather. In it, Jesus agrees with Mary's continued virginity. The text explains the relationship between Jesus and his brothers and sisters by stating that Joseph had four sons named Judas, Justus, James, and Simon and two daughters called Assia and Lydia by a previous marriage.

At age 90, after the death of his first wife, Joseph is given charge of the twelve year old virgin Mary. She lives in his household raising his youngest son James 'the less' along with Judas, until the time she is to be married at age 14.

We must remember that marriage at that time was not like it is today. Marriage had more to do with consummation than living arrangement. Mary may have lived with Joseph at age 12, but they would not have been considered married until they had sex. The exception would be when a man decided to keep a woman as his wife but keep her virginity.

After this basic background, the text proceeds to paraphrase the Gospel of James, stopping at the point of Jesus' birth. The text states that Joseph was miraculously blessed with mental and physical youth, dying at the age of 111.

Joseph's death takes up approximately half of the work. At the conclusion of the text, Jesus affirms that Mary remained a virgin throughout her days by addressing her as "my mother, virgin undefiled." The words "virginity" and "undefiled" in this context must relate to sexual relations and not to the traumas of childbirth.

The Text says "And the holy apostles have preserved this conversation, and have left it written down in the library at Jerusalem."

There are indications that the text was written in Egypt in the 5th century AD. Two versions survive, one in Coptic, the other in Arabic, with the Coptic version likely being the original. Much of the text is based on material in the Gospel of James.

The source used here is, The History of Joseph The Carpenter, Translated by Alexander Walker. From <u>Ante-Nicene Fathers</u>, Vol. 8. Edited by Alexander Roberts, James Donaldson, and A. Cleveland Coxe. (Buffalo, NY: Christian Literature Publishing Co., 1886.)

The Life of Saint Issa

In 1894 Nicolas Notovitch published a book called The Unknown Life of Christ. He was a Russian doctor who journeyed extensively throughout Afghanistan, India, and Tibet.

During one of his jouneys he was visiting Leh, the capital of Ladak, near the buddhist convent Himis. He had an accident that resulted in his leg being broken. This gave him the unscheduled opportunity to stay awhile at the Himis convent.

While convalescing, Notovitch was told of an ancient record of the life of Jesus known as "The Life of St. Issa."

Notovitch enlisted a member of his party to translate the Tibetan volumes while he carefully noted each verse in the back pages of his journal.

When he returned to the western world there was much controversy as to the authenticity of the document. He was accused of creating a hoax and was ridiculed as an imposter. In his defense he encouraged a scientific expedition to prove the original Tibetan documents existed.

Archibald Douglas and Max Müller recognized Notovitch's work as fraudulent, although it was not immediately clear (to Müller, at least) what the source of the fraud was. Perhaps the best thing is to read excerpts from the original, absolutely scathing account, from the Nineteenth Century academic journal itself (long out of copyright):

(from The Nineteenth Century, 39 (January-June 1896) pp. 667-677
THE CHIEF LAMA OF HIMIS ON THE ALLEGED 'UNKNOWN LIFE OF CHRIST')

"I was resident in Madras during the whole of last year, and did not expect to have an opportunity of investigating the facts respecting the Unknown Life of Christ at so early a date. Removing to the North-West Provinces in the early part of the present year, I | 668 found that it would be practicable during the three months of the University vacation to travel through Kashmir to Ladakh, following the route taken by M. Notovitch, and to spend sufficient time at the monastery at Himis to learn the truth on this important question. I may here mention, en passant, that I did not find it necessary to break even a little finger, much less a leg, in order to gain admittance to Himis Monastery, where I am now staying for a few days, enjoying the kind hospitality of the Chief Lama (or Abbot), the same gentleman who, according to M. Notovitch, nursed him so kindly under the painful circumstances connected with his memorable visit.

Coming to Himis with an entirely open mind on the question, and in no way biassed by the formation of a previous judgment, I was fully prepared to find that M. Notovitch's narrative was correct, and to congratulate him on his marvellous discovery. One matter of detail, entirely unconnected with the genuineness of the Russian traveller's literary discovery, shook my faith slightly in the general veracity of the discoverer....

...I will now call attention to several leading statements in M. Notovitch's book, all of which will be found to be definitely contradicted in the document signed by the Chief Superior of Himis Monastery, and sealed with his official seal. This statement I have sent to Professor Max Müller for inspection, together with the subjoined declaration of Mr. Joldan, an educated Tibetan gentleman, to whose able assistance I am deeply indebted.

A more patient and painstaking interpreter could not be found, nor one better fitted for the task.

The extracts from M. Notovitch's book were slowly translated to the Lama, and were thoroughly understood by him. The questions and answers were fully discussed at two lengthy interviews before being prepared as a document for signature, and when so prepared were carefully translated again to the Lama by Mr. Joldan, and discussed by him with that gentleman, and with a venerable monk who appeared to act as the Lama's private secretary.

I may here say that I have the fullest confidence in the veracity and honesty of this old and respected Chief Lama, who appears to be held in the highest esteem, not only among Buddhists, but by all Europeans who have made his acquaintance. As he says, he has nothing whatever to gain by the concealment of facts, or by any departure from the truth.

His indignation at the manner in which he has been travestied by the ingenious author was of far too genuine a character to be feigned, and I was much interested when, in our final interview, he asked me if in Europe there existed no means of punishing a person | 670 who told such untruths. I could only reply that literary honesty is taken for granted to such an extent in Europe, that literary forgery of the nature committed by M. Notovitch could not, I believed, be punished by our criminal law.

With reference to M. Notovitch's declaration that he is going to Himis to verify the statements made in his book, I would take the liberty of earnestly advising him, if he does so, to disguise himself at least as effectually as on the occasion of his former visit. M. Notovitch will not find himself popular at Himis, and might not gain admittance, even on the pretext of having another broken leg.

The following extracts have been carefully selected from the Unknown Life of Christ, and are such that on their truth or falsehood may be said to depend the value of M. Notovitch's story.

After describing at length the details of a dramatic performance, said to have been witnessed in the courtyard of Himis Monastery, M. Notovitch writes:

After having crossed the courtyard and ascended a staircase lined with prayer-wheels, we passed through two rooms encumbered with idols, and came out upon the terrace, where I seated myself on a bench opposite the venerable Lama, whose eyes flashed with intelligence (p. 110).

(This extract is important as bearing on the question of identification; see Answers 1 and 2 of the Lama's statement: and it may here be remarked that the author's account of the approach to the Chief Lama's reception room and balcony is accurate.) Then follows a long résumé of a conversation on religious matters, in the course of which the Abbot is said to have made the following observations amongst others:

We have a striking example of this (Nature-worship) in the ancient Egyptians, who worshipped animals, trees, and stones, the winds and the rain (p. 114).

The Assyrians, in seeking the way which should lead them to the feet of the Creator, turned their eyes to the stars (p. 115).

Perhaps the people of Israel have demonstrated in a more flagrant manner than any other, man's love for the concrete (p. 115).

The name of Issa is held in great respect by the Buddhists, but little is known about him save by the Chief Lamas who have read the scrolls relating to his life (p. 120).

The documents brought from India to Nepal, and from Nepal to Tibet, concerning Issa's existence, are written in the Pâli language, and are now in Lassa; but a copy in our language----that is, the Tibetan----exists in this convent (p. 123).

Two days later I sent by a messenger to the Chief Lama a present comprising an alarm, a watch, and a thermometer (p. 125).

We will now pass on to the description given by the author of his re-entry into the monastery with a broken leg:

I was carried with great care to the best of their chambers, and placed on a bed of soft materials, near to which stood a prayer-wheel. All this took place under the immediate surveillance of the Superior, who affectionately pressed the hand I offered him in gratitude for his kindness (p. 127).

While a youth of the convent kept in motion the prayer-wheel near my bed, the venerable Superior entertained me with endless stories, constantly taking my alarm and watch from their cases, and asking me questions as to their uses, and the way they should be worked. At last, acceding to my earnest entreaties, he ended by bringing me two large bound volumes, with leaves yellowed by time, and from them he read to me, in the Tibetan language, the biography of Issa, which I carefully noted in my carnet de voyage, as my interpreter translated what he said (p. 128).

This last extract is in a sense the most important of all, as will be seen when it is compared with Answers 3, 4, and 5 in the statement of the Chief Superior of Himis Monastery. That statement I now append. The original is in the hands of Professor Max Müller, as I have said, as also is the appended declaration of Mr. Joldan, of Leh.

The statement of the Lama, if true----and there is every reason to believe it to be so----disposes once and for ever of M. Notovitch's claim to have discovered a Life of Issa among the Buddhists of

Ladakh. My questions to the Lama were framed briefly, and with as much simplicity as possible, so that there might be no room for any mistake or doubt respecting the meaning of these questions.

My interpreter. Mr. Joldan, tells me that he was most careful to translate the Lama's answers verbally and literally, to avoid all possible misapprehension. The statement is as follows:

Question 1. You are the Chief Lama (or Abbot) of Himis Monastery?

Answer 1. Yes.

Question 2. For how long have you acted continuously in that capacity?

Answer 2. For fifteen years.

Question 3. Have you or any of the Buddhist monks in this monastery ever seen here a European with an injured leg?

Answer 3. No, not during the last fifteen years. If any sahib suffering from serious injury had stayed in this monastery it would have been my duty to report the matter to the Wazir of Leh. I have never had occasion to do so.

Question 4. Have you or any of your monks ever shown any Life of Issa to any sahib, and allowed him to copy and translate the same?

Answer 4. There is no such book in the monastery, and during my term of office no sahib has been allowed to copy or translate any of the manuscripts in the monastery.

Question 5. Are you aware of the existence of any book in any of the Buddhist monasteries of Tibet bearing on the life of Issa?

Answer 5. I have been for forty-two years a Lama, and am well acquainted with all the well-known Buddhist books and manuscripts, and I have never heard of one which mentions the name of Issa, and it is my firm and honest belief that none such exists. I have inquired of our principal Lamas in other monasteries of

Tibet, and they are not acquainted with any books or manuscripts which mention the name of Issa.

Question 6. M. Nicolas Notovitch, a Russian gentleman who visited your monastery between seven and eight years ago, states that you discussed with him the religions of the ancient Egyptians, Assyrians, and the people of Israel.

Answer 6. I know nothing whatever about the Egyptians, Assyrians, and the people of Israel, and do not know anything of their religions whatsoever. I have never mentioned these peoples to any sahib.

[I was reading M. Notovitch's book to the Lama at the time, and he burst out with, 'Sun, sun, sun, manna mi dug!' which is Tibetan for, 'Lies, lies, lies, nothing but lies!' I have read this to him as part of the statement, which he is to sign----as his deliberate opinion of M. Notovitch's book. He appears perfectly satisfied on the matter. J. A. D.]...

Regarded, then, in the light of a work of the imagination, M. Notovitch's book fails to please, because it does not present that most fascinating feature of fiction, a close semblance of probability.

And yet, if I am rightly informed, the French version has gone through eleven editions; so M. Notovitch's effort of imagination has found, doubtless, a substantial reward. In face of the evidence adduced, we must reject the theory generously put forward by Professor Max Müller, that M. Notovitch was the victim of a cunning 'hoax ' on the part of the Buddhist monks of Himis.

...I do not believe that the venerable monk who presides over Himis Monastery would have consented to the practice of such a deception, and I do not think that any of the monks are capable of carrying out such a deception successfully. The departures from truth, on other points, which can be proved against M. Notovitch render such a solution highly improbable....

...I have visited Himis, and have endeavoured by patient and impartial inquiry to find out the truth respecting M. Notovitch's remarkable story, with the result that, while I have not found one single fact to support his statements, all the weight of evidence goes to disprove them beyond all shadow of doubt. It is certain that no such passages as M. Notovitch pretends to have translated exist in the monastery of Himis, and therefore it is impossible that he could have 'faithfully reproduced' the same.

The following "postscript" was amended to the article by Max Müller himself:

"...After having read, however, the foregoing article by Professor Douglas, I feel bound most humbly to apologize to the excellent Lamas of that monastery for having thought them capable of such frivolity. After the complete refutation, or, I should rather say, annihilation, of M. Notovitch by Professor A. Douglas, there does not seem to be any further necessity----nay, any excuse----for trying to spare the feelings of that venturesome Russian traveler. He was not hoaxed, but he tried to hoax us. Mr. Douglas has sent me the original papers, containing the depositions of the Chief Priest of the Monastery of him is and of his interpreter, and I gladly testify that they entirely agree with the extracts given in the article, and are signed and sealed by the Chief Lama and by Mr. Joldan, formerly Postmaster of Ladakh, who acted as interpreter between the priests and Professor A. Douglas. The papers are dated Himis Monastery, Little Tibet, June 3, 1894.

I ought perhaps to add that I cannot claim any particular merit in having proved the Vie inconnue de Jésus-Christ----that is, the Life of Christ taken from MSS. in the monasteries of Tibet----to be a mere fiction. I doubt whether any Sanskrit or Pâli scholar, in fact any serious student of Buddhism, was taken in by M. Notovitch. One might as well look for the waters of Jordan in the Brahmaputra as. for a Life of Christ in Tibet.

F. Max Müller.

November 15, 1895."

Another one of his skeptics was Swami Abhedananda. Abhedananda, who journeyed into the arctic region of the Himalayas, determined to find a copy of the Himis manuscript or to expose the fraud. His book of travels, entitled Kashmir O Tibetti, tells of a visit to the Himis gonpa and includes a Bengali translation of two hundred twenty-four verses essentially the same as the Notovitch text. Abhedananda was thereby convinced of the authenticity of the Issa legend.

In 1925, another Russian named Nicholas Roerich arrived at Himis. Roerich, was a philosopher and a distinguished scientist. He apparently saw the same documents as Notovitch and Abhedananda. And he recorded in his own travel diary the same legend of St. Issa. Speaking of Issa, Roerich quotes legends which have the estimated antiquity of many centuries.

... He passed his time in several ancient cities of India such as Benares. All loved him because Issa dwelt in peace with Vaishas and Shudras whom he instructed and helped. But the Brahmins and Kshatriyas told him that Brahma forbade those to approach who were created out of his womb and feet. The Vaishas were allowed to listen to the Vedas only on holidays and the Shudras were forbidden not only to be present at the reading of the Vedas, but could not even look at them.

Issa said that man had filled the temples with his abominations. In order to pay homage to metals and stones, man sacrificed his fellows in whom dwells a spark of the Supreme Spirit. Man demeans those who labor by the sweat of their brows, in order to gain the good will of the sluggard who sits at the lavishly set board. But they who deprive their brothers of the common blessing shall be themselves stripped of it.

Vaishas and Shudras were struck with astonishment and asked what they could perform. Issa bade them "Worship not the idols. Do not consider yourself first. Do not humiliate your neighbor. Help the poor. Sustain the feeble. Do evil to no one. Do not covet that which you do not possess and which is possessed by others."

Many, learning of such words, decided to kill Issa. But Issa,

forewarned, departed from this place by night.
Afterward, Issa went into Nepal and into the Himalayan mountains....

"Well, perform for us a miracle," demanded the servitors of the Temple. Then Issa replied to them: "Miracles made their appearance from the very day when the world was created. He who cannot behold them is deprived of the greatest gift of life. But woe to you, enemies of men, woe to you, if you await that He should attest his power by miracle."

Issa taught that men should not strive to behold the Eternal Spirit with one's own eyes but to feel it with the heart, and to become a pure and worthy soul....

"Not only shall you not make human offerings, but you must not slaughter animals, because all is given for the use of man. Do not steal the goods of others, because that would be usurpation from your near one. Do not cheat, that you may in turn not be cheated.
"Beware, you, who divert men from the true path and who fill the people with superstitions and prejudices, who blind the vision of the seeing ones, and who preach subservience to material things."
Issa taught: "Do not seek straight paths in darkness, possessed by fear. But gather force and support each other. He who supports his neighbor strengthens himself

"I tried to revive the laws of Moses in the hearts of the people. And I say to you that you do not understand their true meaning because they do not teach revenge but forgiveness. But the meaning of these laws is distorted."

Then the ruler sent to Issa his disguised servants that they should watch his actions and report to him about his words to the people. "You just man, "said the disguised servant of the ruler of Jerusalem approaching Issa, "Teach us, should we fulfill the will of Caesar or await the approaching deliverance?" But Issa, recognizing the disguised servants, said, "I did not foretell to you that you would be delivered from Caesar; but I said that the soul which was immersed in sin would be delivered from sin."

At this time, an old woman approached the crowd, but was pushed back. Then Issa said, "Reverence Woman, mother of the universe,' in her lies the truth of creation. She is the foundation of all that is good and beautiful. She is the source of life and death. Upon her depends the existence of man, because she is the sustenance of his labors. She gives birth to you in travail, she watches over your growth. Bless her. Honor her. Defend her. Love your wives and honor them, because tomorrow they shall be mothers, and later-progenitors of a whole race. Their love ennobles man, soothes the embittered heart and tames the beast. Wife and mother, they are the adornments of the universe."

"As light divides itself from darkness, so does woman possess the gift to divide in man good intent from the thought of evil. Your best thoughts must belong to woman. Gather from them your moral strength, which you must possess to sustain your near ones. Do not humiliate her, for therein you will humiliate yourselves. And all which you will do to mother, to wife, to widow or to another woman in sorrow, that shall you also do for the Spirit."
So taught Issa; but the ruler Pilate ordered one of his servants to make accusation against him.
Said Issa: "Not far from here is the time when by the Highest Will the people will become purified and united into one family."
And then turning to the ruler, he said, "Why demean your dignity and teach your subordinates to live in deceit when even without this you could also have had the means of accusing an innocent one?"
From another version of the legend, Roerich quotes fragments of thought and evidence of the miraculous.

Near Lhasa was a temple of teaching with a wealth of manuscripts. Jesus was to acquaint himself with them. Meng-ste, a great sage of all the East, was in this temple.

Finally Jesus reached a mountain pass and in the chief city of Ladak, Leh, he was joyously accepted by monks and people of the lower class. And Jesus taught in the monasteries and in the bazaars (the market places); wherever the simple people gathered, there he taught.

Not far from this place lived a woman whose son had died and she brought him to Jesus. And in the presence of a multitude, Jesus laid his hand on the child, and the child rose healed. And many brought their children and Jesus laid his hands upon them, healing them.

Among the Ladakis, Jesus passed many days, teaching them. And they loved him and when the time of his departure came they sorrowed as children.

Letter of Herod To Pilate The Governor

And

Letter of Pilate To Herod

These letters connect Roman history with the death of Jesus at Jerusalem. Two copies were found. The letters located in the British Museum were written in Syriac and dated to the sixth or seventh century A.D. Those located in a Paris museum are written in Greek. The letter of Herod to Pilate The Governor gives us a detailed overview of what befell Herod after the crucifixion of Christ.

The letter written by Pilate the Governor of Judea is in response to the letter written by Herod in which Herod describes all the ills that have befallen him and his household since the crucifixion of Christ. Pilate speaks of the many supernatural occurrences he himself had confirmed concerning the death and subsequent resurrection of Jesus.

The Epistle of Pontius Pilate

The Epistle of Pontius Pilate was written as a report to Tiberius Caesar, Emperor of Rome concerning the crucifixion of Jesus. The Epistle, speaks of supernatural events connected with the death of Christ.

The Report of Pontius Pilate to Tiberius

The Report of Pontius Pilate to Tiberus was regarded as genuine by the early church fathers. It consists of a letter written by Pontius Pilate, Procurator of Judea, to Tiberius Caesar, the Emperor of Rome. The letter goes into great detail about the circumstances of the crucifixion of Christ and events immediately following Christ's death. In this letter, Pontius Pilate, an eyewitness to these events, relates many of the miracles performed by Christ. But, most importantly, it describes in detail the supernatural happenings at the time Christ was crucified.

Letters Between Pilate and Seneca

Historically, little is known about Pontius Pilate. He was Procurator of Judaea from A.D. 26 to 36 and was recalled in the year in which the Emperor Tiberius died.

He was recalled because he was considered a failure in the position of Procurator. Although history does not give us much to go on, it is known that men caught in this position usually commit suicide because to do so was considered an honorable way out so their family could inherit their property. If prosecuted, all possessions would have been confiscated by the state.

The activities of John the Baptist and Jesus of Nazareth took place towards the end of the first half of his term of office. There are references to him in the Jewish historian Josephus and the Jewish philosopher Philo of Alexandria, and there are the accounts of the trial of Jesus, which are offered by the writers of the Gospels.

The 'Letters' were addressed by Pilate to his friend Lucius Annaeus Seneca the younger, who was later to be the tutor of the young Emperor Nero (and to commit suicide at his order), and who is known to posterity as a liberal philosopher and writer of moral essays and tragedies which few men read. It appears from the 'Letters' that even in his early manhood Seneca was interested in the difficult problem which Pilate had to handle: the problem of a militant Power ruling a subject people whose religion not only was the prime object of its loyalty, but actually rejected the idea of a foreign over-lordship and its symbols.

The letters give insight into the political climate and how Pilate approached his task as Procurator. He confronts the uprisings of John the Baptist and Jesus with the same attitude and conclusion.

It is for the reader to say how far they may be regarded as authentic; how far, that is, they can be accepted as an account of the period which is not only credible in itself, but at important points more credible than the existing narratives.

Letters of Pontius Pilate, written during his Governorship of Judaea to his friend Seneca in Rome, Edited by W. P. CROZIER (formerly Scholar of Trinity College, Oxford), JONATHAN CAPE, Thirty Bedford Square, London. First Published 1928

Appendix

THE ARABIC GOSPEL OF THE INFANCY OF THE SAVIOUR

In the name of the Father, and the Son, and the Holy Spirit, one God.

With the help and favor of the Most High we begin to write a book of the miracles of our Lord and Master and Savior Jesus Christ, which is called the Gospel of the Infancy: in the peace of the Lord. Amen.

1. We find what follows in the book of Joseph the high priest, who lived in the time of Christ. Some say that he is Caiaphas. He has said that Jesus spoke, and, indeed, when He was lying in His cradle said to Mary His mother: I am Jesus, the Son of God, the Logos, whom you have brought forth, as the Angel Gabriel announced to you; and my Father has sent me for the salvation of the world.

2. In the three hundred and ninth year of the era of Alexander, Augustus put forth an edict, that every man should be enrolled in his native place. Joseph therefore arose, and taking Mary his spouse, went away to (3) Jerusalem, and came to Bethlehem, to be enrolled along with his family in his native city. And having come to a cave, Mary told Joseph that the time of the birth was at hand, and that she could not go into the city; but, said she, let us go into this cave. This took place at sunset. And Joseph went out in haste to go for a woman to be near her. When, therefore, he was busy about that, he saw a Hebrew old woman belonging to Jerusalem, and said: Come here, my good woman, and go into this cave, in which there is a woman near her time.

3. Therefore, after sunset, the old woman, and Joseph with her, came to the cave, and they both went in. And, behold, it was filled with lights more beautiful than the gleaming of lamps and candles, (4) and more splendid than the light of the sun. The child, enwrapped in swaddling clothes, was sucking the breast of the Lady Mary His mother, being placed in a stall. And when both were wondering at

this light, the old woman asks the Lady Mary: Are you the mother of this Child? And when the Lady Mary gave her assent, she said: You are not at all like the daughters of Eve. The Lady Mary said: As my son has no equal among children, so his mother has no equal among women. The old woman replied: My mistress, I came to get payment; I have been for a long time affected with palsy. Our mistress the Lady Mary said to her: Place your hands upon the child. And the old woman did so, and was immediately cured. Then she went forth, saying: Henceforth I will be the attendant and servant of this child all the days of my life.

4. Then came shepherds; and when they had lighted a fire, and were rejoicing greatly, there appeared to them the hosts of heaven praising and celebrating God Most High. And while the shepherds were doing the same, the cave was at that time made like a temple of the upper (heavenly) world, since both heavenly and earthly voices glorified and magnified God on account of the birth of the Lord Christ. And when that old Hebrew woman saw the manifestation of those miracles, she thanked God, saying: I give You thanks, O God, the God of Israel, because my eyes have seen the birth of the Savior of the world.

5. Then the time of circumcision on the eighth day was at hand and the child was to be circumcised according to the law. Therefore they circumcised Him in the cave. And the old Hebrew woman took the piece of skin; but some say that she took the navel-string, and laid it past in a jar of old oil of nard. And she had a son, a dealer in ointments, and she gave it to him, saying: See that you do not sell this jar of ointment of nard (Himalayan Spikenard), even although three hundred denarii should be offered you for it. And this is that jar which Mary the sinner bought and poured upon the head and feet of our Lord Jesus Christ, which thereafter she wiped with the hair of her head. Ten days after, they took Him to Jerusalem; and on the fortieth day after His birth they carried Him into the temple, and set Him before the Lord, and offered sacrifices for Him, according to the command-meet of the law of Moses, which is: Every male that opens the womb shall be called the holy of God.

6. Then old Simeon saw Him shining like a pillar of light, when the Lady Mary, His virgin mother, rejoicing over Him, was carrying Him

in her arms. And angels, praising Him, stood round Him in a circle, like life guards standing by a king. Simeon therefore went up in haste to the Lady Mary, and, with hands stretched out before her, said to the Lord Christ: Now, O my Lord, let Your servant depart in peace, according to Your word; for my eyes have seen Your compassion, which You have prepared for the salvation of all peoples, a light to all nations, and glory to Your people Israel. Hanna also, a prophetess, was present, and came up, giving thanks to God, and calling the Lady Mary blessed.

7. And it came to pass, when the Lord Jesus was born at Bethlehem of Judaea, in the time of King Herod, behold, magi came from the east to Jerusalem, as Zeraduscht (Zarathustra / Zoroaster) had predicted; and there were with them gifts, gold, and frankincense, and myrrh. And they adored Him, and presented to Him their gifts. Then the Lady Mary took one of the swaddling-bands, and, on account of the smallness of her means, gave it to them; and they received it from her with the greatest marks of honor. And in the same hour there appeared to them an angel in the form of that star which had before guided them on their journey; and they went away, following the guidance of its light, until they arrived in their own country.

8. And their kings and chief men came together to them, asking what they had seen or done, how they had gone and come back, what they had brought with them. And they showed them that swathing-cloth which the Lady Mary had given them. Therefore they celebrated a feast, and, according to their custom, lighted a fire and worshipped it, and threw that swathing-cloth into it; and the fire laid hold of it, and enveloped it. And when the fire had gone out, they took out the swathing-cloth exactly as it had been before, just as if the fire had not touched it. Therefore they began to kiss it, and to put it on their heads and their eyes, saying: This truly is the truth without doubt. Assuredly it is a great thing that the fire was not able to burn or destroy it. Then they took it, and with the greatest honor laid it up among their treasures.

9. And when Herod saw that the magi had left him, and not come back to him, he summoned the priests and the wise men, and said to them: Show me where Christ is to be born. And when they answered, In Bethlehem of Judaea, he began to think of putting the Lord Jesus

Christ to death. Then appeared an angel of the Lord to Joseph in his sleep, and said: Rise, take the boy and His mother, and go away into Egypt. (7) He rose, therefore, towards cockcrow, and set out.

10. While he is reflecting how he is to set about his journey, morning came upon him after he had gone a very little way. And now he was approaching a great city, in which there was an idol, to which the other idols and gods of the Egyptians offered gifts and vows. And there stood before this idol a priest ministering to him, who, as often as Satan spoke from that idol, reported it to the inhabitants of Egypt and its territories. This priest had a son, three years old, beset by several demons; and he made many speeches and utterances; and when the demons seized him, he tore his clothes, and remained naked, and threw stones at the people. And there was a place of healing in that city dedicated to that idol. And when Joseph and the Lady Mary had come to the city, and had turned aside into that place of healing, the citizens were very much afraid; and all the chief men and the priests of the idols came together to that idol, and said to it: What agitation and commotion is this that has arisen in our land? The idol answered them: A God has come here in secret, who is God indeed; nor is any god besides Him worthy of divine worship, because He is truly the Son of God. And when this land became aware of His presence, it trembled at His arrival, and was moved and shaken; and we are exceedingly afraid from the greatness of His power. And in the same hour that idol fell down, and at its fall, all inhabitants of Egypt and others, ran together.

11. And the son of the priest, his usual disease having come upon him, entered the place of healing, and there came upon Joseph and the Lady Mary, from whom all others had fled. The Lady Mary had washed the cloths of the Lord Christ, and had spread them over some wood. That demoniac boy, therefore, came and took one of the cloths, and put it on his head. Then the demons, fleeing in the shape of ravens and serpents, began to go forth out of his mouth. The boy, being immediately healed at the command of the Lord Christ, began to praise God, and then to give thanks to the Lord who had healed him. And when his father saw him restored to health, My son, said he, what has happened to you? and by what means have you been healed? The son answered: When the demons had thrown me on the ground, I went into the place of healing, and there I found an august

woman with a boy, whose newly-washed cloths she had thrown upon some wood: one of these I took up and put upon my head, and the demons left me and fled. At this the father rejoiced greatly, and said: My son, it is possible that this boy is the Son of the living God who created the heavens and the earth: for when he came over to us, the idol was broken, and all the gods fell, and perished by the power of his magnificence.

12. Here was fulfilled the prophecy which says, Out of Egypt have I called my son. (1) Joseph indeed, and Mary, when they heard that that idol had fallen down and perished, trembled, and were afraid. Then they said: When we were in the land of Israel, Herod thought to put Jesus to death, and on that account slew all the children of Bethlehem and its confines; and there is no doubt that the Egyptians, as soon as they have heard that this idol has been broken, will burn us with fire. (2)

13. Going out from there, they came to a place where there were robbers who had plundered several men of their baggage and clothes, and had bound them. Then the robbers heard a great noise, like the noise of a magnificent king going out of his city with his army, and his chariots and his drums; and at this the robbers were terrified, and left all their plunder. And their captives rose up, loosed each other's bonds, recovered their baggage, and went away. And when they saw Joseph and Mary coming up to the place, they said to them: Where is that king, at the hearing of the magnificent sound of whose approach the robbers have left us, so that we have escaped safe? Joseph answered them: He will come behind us.

14. Thereafter they came into another city, where there was a demoniac woman whom Satan, accursed and rebellious, had beset, when on one occasion she had gone out by night for water. She could neither bear clothes, nor live in a house; and as often as they tied her up with chains and leather straps, she broke them, and fled naked into waste places; and, standing in cross-roads and cemeteries, she kept throwing stones at people, and brought very heavy calamities upon her friends. And when the Lady Mary saw her, she pitied her; and upon this Satan immediately left her, and fled away in the form of a young man, saying: Woe to me from you, Mary, and from your son. So that woman was cured of her torment, and being restored to

her senses, she blushed on account of her nakedness; and shunning the sight of men, went home to her friends. And after she put on her clothes, she gave an account of the matter to her father and her friends; and as they were the chief men of the city, they received the Lady Mary and Joseph with the greatest honor and hospitality.

15. On the day after, being supplied by them with provision for their journey, they went away, and on the evening of that day arrived at another town, in which they were celebrating a marriage; but, by the arts of accursed Satan and the work of enchanters, the bride had become dumb, and could not speak a word. And after the Lady Mary entered the town, carrying her son the Lord Christ, that dumb bride saw her, and stretched out her hands towards the Lord Christ, and drew Him to her, and took Him into her arms, and held Him close and kissed Him, and leaned over Him, moving His body back and forwards. Immediately the knot of her tongue was loosened, and her ears were opened; and she gave thanks and praise to God, because He had restored her to health. And that night the inhabitants of that town exulted with joy, and thought that God and His angels had come down to them.

16. There they remained three days, being held in great honor, and living splendidly. Thereafter, being supplied by them with provision for their journey, they went away and came to another city, in which, because it was very populous, they thought of passing the night. And there was in that city an excellent woman: and once, when she had gone to the river to bathe, lo, accursed Satan, in the form of a serpent, had leapt upon her, and twisted himself round her belly; and as often as night came on, he tyrannically tormented her. This woman, seeing the mistress the Lady Mary, and the child, the Lord Christ, in her bosom, was struck with a longing for Him, and said to the mistress the Lady Mary: O mistress, give me this child, that I may carry him, and kiss him. She therefore gave Him to the woman; and when He was brought to her, Satan let her go, and fled and left her, nor did the woman ever see him after that day. Therefore all who were present praised God Most High, and that woman bestowed on them liberal gifts.

17. On the day after, the same woman took scented water to wash the Lord Jesus; and after she had washed Him, she took the water with

which she had done it, and poured part of it upon a girl who was living there, whose body was white with leprosy, and washed her with it. And as soon as this was done, the girl was cleansed from her leprosy. And the towns-people said: There is no doubt that Joseph and Mary and that boy are gods, not men. And when they were getting ready to go away from them, the girl who had labored under the leprosy came up to them, and asked them to let her go with them.

18. When they had given her permission, she went with them. And afterwards they came to a city, in which was the castle of a most illustrious prince, who kept a house for the entertainment of strangers. They turned into this place; and the girl went away to the prince's wife; and she found her weeping and sorrowful, and she asked why she was weeping. Do not be surprised, said she, at my tears; for I am overwhelmed by a great affliction, which as yet I have not endured to tell to any one. Perhaps, said the girl, if you reveal it and disclose it to me, I may have a remedy for it. Hide this secret, then, replied the princess, and tell it to no one. I was married to this prince, who is a king and ruler over many cities, and I lived long with him, but by me he had no son. And when at length I produced him a son, he was leprous; and as soon as he saw him, he turned away with loathing, and said to me: Either kill him, or give him to the nurse to be brought up in some place from which we shall never hear of him more. After this I can have nothing to do with you, and I will never see you more. On this account I know not what to do, and I am overwhelmed with grief. Alas! my son. Alas! my husband. Did I not say so? said the girl. I have found a cure for your disease, and I shall tell it you. For I too was a leper; but I was cleansed by God, who is Jesus, the son of the Lady Mary. And the woman asking her where this God was whom she had spoken of, Here, with you, said the girl; He is living in the same house. But how is this possible? said she. Where is he? There, said the girl, are Joseph and Mary; and the child who is with them is called Jesus; and He it is who cured me of my disease and my torment. But by what means, said she, were you cured of your leprosy? Will you not tell me that? Why not? said the girl. I got from His mother the water in which He had been washed, and poured it over myself; and so I was cleansed from my leprosy. Then the princess rose up, and invited them to avail themselves of her hospitality. And she prepared a splendid banquet for Joseph in a great assembly of the men of the place. And on the following day she

took scented water with which to wash the Lord Jesus, and thereafter poured the same water over her son, whom she had taken with her; and immediately her son was cleansed from his leprosy. Therefore, singing thanks and praises to God, she said: Blessed is the mother who bore you, O Jesus; do you so cleanse those who share the same nature with you with the water in which your body has been washed? Besides, she bestowed great gifts upon the mistress the Lady Mary, and sent her away with great honor.

19. Coming thereafter to another city, they wished to spend the night in it. They turned aside, therefore, to the house of a man newly married, but who, under the influence of witchcraft, was not able to enjoy his wife; and when they had spent that night with him, his bond was loosed. And at daybreak, when they were girding themselves for their journey, the bridegroom would not let them go, and prepared for them a great banquet.

20. They set out, therefore, on the following day; and as they came near another city, they saw three women weeping as they came out of a cemetery. And when the Lady Mary beheld them, she said to the girl who accompanied her: Ask them what is the matter with them, or what calamity has befallen them. And to the girl's questions they made no reply, but asked in their turn: From where are you, and where are you going? for the day is already past, and night is coming on quickly. We are travelers, said the girl, and are seeking a house of entertainment in which we may pass the night. They said: Go with us, and spend the night with us. They followed them, therefore, and were brought into a new house with splendid decorations and furniture. Now it was winter; and the girl, going into the chamber of these women, found them again weeping and lamenting. There stood beside them a mule, covered with housings of cloth of gold, and sesame was put before him; and the women were kissing him, and giving him food. And the girl said: What is all the ado, my ladies, about this mule? They answered her with tears, and said: This mule, which you see, was our brother, born of the same mother with ourselves. And when our father died, and left us great wealth, and this only brother, we did our best to get him married, and were preparing his nuptials for him, after the manner of men. But some women, moved by mutual jealousy, bewitched him unknown to us; and one night, a little before daybreak, when the door of our house

was shut, we saw that this our brother had been turned into a mule, as you now behold him. And we are sorrowful, as you see, having no father to comfort us: there is no wise man, or magician, or enchanter in the world that we have omitted to send for; but nothing has done us any good. And as often as our hearts are overwhelmed with grief, we rise and go away with our mother here, and weep at our father's grave, and come back again.

21. And when the girl heard these things, Be of good courage, said she, and weep not: for the cure of your calamity is near; yea, it is beside you, and in the middle of your own house. For I also was a leper; but when I saw that woman, and along with her that young child, whose name is Jesus, I sprinkled my body with the water with which His mother had washed Him, and I was cured. And I know that He can cure your affliction also. But rise, go to Mary my mistress; bring her into your house, and tell her your secret; and entreat and supplicate her to have pity upon you. After the woman had heard the girl's words, they went in haste to the Lady Mary, and brought her into their chamber, and sat down before her weeping, and saying: O our mistress, Lady Mary, have pity on your hand-maidens; for no one older than ourselves, and no head of the family, is left, neither father nor brother, to live with us; but this mule which you see was our brother, and women have made him such as you see by witchcraft. We beg you, therefore, to have pity upon us. Then, grieving at their lot, the Lady Mary took up the Lord Jesus, and put Him on the mule's back; and she wept as well as the women, and said to Jesus Christ: Alas! my son, heal this mule by Your mighty power, and make him a man endowed with reason as he was before. And when these words were uttered by the Lady Mary, his form was changed, and the mule became a young man, free from every defect. Then he and his mother and his sisters adored the Lady Mary, and lifted the boy above their heads, and began to kiss Him, saying: Blessed is she that bore You, O Jesus, O Savior of the world; blessed are the eyes which enjoy the felicity of seeing You.

22. Moreover, both the sisters said to their mother: Our brother indeed, by the aid of the Lord Jesus Christ, and by the salutary intervention of this girl, who pointed out to us Mary and her son, has been raised to human form. Now, indeed, since our brother is unmarried, it would do very well for us to give him as his wife this

girl, their servant. And having asked the Lady Mary, and obtained her consent, they made a splendid wedding for the girl; and their sorrow being changed into joy, and the beating of their breasts into dancing, they began to be glad, to rejoice, to exult, and sing, adorned, on account of their great joy, in most splendid and gorgeous attire. Then they began to recite songs and praises, and to say: O Jesus, son of David, who turns sorrow into gladness, and lamentations into joy! And Joseph and Mary remained there ten days. Thereafter they set out, treated with great honors by these people, who bade them farewell, and from bidding them farewell returned weeping, especially the girl.

23. And turning away from this place, they came to a desert; and hearing that it was infested with robbers, Joseph and the Lady Mary resolved to cross this region by night. But as they go along, behold, they see two robbers lying in the way, and along with them a great number of robbers, who were their associates, sleeping. Now those two robbers, into whose hands they had fallen, were Titus and Dumachus. Titus therefore said to Dumachus: I beg you to let these persons go freely, and so that our comrades may not see them. And as Dumachus refused, Titus said to him again: Take to yourself forty drachmas from me, and hold this as a pledge. At the same time he held out to him the belt which he had about his waist, to keep him from opening his mouth or speaking. And the Lady Mary, seeing that the robber had done them a kindness, said to him: The Lord God will sustain you by His right hand, and will grant you remission of your sins. And the Lord Jesus answered, and said to His mother: Thirty years from now, O my mother, the Jews will crucify me at Jerusalem, and these two robbers will be raised upon the cross along with me, Titus on my right hand and Dumachus on my left; and after that day Titus shall go before me into Paradise. And she said: God keep this from you, my son. And they went from there towards a city of idols, which, as they came near it, was changed into sand-hills.

24. Then they turned aside to that sycamore which is now called Matarea,[1] and the Lord Jesus brought forth in Matarea a fountain in which the Lady Mary washed His shirt. And from the sweat of the Lord Jesus which she sprinkled there, balsam was produced in that region.

25. From there they came down to Memphis, and saw Pharaoh, and remained three years in Egypt; and the Lord Jesus did in Egypt very many miracles which are recorded neither in the Gospel of the Infancy nor in the perfect Gospel.

26. And at the end of the three years He came back out of Egypt, and returned. And when they had arrived at Judaea, Joseph was afraid to enter it; but hearing that Herod was dead, and that Archelaus his son had succeeded him, he was afraid indeed, but he went into Judaea. And an angel of the Lord appeared to him, and said: O Joseph, go into the city of Nazareth, and there abide. Wonderful indeed, that the Lord of the world should be thus borne and carried about through the world!

27. Thereafter, going into the city of Bethlehem, they saw there many and grievous diseases infesting the eyes of the children, who were dying in consequence. And a woman was there with a sick son, whom, now very near death, she brought to the Lady Mary, who saw him as she was washing Jesus Christ. Then said the woman to her: O my Lady Mary, look upon this son of mine, who is laboring under a grievous disease. And the Lady Mary listened to her, and said: Take a little of that water in which I have washed my son, and sprinkle him with it. She therefore took a little of the water, as the Lady Mary had told her, and sprinkled it over her son. And when this was done his illness abated; and after sleeping a little, he rose up from sleep safe and sound. His mother rejoicing at this, again took him to the Lady Mary. And she said to her: Give thanks to God, because He has healed this your son.

28. There was in the same place another woman, a neighbor of her whose son had lately been restored to health. And as her son was laboring under the same disease, and his eyes were now almost blinded, she wept night and day. And the mother of the child that had been cured said to her: Why do you not take your son to the Lady Mary, as I did with mine when he was nearly dead? And he got well with that water with which the body of her son Jesus had been washed. And when the woman heard this from her, she too went and got some of the same water, and washed her son with it, and his body and his eyes were instantly made well. Her also, when she had brought her son to her, and disclosed to her all that had happened,

the Lady Mary ordered to give thanks to God for her son's restoration to health, and to tell nobody of this matter.

29. There were in the same city two women, wives of one man, each having a son ill with fever. The one was called Mary, and her son's name was Cleopas. She rose and took up her son, and went to the Lady Mary, the mother of Jesus, and offering her a beautiful scarf, said: O my Lady Mary, accept this scarf, and for it give me one small bandage. Mary did so, and the mother of Cleopas went away, and made a shirt of it, and put it on her son. So he was cured of his disease; but the son of her rival died. Then there sprung up hatred between them; and as they did the house-work week about, and as it was the turn of Mary the mother of Cleopas, she heated the oven to bake bread; and going away to bring the lump that she had kneaded, she left her son Cleopas beside the oven. Her rival seeing him alone-- and the oven was very hot with the fire blazing under it--seized him and threw him into the oven, and ran off. Mary coming back, and seeing her son Cleopas lying in the oven laughing, and the oven quite cold, as if no fire had ever come near it, knew that her rival had thrown him into the fire. She drew him out, therefore, and took him to the Lady Mary, and told her of what had happened to him. And she said: Keep silence, and tell nobody of the affair; for I am afraid for you if you divulge it. After this her rival went to the well to draw water; and seeing Cleopas playing beside the well, and nobody near, she seized him and threw him into the well, and went home herself. And some men who had gone to the well for water saw the boy sitting on the surface of the water; and so they went down and drew him out. And they were seized with a great admiration of that boy, and praised God. Then came his mother, and took him up, and went weeping to the Lady Mary, and said: O my lady, see what my rival has done to my son, and how she has thrown him into the well; she will be sure to destroy him some day or other. The Lady Mary said to her: God will avenge you upon her. Thereafter, when her rival went to the well to draw water, her feet got entangled in the rope, and she fell into the well. Some men came to draw her out, but they found her skull fractured and her bones broken. Thus she died a miserable death, and in her came to pass that saying: They have dug a well deep, but have fallen into the pit which they had prepared.[1]

30. Another woman there had twin sons who had fallen into disease,

and one of them died, and the other was at his last breath. And his mother, weeping, lifted him up, and took him to the Lady Mary, and said: O my lady, aid me and comfort me. For I had two sons, and I have just buried the one, and the other is at the point of death. See how I am going to entreat and pray to God. And she began to say: O Lord, You are compassionate, and merciful, and full of affection. You gave me two sons, of whom You have taken away the one: this one at least leave to me. Therefore the Lady Mary, seeing the fervour of her weeping, had compassion on her, and said: Put your son in my son's bed, and cover him with his clothes. And when she had put him in the bed in which Christ was lying, he had already closed his eyes in death; but as soon as the smell of the clothes of the Lord Jesus Christ reached the boy, he opened his eyes, and, calling upon his mother with a loud voice, he asked for bread, and took it and sucked it. Then his mother said: O Lady Mary, now I know that the power of God dwells in you, so that your son heals those that partake of the same nature with himself, as soon as they have touched his clothes. This boy that was healed is he who in the Gospel is called Bartholomew.

31. Moreover, there was there a leprous woman, and she went to the Lady Mary, the mother of Jesus, and said: My lady, help me. And the Lady Mary answered: What help do you seek? Is it gold or silver? or is it that your body be made clean from the leprosy? And that woman asked: Who can grant me this? And the Lady Mary said to her: Wait a little, until I shall have washed my son Jesus, and put him to bed. The woman waited, as Mary had told her; and when she had put Jesus to bed, she held out to the woman the water in which she had washed His body, and said: Take a little of this water, and pour it over your body. And as soon as she had done so, she was cleansed, and gave praise and thanks to God.

32. Therefore, after staying with her three days, she went away; and coming to a city, saw there one of the chief men, who had married the daughter of another of the chief men. But when he saw the woman, he beheld between her eyes the mark of leprosy in the shape of a star; and so the marriage was dissolved, and became null and void. And when that woman saw them in this condition, weeping and overwhelmed with sorrow, she asked the cause of their grief. But they said: Inquire not into our condition, for to no one living can we tell our grief, and to none but ourselves can we disclose it. She urged

them, however, and entreated them to entrust it to her, saying that she would perhaps be able to tell them of a remedy. And when they showed her the girl, and the sign of leprosy which appeared between her eyes, as soon as she saw it, the woman said: I also, whom you see here, labored under the same disease, when, upon some business which happened to come in my way, I went to Bethlehem. There going into a cave, I saw a woman named Mary, whose son was he who was named Jesus; and when she saw that I was a leper, she took pity on me, and handed me the water with which she had washed her son's body. With it I sprinkled my body, and came out clean. Then the woman said to her: Will you not, O lady, rise and go with us, and show us the Lady Mary? And she assented; and they rose and went to the Lady Mary, carrying with them splendid gifts. And when they had gone in, and presented to her the gifts, they showed her the leprous girl whom they had brought. The Lady Mary therefore said: May the compassion of the Lord Jesus Christ descend upon you; and handed to them also a little of the water in which she had washed the body of Jesus Christ, she ordered the wretched woman to be bathed in it. And when this had been done, she was immediately cured; and they, and all standing by, praised God. Joyfully therefore they returned to their own city, praising the Lord for what He had done. And when the chief heard that his wife had been cured, he took her home, and made a second marriage, and gave thanks to God for the recovery of his wife's health.

33. There was there also a young woman afflicted by Satan; for that accursed wretch repeatedly appeared to her in the form of a huge dragon, and prepared to swallow her. He also sucked out all her blood, so that she was left like a corpse. As often as he came near her, she, with her hands clasped over her head, cried out, and said: Woe, woe's me, for nobody is near to free me from that accursed dragon. And her father and mother, and all who were about her or saw her, bewailed her lot; and men stood round her in a crowd, and all wept and lamented, especially when she wept, and said: Oh, my brethren and friends, is there no one to free me from that murderer? And the daughter of the chief who had been healed of her leprosy, hearing the girl's voice, went up to the roof of her castle, and saw her with her hands clasped over her head weeping, and all the crowds standing round her weeping as well. She therefore asked the demoniac's husband whether his wife's mother were alive. And

when he answered that both her parents were living, she said: Send for her mother to come to me. And when she saw that he had sent for her, and she had come, she said: Is that deranged girl your daughter? Yes, O lady, said that sorrowful and weeping woman, she is my daughter. The chiefs daughter answered: Keep my secret, for I confess to you that I was formerly a leper; but now the Lady Mary, the mother of Jesus Christ, has healed me. But if you wish your daughter to be healed, take her to Bethlehem, and seek Mary the mother of Jesus, and believe that your daughter will be healed; I indeed believe that you will come back with joy, with your daughter healed. As soon as the woman heard the words of the chief's daughter, she led away her daughter in haste; and going to the place indicated, she went to the Lady Mary, and revealed to her the state of her daughter. And the Lady Mary hearing her words, gave her a little of the water in which she had washed the body of her son Jesus, and ordered her to pour it on the body of her daughter. She gave her also from the clothes of the Lord Jesus a swathing-cloth, saying: Take this cloth, and show it to your enemy as often as you shall see him. And she saluted them, and sent them away.

34. When, therefore, they had gone away from her, and returned to their own district, and the time was at hand at which Satan was wont to attack her, at this very time that accursed one appeared to her in the shape of a huge dragon, and the girl was afraid at the sight of him. And her mother said to her: Fear not, my daughter; allow him to come near you, and then show him the cloth which the Lady Mary has given us, and let us see what will happen. Satan, therefore, having come near in the likeness of a terrible dragon, the body of the girl shuddered for fear of him; but as soon as she took out the cloth, and placed it on her head, and covered her eyes with it, flames and live coals began to dart forth from it, and to be cast upon the dragon. O the great miracle which was done as soon as the dragon saw the cloth of the Lord Jesus, from which the fire darted, and was cast upon his head and eyes! He cried out with a loud voice: What have I to do with you, O Jesus, son of Mary? Where shall I fly from you? And with great fear he turned his back and departed from the girl, and never afterwards appeared to her. And the girl now had rest from him, and gave praise and thanks to God, and along with her all who were present at that miracle.

35. Another woman was living in the same place, whose son was tormented by Satan. He, Judas by name, as often as Satan seized him, used to bite all who came near him; and if he found no one near him, he used to bite his own hands and other limbs. The mother of this wretched creature, then, hearing the fame of the Lady Mary and her son Jesus, rose up and brought her son Judas with her to the Lady Mary. In the meantime, James and Joses had taken the child the Lord Jesus with them to play with the other children; and they had gone out of the house and sat down, and the Lord Jesus with them. And the demoniac Judas came up, and sat down at Jesus' right hand: then, being attacked by Satan in the same manner as usual, he wished to bite the Lord Jesus, but was not able; nevertheless he struck Jesus on the right side, whereupon He began to weep. And immediately Satan went forth out of that boy, fleeing like a mad dog. And this boy who struck Jesus, and out of whom Satan went forth in the shape of a dog, was Judas Iscariot, who betrayed Him to the Jews; and that same side on which Judas struck Him, the Jews ran him through with a lance.

36. Now, when the Lord Jesus had completed seven years from His birth, on a certain day He was occupied with boys of His own age. For they were playing among clay, from which they were making images of asses, oxen, birds, and other animals; and each one boasting of his skill, was praising his own work. Then the Lord Jesus said to the boys: The images that I have made I will order to walk. The boys asked Him whether then he were the son of the Creator; and the Lord Jesus bade them walk. And they immediately began to leap; and then, when He had given them leave, they again stood still. And He had made figures of birds and sparrows, which flew when He told them to fly, and stood still when He told them to stand, and ate and drank when He handed them food and drink. After the boys had gone away and told this to their parents, their fathers said to them: My sons, take care not to keep company with him again, for he is a wizard: flee from him, therefore, and avoid him, and do not play with him again after this.

37. On a certain day the Lord Jesus, running about and playing with the boys, passed the shop of a dyer, whose name was Salem; and he had in his shop many pieces of cloth which he was to dye. The Lord Jesus then, going into his shop, took up all the pieces of cloth, and threw them into a tub full of indigo. And when Salem came and saw

his cloths destroyed, he began to cry out with a loud voice, and to ridicule Jesus, saying: Why have you done this to me, O son of Mary? You have disgraced me before all my townsmen: for, seeing that every one wished the color that suited himself, you indeed have come and destroyed them all. The Lord Jesus answered: I shall change for you the color of any piece of cloth which you shall wish to be changed. And immediately He began to take the pieces of cloth out of the tub, each of them of that color which the dyer wished, until He had taken them all out. When the Jews saw this miracle and prodigy, they praised God.

38. And Joseph used to go about through the whole city, and take the Lord Jesus with him, when people sent for him in the way of his trade to make for them doors, and milk-pails, and beds, and chests; and the Lord Jesus was with him wherever he went. As often, therefore, as Joseph had to make anything a cubit or a span longer or shorter, wider or narrower, the Lord Jesus stretched His hand towards it; and as soon as He did so, it became such as Joseph wished. Nor was it necessary for him to make anything with his own hand, for Joseph was not very skillful in carpentry.

39. Now, on a certain day, the king of Jerusalem sent for him, and said: I wish you, Joseph, to make for me a throne to fit that place in which I usually sit. Joseph obeyed, and began the work immediately, and remained in the palace two years, until he finished the work of that throne. And when he had it carried to its place, he perceived that each side wanted two spans of the prescribed measure. And the king, seeing this, was angry with Joseph; and Joseph, being in great fear of the king, spent the night without supper, nor did he taste anything at all. Then, being asked by the Lord Jesus why he was afraid, Joseph said: Because I have spoiled all the work that I have been two years at. And the Lord Jesus said to him: Fear not, and do not lose heart; but do you take hold of one side of the throne; I shall take the other; and we shall put that to rights. And Joseph, having done as the Lord Jesus had said and each having drawn by his own side, the throne was put to rights, and brought to the exact measure of the place. And those that stood by and saw this miracle were struck with astonishment, and praised God. And the woods used in that throne were of those which are celebrated in the time of Solomon the son of David; that is, woods of many and various kinds.

40. On another day the Lord Jesus went out into the road, and saw the boys that had come together to play, and followed them; but the boys hid themselves from Him. The Lord Jesus, therefore, having come to the door of a certain house, and seen some women standing there, asked them where the boys had gone; and when they answered that there was no one there, He said again: Who are these whom you see in the furnace?' They replied that they were kids of three years old. And the Lord Jesus cried out, and said: Come out here, O kids, to your Shepherd. Then the boys, in the form of kids, came out, and began to dance round Him; and the women, seeing this, were very much astonished, and were seized with trembling, and speedily, supplicated and adored the Lord Jesus, saying: O our Lord Jesus, son of Mary, You are of a truth that good Shepherd of Israel; have mercy on Your handmaidens who stand before You, and who have never doubted: for You have come, O our Lord, to heal, and not to destroy. And when the Lord Jesus answered that the sons of Israel were like the Ethiopians among the nations, the women said: You, O Lord, know all things, nor is anything hid from You; now, indeed, we beg You, and ask You of Your affection to restore these boys Your servants to their former condition. The Lord Jesus therefore said: Come, boys, let us go and play. And immediately, while these women were standing by, the kids were changed into boys.

41. Now in the month Adar, Jesus, after the manner of a king, assembled the boys together. They spread their clothes on the ground, and He sat down upon them. Then they put on His head a crown made of flowers, and, like chamber-servants, stood in His presence, on the right and on the left, as if He were a king. And whoever passed by that way was forcibly dragged by the boys, saying: Come here, and adore the king; then go your way.

42. In the meantime, while these things were going on, some men came up carrying a boy. For this boy had gone into the mountain with those of his own age to seek wood, and there he found a partridge's nest; and when he stretched out his hand to take the eggs from it, a venomous serpent bit him from the middle of the nest, so that he called out for help. His comrades accordingly went to him with haste, and found him lying on the ground like one dead. Then his relations came and took him up to carry him back to the city. And

after they had come to that place where the Lord Jesus was sitting like a king, and the rest of the boys standing round Him like His servants, the boys went hastily forward to meet him who had been bitten by the serpent, and said to his relations: Come and salute the king. But when they were unwilling to go, on account of the sorrow in I which they were, the boys dragged them by force against their will. And when they had come up to the Lord Jesus, He asked them why they were carrying the boy. And when they answered that a serpent had bitten him, the Lord Jesus said to the boys: Let us go and kill that serpent. And the parents of the boy asked leave to go away, because their son was in the agony of death; but the boys answered them, saying: Did you not hear the king saying: Let us go kill the serpent? and will you not obey him? And so, against their will the boy was carried back. And when they came to the nest, the Lord Jesus said to the boys: Is this the serpent's place? They said that it was; and the serpent, at the call of the Lord, came forth without delay, and submitted itself to Him. And He said to it: Go away, and suck out all the poison which you have infused into this boy. And so the serpent crawled to the boy, and sucked out all its poison. Then the Lord Jesus cursed it, and immediately on this being done it burst apart; and the Lord Jesus stroked the boy with his hand, and he was healed. And he began to weep; but Jesus said: Do not weep, for by and by you shall be my disciple. And this is Simon the Cananite,(2) of whom mention is made in the Gospel.(3)

43. On another day, Joseph sent his son James to gather wood, and the Lord Jesus went with him as his companion. And when they had come to the place where the wood was, and James had begun to gather it, behold, a venomous viper bit his hand, so that he began to cry out and weep. The Lord Jesus then, seeing him in this condition, went up to him, and blew upon the place where the viper had bitten him; and this being done, he was healed immediately.

44. One day, when the Lord Jesus was again with the boys playing on the roof of a house, one of the boys fell down from above, and immediately expired. And the rest of the boys fled in all directions, and the Lord Jesus was left alone on the roof. And the relations of the boy came up and said to the Lord Jesus: It was you who did throw our son headlong from the roof. And when He denied it, they cried out, saying: Our son is dead, and here is he who has killed him. And

the Lord Jesus said to them: Do not bring an evil report against me; but if you do not believe me, come and let us ask the boy himself, that he may bring the truth to light. Then the Lord Jesus went down, and standing over the dead body, said, with a loud voice: Zeno, Zeno, who threw you down from the roof? Then the dead boy answered and said: My lord, it was not you who did throw me down, but such a one cast me down from it. And when the Lord commanded those who were standing by to attend to His words, all who were present praised God for this miracle.

45. Once upon a time the Lady Mary had ordered the Lord Jesus to go and bring her water from the well. And when He had gone to get the water, the pitcher already full was knocked against something, and broken. And the Lord Jesus stretched out His handkerchief, and collected the water, and carried it to His mother; and she was astonished at it. And she hid and preserved in her heart all that she saw.

46. Again, on another day, the Lord Jesus was with the boys at a stream of water, and they had again made little fish-ponds. And the Lord Jesus had made twelve sparrows, and had arranged them round His fish-pond, three on each side. And it was the Sabbath-day. Then a Jew, the son of Hanan, coming up, and seeing them thus engaged, said in anger and great indignation: Do you make figures of clay on the Sabbath-day? And he ran quickly, and destroyed their fish-ponds. But when the Lord Jesus clapped His hands over the sparrows which He had made, they flew away chirping. Then the son of Hanan came up to the fish-pond of Jesus also, and kicked it with his shoes, and the water of it vanished away. And the Lord Jesus said to him: As that water has vanished away, so your life shall likewise vanish away. And immediately that boy dried up.

47. At another time, when the Lord Jesus was returning home with Joseph in the evening. He met a boy, who ran up against Him with so much force that He fell. And the Lord Jesus said to him: As you have thrown me down, so you shall fall and not rise again. And the same hour the boy fell down, and expired.

48. There was, moreover, at Jerusalem, a certain man named

Zacchaeus, who taught boys. He said to Joseph: Why, O Joseph, do you not bring Jesus to me to learn his letters? Joseph agreed to do so, and reported the matter to the Lady Mary. They therefore took Him to the master; and he, as soon as he saw Him, wrote out the alphabet for Him, and told Him to say Aleph. And when He had said Aleph, the master ordered Him to pronounce Beth. And the Lord Jesus said to him: Tell me first the meaning of the letter Aleph, and then I shall pronounce Beth. And when the master threatened to flog Him, the Lord Jesus explained to him the meanings of the letters Aleph and Beth; also which figures of the letter were straight, which crooked, which drawn round into a spiral, which marked with points, which without them, why one letter went before another; and many other things He began to recount and to elucidate which the master himself had never either heard or read in any book. The Lord Jesus, moreover, said to the master: Listen, and I shall say them to you. And He began clearly and distinctly to repeat Aleph, Beth, Gimel, Daleth, on to Tau. And the master was astonished, and said: I think that this boy was born before Noah. And turning to Joseph, he said: You have brought to me to be taught a boy more learned than all the masters. To the Lady Mary also be said: This son of yours has no need of instruction.

49. Thereafter they took Him to another and a more learned master, who, when be saw Him, said: Say Aleph. And when He had said Aleph, the master ordered him to pronounce Beth. And the Lord Jesus answered him, and said: First tell me the meaning of the letter Aleph, and then I shall pronounce Beth. And when the master hereupon raised his hand and flogged Him, immediately his hand dried up, and he died. Then said Joseph, to the Lady Mary: From this time we shall not let him go out of the house, since every one who opposes him is struck dead.

50. And when He was twelve years old, they took Him to Jerusalem to the feast. And when the feast was finished, they indeed returned; but the Lord Jesus remained in the temple among the teachers and elders and learned men of the sons of Israel, to whom He put various questions upon the sciences, and gave answers in His turn.(1) For He said to them: Whose son is the Messiahs? They answered Him: The son of David. Then, said He, does he in the Spirit call him his lord, when he says, The Lord said to my lord, Sit at my right hand, that I

may put your enemies under your footsteps?(1) Again the chief of the teachers said to Him: Have you read the books? Both the books, said the Lord Jesus, and the things contained in the books. And He explained the books, and the law, and the precepts, and the statutes, and the mysteries, which are contained in the books of the prophets--things which the understanding of no creature attains to. That teacher therefore said: I hitherto have neither attained to nor heard of such knowledge: Who, pray, do you think that boy will be?

51. And a philosopher who was there present, a skilful astronomer, asked the Lord Jesus whether He had studied astronomy. And the Lord Jesus answered him, and explained the number of the spheres, and of the heavenly bodies, their natures and operations; their opposition; their aspect, triangular, square, and sextile; their course, direct and retrograde; the twenty-fourths,(2) and sixtieths of twenty-fourths; and other things beyond the reach of reason.

52. There was also among those philosophers one very skilled in treating of natural science, and he asked the Lord Jesus whether He had studied medicine. And He, in reply, explained to him physics and metaphysics, hyperphysics and hypophysics, the powers likewise and humors of the body, and the effects of the same; also the number of members and bones, of veins, arteries, and nerves; also the effect of heat and dryness, of cold and moisture, and what these give rise to; what was the operation of the soul upon the body, and its perceptions and powers; what was the operation of the faculty of speech, of anger, of desire; lastly, their conjunction and disjunction, and other things beyond the reach of any created intellect. Then that philosopher rose up, and adored the Lord Jesus, and said: O Lord, from this time I will be your disciple and slave.

53. While they were speaking to each other of these and other things, the Lady Mary came, after having gone about seeking Him for three days along with Joseph. She therefore, seeing Him sitting among the teachers asking them questions, and answering in His turn, said to Him: My son, why have you treated us thus? Behold, your father and I have sought you with great trouble. But He said: Why do you seek me? Do you not know that I ought to occupy myself in my Father's house? But they did not understand the words that He spoke to them. Then those teachers asked Mary whether He were her son; and

when she signified that He was, they said: Blessed are you, O Mary, who have brought forth such a son. And returning with them to Nazareth, He obeyed them in all things. And His mother kept all these words of His in her heart. And the Lord Jesus advanced in stature, and in wisdom, and in favor with God and man.(3)

54. And from this day He began to hide His miracles and mysteries and secrets, and to give attention to the law, until He completed His thirtieth year, when His Father publicly declared Him at the Jordan by this voice sent down from heaven: This is my beloved Son, in whom I am well pleased; the Holy Spirit being present in the form of a white dove.(4)

55. This is He whom we adore with supplications, who has given us being and life, and who has brought us from our mothers' wombs; who for our sakes assumed a human body, and redeemed us, that He might embrace us in eternal compassion, and show to us His mercy according to His liberality, and beneficence, and generosity, and benevolence. To Him is glory, and beneficence, and power, and dominion from this time forth for evermore. Amen. Here ends the whole Gospel of the Infancy, with the aid of God Most High, according to what we have found in the original.

BOOK OF JAMES, OR PROTEVANGELIUM

From "The Apocryphal New Testament"
M.R. James-Translation and Notes
Oxford: Clarendon Press, 1924

I. In the histories of the twelve tribes of Israel it is written that there was one Joakim, exceeding rich: and he offered his gifts twofold, saying: That which is of my superfluity shall be for the whole people, and that which is for my forgiveness shall be for the Lord, for a propitiation to me.

2 Now the great day of the Lord drew near and the children of Israel

offered their gifts. And Reuben stood over against him saying: It is not lawful for you to offer your gifts first, forasmuch as you have gotten no offspring in Israel. And Joakim was very grieved, and went to the record of the twelve tribes of the people, saying: I will look upon the record of the twelve tribes of Israel, whether I only have not gotten offspring in Israel. And he searched, and found concerning all the righteous that they had raised up offspring in Israel. And he remembered the patriarch Abraham, how in the last days God gave him a son, even Isaac. And Joakim was very grieved, and showed not himself to his wife, but he took himself into the wilderness, and pitched his tent there, and fasted forty days and forty nights, saying within himself: I will not go down either for meat or for drink until the Lord my God visit me, and my prayer shall be to me meat and drink.

II Now his wife Anna lamented with two lamentations, and bewailed herself with two wailings, saying: I will bewail my widowhood, and I will bewail my childlessness.

2 And the great day of the Lord drew near, and Judith her handmaid said to her: How long will you humble your soul? The great day of the Lord has come, and it is not lawful for you to mourn: but take this headband, which the mistress of my work gave me, and it is not lawful for me to put it on, forasmuch as I am a handmaid, and it has a mark of royalty. And Anna said: Get you from me. Lo! I have done nothing (or I will not do so) and the Lord has greatly humbled me: peradventure one gave it to you in secret, and you are come to make me partaker in your sin. And Judith said: How shall I curse you, seeing the Lord has shut up your womb, to give you no fruit in Israel?

3 And Anna was very grieved [and mourned with a great mourning because she was looked down on by all the tribes of Israel. And coming to herself she said: What shall I do? I will pray with weeping to the Lord my God that he visit me]. And she put off her mourning garments and cleansed (or adorned) her head and put on her bridal garments: and about the ninth hour she went down into the garden to walk there. And she saw a laurel-tree and sat down underneath it and besought the Lord saying: O God of our fathers, bless me, and listen to my prayer, as you did bless the womb of Sarah, and gave

her a son, even Isaac.

III. 1 And looking up to the heaven she spied a nest of sparrows in the laurel-tree, and made a lamentation within herself, saying: Woe to me, who begat me? And what womb brought me forth for I am become a curse before the children of Israel, and I am looked down on, and they have mocked me forth out of the temple of the Lord? 2 Woe to me, to what am I similar? I am not similar to the fowls of the heaven, for even the fowls of the heaven are fruitful before you, O Lord. Woe to me, to what am I similar? I am not similar to the beasts of the earth, for even the beasts of the earth are fruitful before you, O Lord. Woe to me, to what am I similar? I am not similar to these waters, for even these waters are fruitful before you, O Lord. 3 Woe to me, to what am I similar? I am not similar to this earth, for even this earth brings forth her fruits in due season and blesses you, O Lord.

IV. 1 And behold an angel of the Lord appeared, saying to her: Anna, Anna, the Lord has listened to your prayer, and you shall conceive and bear, and your offspring shall be spoken of in the whole world. And Anna said: As the Lord my God lives, if I bring forth either male or female, I will bring it for a gift to the Lord my God, and it shall be ministering to him all the days of its life. 2 And behold there came two messengers saying to her: Behold Joakim your husband comes with his flocks: for an angel of the Lord came down to him saying: Joakim, Joakim, the Lord God has listened to your prayer. Get you down from here, for behold your wife Anna has conceived. 3 And Joakim sat him down and called his herdsmen saying: Bring me here ten lambs without blemish and without spot, and they shall be for the Lord my God; and bring me twelve tender calves, and they shall be for the priests and for the assembly of the elders; and a hundred kids for the whole people.

4 And behold Joakim came with his flocks, and Anna stood at the gate and saw Joakim coming, and ran and hung upon his neck, saying: Now know I that the Lord God has greatly blessed me: for behold the widow is no more a widow, and she that was childless shall conceive. And Joakim rested the first day in his house.

V. 1 And on the morrow he offered his gifts, saying in himself: If the Lord God be reconciled to me, the plate that is upon the forehead of the priest will make it manifest to me. And Joakim offered his gifts and looked earnestly upon the plate of the priest when he went up to the altar of the Lord, and he saw no sin in himself. And Joakim said: Now know I that the Lord is become propitious to me and has forgiven all my sins. And he went down from the temple of the Lord justified, and went to his house.

2 And her months were fulfilled, and in the ninth month Anna brought forth. And she said to the midwife: what have I brought forth? And she said: A female. And Anna said: My soul is magnified this day, and she laid herself down. And when the days were fulfilled, Anna purified herself and gave suck to the child and called her name Mary.

VI. 1 And day by day the child grew strong, and when she was six months old her mother stood her upon the ground to try if she would stand; and she walked seven steps and returned to her bosom. And she caught her up, saying: As the Lord my God lives, you shall walk no more upon this ground, until I bring you into the temple of the Lord. And she made a sanctuary in her bed chamber and suffered nothing common or unclean to pass through it. And she called for the daughters of the Hebrews that were undefiled, and they carried her here and there.

2 And the first year of the child was fulfilled, and Joakim made a great feast and bade the priests and the scribes and the assembly of the elders and the whole people of Israel. And Joakim brought the child to the priests, and they blessed her, saying: 0 God of our fathers, bless this child and give her a name renowned for ever among all generations. And all the people said: So be it, so be it. Amen. And he brought her to the high priests, and they blessed her, saying: 0 God of the high places, look upon this child, and bless her with the last blessing which has no successor.

3 And her mother caught her up into the sanctuary of her bed chamber and gave her suck.

And Anna made a song to the Lord God, saying:

I will sing a hymn to the Lord my God, because he has visited me and taken away from me the ridicule of my enemies, and the Lord has given me a fruit of his righteousness, single and manifold before him. Who shall declare to the sons of Reuben that Anna gives suck? Listen, listen, you twelve tribes of Israel, that Anna gives suck. And she laid the child to rest in the bed chamber of her sanctuary, and went forth and ministered to them. And when the feast was ended, they got them down rejoicing, and glorifying the God of Israel.

VII. 1 And to the child her months were added: and the child became two years old. And Joakim said: Let us bring her up to the temple of the Lord that we may pay the promise which we promised; lest the Lord require it of us (lit. send to us), and our gift become unacceptable. And Anna said: Let us wait until the third year, that the child may not long after her father or mother. And Joakim said: Let us wait.

2 And the child became three years old, and Joakim said: Call for the daughters of the Hebrews that are undefiled, and let them take every one a lamp, and let them be burning, that the child turn not backward and her heart be taken captive away from the temple of the Lord. And they did so until they were gone up into the temple of the Lord.

And the priest received her and kissed her and blessed her and said: The Lord has magnified your name among all generations: in you in the latter days shall the Lord make manifest his redemption to the children of Israel. And he made her to sit upon the third step of the altar. And the Lord put grace upon her and she danced with her feet and all the house of Israel loved her.

VIII. 1 And her parents got them down marveling, and praising the Lord God because the child was not turned away backward.

And Mary was in the temple of the Lord as a dove that is nurtured: and she received food from the hand of an angel.

2 And when she was twelve years old, there was a council of the priests, saying: Behold Mary is become twelve years old in the temple of the Lord. What then shall we do with her? lest she pollute the sanctuary of the Lord. And they said to the high priest: You stand over the altar of the Lord. Enter in and pray concerning her: And whatsoever the Lord shall reveal to you, that let us do.

3 And the high priest took the vestment with the twelve bells and went in to the Holy of Holies and prayed concerning her. And lo, an angel of the Lord appeared saying to him: Zacharias, Zacharias, go forth and assemble them that are widowers of the people, and let them bring every man a rod, and to whomsoever the Lord shall show a sign, his wife shall she be. And the heralds went forth over all the country round about Judaea, and the trumpet of the Lord sounded, and all men ran thereto.

IX. 1 And Joseph cast down his adze and ran to meet them, and when they were gathered together they went to the high priest and took their rods with them. And he took the rods of them all and went into the temple and prayed. And when he had finished the prayer he took the rods and went forth and gave them back to them: and there was no sign upon them. But Joseph received the last rod: and lo, a dove came forth of the rod and flew upon the head of Joseph. And the priest said to Joseph: Unto you has it fallen to take the virgin of the Lord and keep her for yourself. 2 And Joseph refused, saying: I have sons, and I am an old man, but she is a girl: lest I became a laughing-stock to the children of Israel. And the priest said to Joseph: Hear the Lord your God, and remember what things God did to Dathan and Abiram and Korah, how the earth split and they were swallowed up because of their gainsaying. And now fear you, Joseph, lest it be so in your house. And Joseph was afraid, and took her to keep her for himself. And Joseph said to Mary: Lo, I have received you out of the temple of the Lord: and now do I leave you in my house, and I go away to build my buildings and I will come again to you. The Lord shall watch over you.

X. 1 Now there was a council of the priests, and they said: Let us make a veil for the temple of the Lord. And the priest said: Call to me pure virgins of the tribe of David. And the officers departed and sought and found seven virgins. And the priests called to mind the child Mary, that she was of the tribe of David and was undefiled before God: and the officers went and fetched her. And they brought them into the temple of the Lord, and the priest said: Cast me lots, which of you shall weave the gold and the undefiled (the white) and the fine linen and the silk and the hyacinthine, and the scarlet and the true purple. And the lot of the true purple and the scarlet fell to Mary, and she took them and went to her house. And at that season Zacharias became dumb, and Samuel was in his place until the time when Zacharias spoke again.]But Mary took the scarlet and began to spin it.

XI 1 And she took the pitcher and went forth to fill it with water: and lo a voice saying: Hail, you that are highly favored; the Lord is with you: blessed are you among women.

And she looked about her upon the right hand and upon the left, to see from where this voice should be: and being filled with trembling she went to her house and set down the pitcher, and took the purple and sat down upon her seat and drew out the thread.

2 And behold an angel of the Lord stood before her saying: Fear not, Mary, for you have found grace before the Lord of all things, and you shall conceive of his word. And she, when she heard it, questioned in herself, saying: Shall I truly conceive of the living God, and bring forth after the manner of all women? And the angel of the Lord said: Not so, Mary, for a power of the Lord shall overshadow you: wherefore also that holy thing which shall be born of you shall be called the Son of the Highest. And you shall call his name Jesus: for he shall save his people from their sins. And Mary said: Behold the handmaid of the Lord is before him: be it to me according to your word.

XII 1 And she made the purple and the scarlet and brought them to the priest. And the priest blessed her and said: Mary, the Lord God has magnified your name, and you shall be blessed among all generations of the earth. 2 And Mary rejoiced and went away to Elizabeth her kinswoman: and she knocked at the door. And Elizabeth when she heard it cast down the scarlet (al. the wool) and ran to the door and opened it, and when she saw Mary she blessed her and said: What is this to me that the mother of my Lord should come to me? For behold that which is in me leaped and blessed you. And Mary forgot the mysteries which Gabriel the archangel had told her, and she looked up to the heaven and said: Who am I, Lord, that all the generations of the earth do bless me? 8 And she abode three months with Elizabeth, and day by day her womb grew: and Mary was afraid and departed to her house and hid herself from the children of Israel. Now she was sixteen years old when these mysteries came to pass.

XIII. I Now it was the sixth month with her, and behold Joseph came from his building, and he entered into his house and found her great with child. And he smote his face, and cast himself down upon the ground on sackcloth and wept bitterly, saying: With what countenance shall I look to the Lord my God? And what prayer shall I make concerning this maiden? For I received her out of the temple of the Lord my God a virgin, and have not kept her safe. Who is he that has ensnared me? Who has done this evil in my house and has defiled the virgin? Is not the story of Adam repeated in me? for as at the hour of his giving thanks the serpent came and found Eve alone and deceived her, so has it befallen me also. 2 And Joseph arose from off the sackcloth and called Mary and said to her O you that were cared for by God, why have you done this? You have forgotten the Lord your God. Why have you humbled your soul, you that were nourished up in the Holy of Holies and did receive food at the hand of an angel? 3 But she wept bitterly, saying: I am pure and I know not a man. And Joseph said to her: What then is that which is in your womb? And she said: As the Lord my God lives, I know not from where it is come to me.

XIV. I And Joseph was very afraid and ceased from speaking to her (or left her alone), and pondered what he should do with her. And Joseph said: If I hide her sin, I shall be found fighting against the law of the Lord: and if I manifest her to the children of Israel, I fear lest that which is in her be the offspring of an angel, and I shall be found delivering up innocent blood to the judgment of death. What then shall I do? I will let her go from me privately. And the night came upon him. 2 And behold an angel of the Lord appeared to him in a dream, saying: Fear not this child, for that which is in her is of the Holy Ghost, and she shall bear a son and you shall call his name

Jesus, for he shall save his people from their sins. And Joseph arose from sleep and glorified the God of Israel which had shown this favor to her: and he watched over her.

XV. I Now Annas the scribe came to him and said to him: Why did you not appear in our assembly? and Joseph said to him: I was weary with the journey, and I rested the first day. And Annas turned him about and saw Mary great with child. 2 And he went hastily to the priest and said to him: Joseph, to whom you bear witness [that he is righteous] has sinned grievously. And the priest said: Wherein? And he said: The virgin whom he received out of the temple of the Lord, he has defiled her, and married her by stealth (lit. stolen her marriage), and has not declared it to the children of Israel. And the priest answered and said: Has Joseph done this? And Annas the scribe said: Send officers, and you shall find the virgin great with child. And the officers went and found as he had said, and they brought her together with Joseph to the place of judgment. 3 And the priest said: Mary, wherefore have you done this, and wherefore have you humbled your soul and forgotten the Lord your God, you that were nurtured in the Holy of Holies and did receive food at the hand of an angel and did hear the hymns and did dance before the Lord, wherefore have you done this?

But she wept bitterly, saying: As the Lord my God lives I am pure before him and I know not a man. 4 And the priest said to Joseph: Why have you done this? And Joseph said: As the Lord my God lives I am pure as concerning her. And the priest said: Bear no false witness but speak the truth: you have married her by stealth and have not declared it to the children of Israel, and have not bowed your head under the mighty hand that your offspring should be blessed. And Joseph held his peace.

XVI 1 And the priest said: Restore the virgin whom you did receive out of the temple of the Lord. And Joseph was full of weeping. And the priest said: I will give you to drink of the water of the conviction of the Lord, and it will make manifest your sins before your eyes. 2 And the priest took thereof and made Joseph drink and sent him into the hill-country. And he returned whole. He made Mary also drink and sent her into the hill-country. And she returned whole. And all the people were astonished, because sin appeared not in them. 3 And the priest said: If the Lord God has not made your sin manifest, neither do I condemn you. And he let them go. And Joseph took Mary and departed to his house rejoicing, and glorifying the God of Israel.

XVII. 1 Now there went out a decree from Augustus the king that all that were in Bethlehem of Judaea should be recorded. And Joseph said: I will record my sons: but this child, what shall I do with her? How shall I record her as my wife? nay, I am ashamed. Or as my daughter? But all the children of Israel know that she is not my daughter. This day of the Lord shall do as the Lord wills. 2 And he saddled the she-ass, and set her upon it, and his son led it and Joseph followed after. And they drew near (to Bethlehem) within three miles: and Joseph turned himself about and saw her of a sad countenance and said within himself: Peradventure that which is within her pains her. And again Joseph turned himself about and saw her laughing, and said to her: Mary, what ails you that I see your face at one time laughing and at another time sad? And Mary said to Joseph: It is because I behold two peoples with my eyes, the one weeping and lamenting and the other rejoicing and exulting.

8 And they came to the midst of the way, and Mary said to him: Take me down from the ass, for that which is within me presses me, to come forth. And he took her down from the ass and said to her: Where shall I take you to hide your shame? For the place is desert.

XVIII. I And he found a cave there and brought her into it, and set his sons by her: and he went forth and sought for a midwife of the Hebrews in the country of Bethlehem.

2 Now I Joseph was walking, and I walked not. And I looked up to the air and saw the air in amazement. And I looked up to the pole of the heaven and saw it standing still, and the fowls of the heaven without motion. And I looked upon the earth and saw a dish set, and workmen lying by it, and their hands were in the dish: and they that were chewing chewed not, and they that were lifting the food lifted it not, and they that put it to their mouth put it not thereto, but the faces of all of them were looking upward. And behold there were sheep being driven, and they went not forward but stood still; and

the shepherd lifted his hand to strike them with his staff, and his hand remained up. And I looked upon the stream of the river and saw the mouths of the kids upon the water and they drank not. And of a sudden all things moved onward in their course.

XIX. I And behold a woman coming down from the hillcountry, and she said to me: Man, where go you? And I said: I seek a midwife of the Hebrews. And she answered and said to me: Are you of Israel? And I said to her: Yea. And she said: And who is she that brings forth in the cave? And I said: She that is betrothed to me. And she said to me: Is she not your wife? And I said to her: It is Mary that was nurtured up in the temple of the Lord: and I received her to wife by lot: and she is not my wife, but she has conception by the Holy Ghost.

And the midwife said to him: Is this the truth? And Joseph said to her: Come here and see. And the midwife went with him.

2 And they stood in the place of the cave: and behold a bright cloud overshadowing the cave. And the midwife said: My soul is magnified this day, because my eyes have seen marvelous things: for salvation is born to Israel. And immediately the cloud withdrew itself out of the cave, and a great light appeared in the cave so that our eyes could not endure it. And little by little that light withdrew itself until the young child appeared: and it went and took the breast of its mother Mary.

And the midwife cried aloud and said: Great to me today is this day, in that I have seen this new sight. 3 And the midwife went forth out of the cave and Salome met her. And she said to her: Salome, Salome, a new sight have I to tell you. A virgin has brought forth, which her nature allows not. And Salome said: As the Lord my God lives, if I make not trial and prove her nature I will not believe that a virgin has brought forth.

XX. 1 And the midwife went in and said to Mary: Prepare yourself, for there is no small contention arisen concerning you. And Salome made trial and cried out and said: Woe to my iniquity and my unbelief, because I have tempted the living God, and lo, my hand falls away from me in fire. And she bowed her knees to the Lord, saying: O God of my fathers, remember that I am the offspring of Abraham and Isaac and Jacob: make me not a public example to the children of Israel, but restore me to the poor, for you know, Lord, that in your name did I perform my cures, and did receive my hire of you. 3 And lo, an angel of the Lord appeared, saying to her: Salome, Salome, the Lord has listened to you: bring your hand near to the young child and take him up, and there shall be to you salvation and joy. 4 And Salome came near and took him up, saying: I will do him worship, for a great king is born to Israel. And behold immediately Salome was healed: and she went forth of the cave justified. And lo, a voice saying: Salome, Salome, tell none of the marvels which you have seen, until the child enter into Jerusalem.

XXI 1 And behold, Joseph made him ready to go forth into Judaea. And there came a great tumult in Bethlehem of Judaea; for there came wise men, saying: Where is he that is born king of the Jews? For we have seen his star in the east and are come to worship him. 2 And when Herod heard it he was troubled and sent officers to the wise men. And he sent for the high priests and questioned them, saying: How is it written concerning the Christ, where he is born? They say to him: In Bethlehem of Judaea: for so it is written. And he let them go. And he questioned the wise men, saying to them: What sign saw you concerning the king that is born? And the wise men said: We saw a very great star shining among those stars and dimming them so that the stars appeared not: and thereby knew we that a king was born to Israel, and we came to worship him. And Herod said: Go and seek for him, and if you find him, tell me, that I also may come and worship him. 3 And the wise men went forth. And lo, the star which they saw in the east went before them until they entered into the cave: and it stood over the head of the cave. And the wise men saw the young child with Mary, his mother: and they brought out of their purse-bags gifts, gold-and frankincense and myrrh. 4 And being warned by the angel that they should not enter into Judaea, they went into their own country by another way.

XXII. 1 But when Herod perceived that he was mocked by the wise men, he was angry, and sent murderers, saying to them: Slay the children from two years old and under. 2 And when Mary heard that the children were being slain, she was afraid, and took the young child and wrapped in swaddling clothes and laid him in an ox-manger.

3 But Elizabeth when she heard that they sought for John, took him and went up into the hill-country and looked about her where she should hide him: and there was no hiding-place. And Elizabeth groaned and said with a loud voice: Oh mountain of God, receive you a mother with a child. For Elizabeth was not able to go up. And immediately the mountain split apart and took her in. And there was a light shining always for them: for an angel of the Lord was with them, keeping watch over them.

XXIII. 1 Now Herod sought for John, and sent officers to Zacharias, saying: Where have you hidden your son? And he answered and said to them: I am a minister of God and attend continually upon the temple of the Lord: I know not where my son is. 2 And the officers departed and told Herod all these things. And Herod was angry and said: His son is to be king over Israel. And he sent to him again, saying: Say the truth: where is your son? For you know that your blood is under my hand. And the officers departed and told him all these things. 3 And Zacharias said: I am a martyr of God if you shed my blood: for my spirit the Lord shall receive, because you shed innocent blood in the front court of the temple of the Lord.

And about the dawning of the day Zacharias was slain. And the children of Israel knew not that he was slain.

XXIV. 1 But the priests entered in at the hour of the salutation, and the blessing of Zacharias met them not according to the manner. And the priests stood waiting for Zacharias, to salute him with the prayer, and to glorify the Most High. 2 But as he delayed to come, they were all afraid: and one of them took courage and entered in: and he saw beside the altar congealed blood: and a voice saying: Zacharias has been slain, and his blood shall not be wiped out until his avenger come. And when he heard that word he was afraid, and went forth and told the priests. 3 And they took courage and went in and saw that which was done: and the panels of the temple did wail: and they rent their clothes from the top to the bottom. And his body they found not, but his blood they found turned into stone. And they feared, and went forth and told all the people that Zacharias was slain. And all the tribes of the people heard it, and they mourned for him and lamented him three days and three nights. And after the three days the priests took counsel whom they should set in his place: and the lot came upon Symeon. Now he it was which was warned by the Holy Ghost that he should not see death until he should see the Christ in the flesh.

XXV. 1 Now I, James, which wrote this history in Jerusalem, when there arose a tumult when Herod died, withdrew myself into the wilderness until the tumult ceased in Jerusalem.

Glorifying the Lord God which gave me the gift, and the wisdom to write this history.

2 And grace shall be with those that fear our Lord Jesus Christ: to whom be glory for ever and ever. Amen.

The Infancy Gospel of Thomas, Latin Text

From "The Apocryphal New Testament"
M.R. James-Translation and Notes
Oxford: Clarendon Press, 1924

Here begins a treatise of the Boyhood of Jesus according to Thomas.

I. How Mary and Joseph fled with him into Egypt.

When there was a tumult because search was made by Herod for our Lord Jesus Christ, that he might slay him, then said an angel to Joseph: Take Mary and her child and flee into Egypt from the face of them that seek to slay him. Now Jesus was two years old when he entered into Egypt. And as he walked through a sown field he put forth his hand and took of the ears and put them upon the fire and ground them and began to eat. [And he gave such favor to that field that year by year when it was sown it yielded to the lord of it so many measures of wheat as the number of the grains which he had taken from it.] Now when they had entered into Egypt they took lodging in the house of a certain widow, and abode in the same place one year. And Jesus became three years old. And seeing boys playing he began to play with them. And he took a dried fish and put it into a basin and commanded it to move to and fro, and it began to move. And again he said to the fish: Cast out your salt that is in you and go into the water. And it came to pass. But when the neighbors saw what was done they told it to the widow woman in whose house his mother Mary dwelt. And she when she heard it hasted and cast them out of her house.

II. How a Master cast him out of the city.

1 And as Jesus walked with Mary his mother through the midst of the marketplace of the city, he looked about and saw a master teaching his pupils. And behold twelve sparrows which were quarrelling one with another fell from the wall into the lap of the master who taught the boys. And when Jesus saw it he laughed and stood still. 2 Now when that teacher saw him laughing, he said to his pupils in great anger: Go, bring him here to me. And when they had brought him, the master took hold on his ear and said: What saw you that you laughed? And he said to him: Master, see, my hand was full of corn, and I showed it to them, and scattered the corn, which they are carrying away in danger: for this cause they fought with one another that they might partake of the corn. 3 And Jesus left not the place until it was accomplished. And for this cause the master labored to cast him out of the city together with his mother.

III. How Jesus came out of Egypt.

1 And behold, an angel of the Lord met with Mary and said to her: Take the child and return into the land of the Jews: for they are dead which sought his life. So Mary arose with Jesus, and they went into the city Nazareth, which is in the inheritance of his (her?) father. 2 But when Joseph departed out of Egypt after the death of Herod, he took Jesus into the wilderness until there was quiet in Jerusalem from them that sought the life of the child. And he gave thanks to God for that he had given him understanding, and because he had found grace before the Lord God. Amen.

After these things an angel of the Lord came to Joseph and to Mary the mother of Jesus and said to them: Take the child, return into the land of Israel, for they are dead that sought the life of the child. And they arose and went to Nazareth where Joseph possessed the goods of his father. 2 And when Jesus was seven years old, there was quiet in the realm of Herod from all them that sought the life of the child. And they returned to Bethlehem and abode there.

IV. What Jesus did in the city of Nazareth.

It is a glorious work for Thomas the Israelite (Ismaelite) the apostle of the Lord to tell of the works of Jesus after he came out of Egypt to Nazareth. Hear (understand) therefore all of you beloved brethren, the signs which the Lord Jesus did when he was in the city of Nazareth: as it is said in the first chapter.

1 Now when Jesus was five years old there was a great rain upon the earth, and the child Jesus walked about therein. And the rain was very terrible: and he gathered the water together into a pool and commanded with a word that it should become clear: and immediately it did so.

2 Again, he took of the clay which came of that pool and made thereof to the number of twelve sparrows. Now it was the Sabbath day when Jesus did this among the children of the Hebrews: and the children of the Hebrews went and said to Joseph his father: Look, your son was playing with us and he took clay and made sparrows which it was not right to do upon the Sabbath, and he has broken it. And Joseph went to the child Jesus, and said to him: Why have you done this which it was not right to do on the Sabbath? But Jesus spread forth (opened) his hands and commanded the sparrows, saying: Go forth into the height and fly: you shall not meet death at any man's hands. And they flew and began to cry out and praise almighty God. But when the Jews saw what was done they were astonished and departed, proclaiming the signs which Jesus did.

3 But a Pharisee which was with Jesus took a branch of an olive tree and began to empty the pool which Jesus had made. And when Jesus saw it he was vexed and said to him: O you of Sodom, ungodly and ignorant, what hurt did the fountain of water do you, which I made? Lo, you shall become like a dry tree which has neither roots nor leaf nor fruit. And straightway he was dried up and fell to the earth and died: but his parents carried him away dead and reviled Joseph, saying: Behold what your son has done: teach you him to pray and not to blaspheme.

V. How the people of the city were grieved against Joseph because of that which Jesus did.

1 And after some days as Jesus walked with Joseph through the city, there ran one of the children and smote Jesus on the arms: but Jesus said to him: So finish you your course. And immediately he fell to the earth and died. But they when they saw this wonder, cried out saying: From from where comes this child? And they said to Joseph: It is not right that such a child should be among us. And he departed and took him with him. And they said to him: Depart out of this place; and if you must be with us, teach him to pray and not to blaspheme: for our sons are put to death by him (lit. lose their senses). 2 And Joseph called Jesus and began to admonish him, saying: Why do you blaspheme? They that dwell in this place conceive hatred against us. But Jesus said: I know that these words are not mine but yours: yet for your sake I will hold my peace: But let them see and bear their own foolishness. And straightway they that spoke against Jesus were made blind, and as they walked to and fro they said: Every word that comes out of his mouth has fulfillment. 3 And when Joseph saw what Jesus had done he took hold on him by his ear in anger: but Jesus was vexed and said to Joseph: It suffices you to see me and not to touch me. For you know not who I am, which if you knew, you would not grieve me. And albeit I am with you now, yet was I made before you.

VI. How Jesus was treated by the Master.

1 There was therefore a man named Zacheus who heard all that Jesus said to Joseph, and he were astonished in himself and said: I have never beheld such a child that spoke so. And he came near to Joseph and said to him: You have a wise child: deliver him to me to learn letters, and when he is learned in the study of the letters, I will teach him reverently that he become not foolish. Joseph answered and said to him: No man is able to teach him but God only. Think you that this young child will be the occasion to us of little torment, my brother? Think you that he is worthy to receive a little cross?

2 But when Jesus heard Joseph saying these things, he said to Zacheus: Truly, O master, all things that proceed out of my mouth are true. And I am before all men, and I am Lord, but you are the children of strangers: for to me is given the glory of them or of the worlds but to you nothing is given: for I am before all worlds. And I know how many are the years of your life, and when you shall raise that standard of the cross whereof my father spoke, then shall you understand that all things that proceed out of my mouth are true.

3 But the Jews which stood by and heard the words which Jesus spoke, were astonished and said: Now have we seen such wonders and heard such words from this child, as we have never heard neither shall hear from any other man, neither from the chief priests nor the doctors nor the Pharisees. 4 Jesus answered and said to them: Why marvel you? Do you think it a thing incredible that I have told you the truth? I know when you were born, and your fathers: and if I should say more to you, I know when the world was created, and who sent me to you.

When the Jews heard the word which the child spoke, they were angry because they were not able to answer him. And the child turned himself about and rejoiced and said: I spoke to you a proverb; but I know that you are weak and know not anything.

5 Now that master said to Joseph: Bring him to me and I will teach him letters. And Joseph took the child Jesus and brought him to the house [of a certain master] where other children also were taught. But the master began to teach him the letters with sweet speech, and wrote for him the first line which goes from A to Z, and began to flatter him and to teach him (and commanded him to say the letters:) but the child held his peace. 6 Then that teacher smote the child on the head and when the child received the blow, he said to him: I ought to teach you and not you to teach me. I know the letters which you would teach me, and I know that you are to me as vessels out of which comes nothing but sound, and neither wisdom nor salvation of the soul. And beginning the line he spoke all the letters from A even to T fully with much quickness: and he looked upon the master and said: But you know not how to interpret A and B: how would you teach others? You hypocrite, if you know and can tell me concerning A, then will I tell you concerning B. But when the teacher began to expound concerning the first letter, he was not able to give any answer.

7 Then said Jesus to Zacheus: Listen to me, O master and understand the first letter. Give ear to me, how that it has two lines (eight quite unintelligible descriptive phrases follow).

8 Now when Zacheus saw that he so divided the first letter he was confounded at such names, and at his teaching, and cried out and said: Woe is me, for I am confounded: I have hired shame to myself by means of this child. And he said to Joseph: I beg you earnestly, my brother, take him away from me: for I cannot look upon his face nor hear his mighty words. For this child is able to subdue the fire and to restrain the sea, for he was born before the worlds. What womb bare him or what manner of mother brought him up I know not. 10 O my friends, I am astray in my wits, I am mocked, wretched man that I am. I said that I had a disciple, but he is found to be my master. I cannot overcome my shame, for I am old, and I cannot find wherewithal to answer him, so that I am like to fall into heavy sickness and depart out of the world or go away from this city, for all men have seen my shame, that a child has ensnared me. What can I answer any man, or what words can I speak, for he has overcome me at the first letter! I am confounded, O you my friends and acquaintances, and I can find neither first nor last to answer him. 11

And now I beg you brother Joseph, remove him from me and take him to your house, for either he is a sorcerer or a god (Lord) or an angel, and what to say I know not.

12 And Jesus turned himself to the Jews that were with Zacheus and said to them: Now let all them that see not see and let them understand which understand not, and let the deaf hear, and let them arise which have died by my means, and let me call them that are high to that which is higher, even as he that sent me to you has commanded me. And when the child Jesus ceased speaking, all the afflicted were made whole, as many as had been afflicted at his word. And they dare not speak to him.

VII. How Jesus raised up a boy.

1 Now on a day, when Jesus climbed up upon a house with the children, he began to play with them: but one of the boys fell down through the door out of the upper chamber and died straightway. And when the children saw it they fled all of them, but Jesus remained alone in the house. 2 And when the parents of the child which had died came they spoke against Jesus saying: Of a truth you made him fall. But Jesus said: I never made him fall: nevertheless they accused him still. Jesus therefore came down from the house and stood over the dead child and cried with a loud voice, calling him by his name: Zeno, Zeno, arise and say if I made you fall. And suddenly he arose and said: Nay, Lord. And when his parents saw this great miracle which Jesus did, they glorified God, and worshipped Jesus.

VIII. How Jesus healed the foot of a boy.

1 And after a few days a certain boy of that village was cleaving wood, and smote his foot. 2 And when much people came to him, Jesus also came with them. And he touched the foot which was hurt, and forthwith it was made whole. And Jesus said to him: Arise and cleave the wood and remember me. But when the multitude that were with him saw the signs which were done they worshipped Jesus and said: of a truth we believe surely that you are God.

IX. How Jesus bare water in his cloak.

1 And when Jesus was six years old, his mother sent him to draw water. And when Jesus was come to the well there was much people there and they brake his pitcher. 2 But he took the cloak which he had upon him and filled it with water and brought it to Mary his mother. And when his mother saw the miracle that Jesus did she kissed him and said: Lord, listen to me and save my son.

X. How Jesus sowed wheat.

1 Now when it was seed time, Joseph went forth to sow corn, and Jesus followed after him. And when Joseph began to sow, Jesus put forth his hand and took of the corn so much as he could hold in his hand, and scattered it. 2 Joseph therefore came at the time of harvest to reap his harvest. And Jesus also came and gathered the ears which he had sown, and they made a hundred measures of good corn: and he called the poor and the widows and fatherless and gave them the corn which he had gained, save that Joseph took a little thereof to his house for a blessing [of Jesus].

XI. How Jesus made a short beam even with a long one.

1 And Jesus came to be eight years old. Now Joseph was a builder and wrought ploughs and yokes for oxen. And on a day a certain rich man said to Joseph: Sir, make me a bed serviceable and comely. But Joseph was troubled because the beam which he had made ready for the work was short. 2 Jesus said to him: Be not troubled, but take you hold of this beam by the one end and I by the other, and let us draw it out. And so it came to pass, and forthwith Joseph found it serviceable for that which he desired. And he said to Joseph: Behold, fashion that you will. But Joseph when he saw what was done embraced him and said: Blessed am I for that God has given me such a son.

XII. How Jesus was delivered over to learn letters.

1 And when Joseph saw that he had so great grace and that he increased in stature, he thought to deliver him over to learn letters. And he delivered him to another doctor that he should teach him. Then said that doctor to Joseph: What manner of letters would you teach this child? Joseph answered and said: Teach him first the letters of the Gentiles and after that the Hebrew. Now the doctor knew that he was of an excellent understanding, and received him gladly. And when he had written for him the first line, that is to say A and B, he taught him for the space of some hours: but Jesus held his peace and answered nothing. 2 At the last Jesus said to the master: If you be truly a master and indeed know the letters, tell me the power of A and I will tell you the power of B. Then was the master filled with indignation and smote him on the head. But Jesus was angry and cursed him, and on a sudden he fell down and died. 3 But Jesus returned to his own home. And Joseph enjoined Mary his mother that she should not let him go out of the court of the house.

XIII. How he was delivered to another master.

1 After many days there came another doctor which was a friend of Joseph and said to him: Deliver him to me and I will teach him letters with much gentleness. And Joseph said to him: If you are able, take him and teach him, and it shall be done gladly. And when the doctor received Jesus, he went with fear and great boldness and took him rejoicing. 2 And when he was come to the house of the doctor, he found a book lying in that place and took it and opened it, and read not those things which were written therein, but opened his mouth and spoke by the Holy Ghost and taught the law: and all that stood by listened attentively, and the teacher sat by him and heard him gladly and entreated him to continue teaching. And much people gathered together and heard all the holy doctrine which he taught and the beloved words which proceeded out of his mouth marveling that he being a little child spoke such things.

3 But when Joseph heard, he was afraid and ran to the place where Jesus was; and the master said to Joseph: Know my brother, that I received your child to teach him and instruct him, but he is filled with great grace and wisdom. Therefore behold now, take him to your house with joy, because the grace which he has is given him of the Lord. 4 And when Jesus heard the master speak thus he was joyful and said: Lo, now you have well said, O master: for your sake shall he rise again who was dead. And Joseph took him to his own home.

XIV. How Jesus made James whole of the bite of a serpent.

Now Joseph sent James to gather straw, and Jesus followed after him. And as James gathered straw, a viper bit him and he fell to the earth as dead by means of the venom. But when Jesus saw that, he breathed upon his wound and forthwith James was made whole, and the viper died.

XV. How Jesus raised up a boy.

After a few days a child that was his neighbor died, and his mother mourned for him very much; and when Jesus heard, he went and stood over the child, and smote him on the breast and said: Child, I say to you, die not, but live. And immediately the child arose: and Jesus said to the mother of the child: Take up your son and give him suck, and remember me. 2 But the multitudes when they saw that miracle said: Of a truth this child is from heaven, for now has he set free many souls from death and has saved all them that hoped in him.

[A gap in all the Latin MSS. filled by the Greek text A, cap. 19,1-3 Jesus and the doctors in the Temple.]

3 The Scribes and Pharisees said to Mary: Are you the mother of this child? and Mary said: Of a truth I am. And they said to her: Blessed are you among women, because God has blessed the fruit of your womb in that he has given you a child so glorious: for so great gifts of wisdom we have never seen nor heard in any.

4 And Jesus arose and followed his mother. But Mary kept in her heart all the great signs which Jesus wrought among the people, in healing many that were sick. And Jesus increased in stature and wisdom, and all that saw him glorified God the Father Almighty: Who is blessed for ever and ever. Amen.

All these things have I, Thomas the Israelite (Ismaelite), written and recorded for the Gentiles and for our brethren, and likewise many other things which Jesus did, which was born in the land of Juda (Judah). Behold, the house of Israel has seen all these from the first even to the last, even how great signs and wonders Jesus did among them, which were good exceedingly. And this is he which shall judge the world according to the will of his Father, immortal and invisible, as the holy Scripture declares and as the prophets have testified of his works among all the peoples of Israel: for he is the Son of God throughout all the World. And to him belongs all glory and honor everlastingly, who lives and reigns with God, world without end. Amen.

Look for other fine books by Joseph Lumpkin.

The Lost Book Of Enoch: A Comprehensive Transliteration,
ISBN: 0974633666

The Gospel of Thomas: A Contemporary Translation
ISBN: 0976823349

Fallen Angels, The Watchers, and the Origins of Evil:
ISBN: 1933580100

The Book of Jubilees; The Little Genesis, The Apocalypse of Moses
ISBN-13: 978-1933580098

The Lost Books of the Bible: The Great Rejected Texts
ISBN-13: 978-1933580661

The Books of Enoch: A Complete Volume Containing 1 Enoch (The Ethiopic Book of Enoch), 2 Enoch (The Slavonic Secrets of Enoch), and 3 Enoch (The Hebrew Book of Enoch)
ISBN-13: 978-1933580807

Joseph Lumpkin

The Life and Times of Jesus: From Child to God

Joseph Lumpkin

www.ingramcontent.com/pod-product-compliance
Lightning Source LLC
Chambersburg PA
CBHW070722160426

43192CB00009B/1282